PUBLIC ENEMIES

PUBLIC ENEMIES

Russell 'Mad Dog' Cox, Ray Denning and the Golden Age of Armed Robbery

MARK DAPIN

ALLEN&UNWIN
SYDNEY • MELBOURNE • AUCKLAND • LONDON

First published in 2020

Allen & Unwin
83 Alexander Street
Crows Nest NSW 2065
Australia
Phone: (61 2) 8425 0100
Email: info@allenandunwin.com
Web: www.allenandunwin.com

NATIONAL LIBRARY OF AUSTRALIA

A catalogue record for this book is available from the National Library of Australia

ISBN 978 1 76029 535 6

Set in 13/17 pt Adobe Caslon Pro by Midland Typesetters, Australia
Printed and bound in Australia by McPhersons Printing Group

10 9 8 7 6 5 4 3 2

FSC www.fsc.org MIX Paper from responsible sources FSC® C001695

The paper this book is printed on is certified against the Forest Stewardship Council® Standards. McPherson's Printing Group holds FSC® chain of custody certification SA-COC-005379. FSC® promotes environmentally responsible, socially beneficial and economically viable management of the world's forests

The earlier quotes from Ray Denning in this book come largely from a statement presented to the Royal Commission into NSW Prisons circa 1978 and the cassette tapes sent by Denning to the ABC in 1980. Later quotes come from his records of interview with Ron Woodham and Ian Teasdale (21, 22 February 1988) and statements made to police about Tim Anderson (1 March 1989, 23 May 1989), Ray Carrion (20 April 1989), Roy Pollitt (May 1990) and Russell Cox (undated).

The quotes from Russell Cox come from a statement made to the Royal Commission into NSW Prisons in 1978, and a document written for Justice Badgery-Parker and quoted in *R v Russell John Cox*, 13 May 1997, 19 June 1997.

Other sources are available on application by email to public.enemiesoz@gmail.com.

Preface

The Golden Age of Armed Robbery ended at about 5 p.m. on 23 July 1991, fifteen minutes after a middle-aged man waving a tomahawk burst into the Advance Bank at St Leonards, Sydney, and leaped the counter. A bank teller activated his bulletproof-glass security screen, and the rising shield caught the bandit mid-flight and jammed his head against the ceiling.

The man's accomplice ran off, robbing a customer on his way out. The bank staff fled the building and left the trapped raider suspended by his skull, crying for help until he passed out. It was a quarter of an hour before the ambos turned up and drove him to Royal North Shore Hospital, where he was declared dead on arrival.

The Golden Age of Armed Robbery was over. The risks finally outweighed the rewards.

1

The Sins of the Fathers

In the glory days of armed robbery in Australia, two fit, handsome, jail-hardened outlaws became notorious for their guts and dash—Russell 'Mad Dog' Cox from Queensland and Raymond John Denning from New South Wales. Both men were serial prison escapers. Cox had broken out of Australia's only 'escape-proof' jail, then broken back in to try to free his mates. Denning had taunted Sydney cops while he was on the run, leaving signed handprints on the doors of their HQ, and terrorised prison warders by shooting at them in their own gun tower.

They were both popular men in prison: natural leaders, charismatic, likeable and tough. But each had grown up without a father, in boys' homes where children were battered and tortured and worse. Their dads were hapless, bungling petty crims—a drunken sausage thief and a failed bingo bandit respectively—but Cox and Denning were the real deal, planning heists, storming banks, firing into the air. *Everybody get down and nobody gets hurt.* Guns and gloves and bags full of money. Tearful tellers, confused detectives, speeding getaway cars, hostages and corpses.

Because, yes, both men had blood on their hands.

But we'll get to that. Like we'll get to the banks and the factories and the security vans, and the pistols and the masks and the graves.

First, I want you to imagine a ten-year-old's idea of a hell.

There's a fire burning in a locked building and a woman screaming. You're Ray Denning and the screaming woman is your mother, a human candle, hurtling from room to room, setting the furniture alight. There are the sounds of her fear and the sweet scent of burning fibres—the threads of her clothes, the strands of her hair—and the cooking smell of searing skin. The flesh that bore you, the body that gave you life, is blistering, blackening, boiling. She's the only parent you've truly known and she's killing herself before your horrified eyes.

Now, hold that thought. Let's look at your father. Because he's still alive and he's not even in jail, for once. It's 1961 and he's just got out. And he's no fucking good, Jack the Hat. But you can't be too hard on the old fella because he's your dad—aside from your sister, he's all you've got left—and, after all, he was only eight when his own mother died. Maybe she didn't kill herself because of him, but she died because she couldn't afford another kid, a brother or sister for Jack.

Jack the Hat's mother, Pretoria Denning (nee Ayliffe), died of septicaemia in Sydney in 1934, after what was described in the press as 'a certain event at her home'. Abortion was illegal in Australia in 1934. A wealthy woman—embarrassed or burdened by an unwanted pregnancy—might make a discreet visit to a private gynaecologist who could perform a dilation and curettage, as if to ease a heavy period. A poor girl who couldn't house or feed a baby would visit a local backyard abortionist—he might be an unregistered doctor, or an enterprising butcher—who would show her to his kitchen table and lie her down with a rag in her mouth to stifle her screams. And he might rupture her uterus. And she might contract septicaemia and die.

Twenty-six-year-old Pretoria already had four children with her husband, Stanley George Denning, an unemployed labourer. Stan put Pretoria's death down to physical weakness caused by poverty. 'I was worried about my wife,' he told the coroner, 'as we could not get enough to eat.

'Neither she nor myself had said we did not want any more children,' he added.

The coroner returned an open verdict.

After Pretoria died, Stan moved across Sydney from Arncliffe to Erskineville, an industrial suburb known for murder. There were 'murders' of the familiar sort in Erskineville in the early 1930s: dressmaker Isabella Foreman and an accomplice were charged with the murder of Dorothy May Thornton, who died 'as the result of an illegal operation'. The police said they had 'used an instrument on the girl for a certain purpose'. Then there was gang trouble: twenty-year-old Erskineville man Reginald Bell got into a fight in a pub in Alexandria, came back to the hotel with a pistol and shot a man dead under the awning. Bell was a married father with a baby. The press called him a 'boy husband'. He was sentenced to death, then his daughter died of pneumonia.

There was a razor murder that sickened Sydney when Catherine Sims had her throat slit in her home by a jealous 'lover' who tried to cut out her heart.

Erskineville was not the kind of place you would choose to raise children unless you couldn't afford to live anywhere else. And Jack was Stan Denning's eldest child, born in 1926. By the time he was fifteen, and the world was wracked by war, Jack had collected convictions for evading a train fare; stealing; breaking and entering; and being an uncontrollable child. Because it was a crime to be an uncontrollable child in Australia in the war years.

According to the *Neglected Children and Juvenile Offenders Act* of 1905, children taken into custody for wandering the streets, sleeping rough or lacking any visible means of support could be found to be uncontrollable, sentenced to a period of probation, committed to an asylum, or sent to an institution. It stood to reason that uncontrollable children had to be disciplined, controlled. So it was a good thing there were places like Gosford Farm Home to teach the motherless children of the hopelessly poor some proper fucking manners.

Gosford Farm Home for Boys was established in 1913 as an industrial school for the reception and treatment of young offenders whose delinquency was 'so persistent, or of such a nature' that only a 'period of detention, with discipline' would 'produce a lasting effect on their characters'. At Gosford, uncontrollable boys would learn to raise crops and work with livestock. They would resume their interrupted education. They would be given moral and religious instruction. They would submit to control, and they would emerge better citizens for it.

The farm home was built on wasteland on an escarpment about five kilometres west of Gosford, with views of the township, Brisbane Water, and over the hills to the ocean. The institution opened with the best of objectives: to offer sympathy as well as discipline, to promote individuality alongside obedience, to listen and encourage while teaching and guiding.

The early good intentions paved a dour, familiar road. The boys lived in dormitories, which were numbered as military companies. They wore naval-style uniforms—a remnant of an older system of juvenile reform, based around training ships. A boy progressed from Number 1 company in Dormitory 1 to Number 4 company in Dormitory 4, acquiring rank and privilege until he reached the heights of chief petty officer.

All the boys had to obey their guards ('officers') unquestioningly. They were not permitted to speak without permission. For the first month, they were not allowed to speak at all. They had one visit a month from their parents—if their parents made the journey. Until at least 1939, the officers punished the boys with wild canings across their bare buttocks until they raised red and blue welts. Bedwetters were forced to carry their sheets out on parade. The names of boys caught masturbating in the dormitory were read out in front of the whole company. Boys were encouraged to settle their differences in the boxing ring, but absconders ('dingoes') and 'sexual offenders' (probably masturbators) were bashed in the 'bag room' by senior boys.

A punishment called 'holystoning' was another leftover from the nautical days. A boy on his hands and knees had to rub a sandstone or pumice back and forward across a timber floor, as if he were dry scrubbing the deck of a ship. At Gosford, the boys holystoned the superintendent's verandah until it shone as if it had been varnished, and until their knees opened up and bled.

In 1934, an inquiry into the NSW *Child Welfare Act* with special reference to state welfare institutions reported that the general atmosphere at Gosford was 'capable of marked improvement' and it was 'not possible definitely to ascertain the results which have been achieved in reformation and character building'. Several officers were sacked and management made attempts to recruit a better class of guard—then, in 1939, the Second World War had broken out, and those who fancied their chances in a real fight left to join the military, along with the heroes who hoped to stop fascism or later to save Australia from the Japanese.

But not every bloke can be a hero, or else they wouldn't be called 'heroes', they'd just be blokes. And the guards at Gosford had their own ranks, their own duties, their own enemies. While other men were waiting for the Imperial Japanese Army in Malaya, the guards at Gosford chased frightened children halfway to Terrigal. *And just you wait until you see what we do when we catch you, son. You'll wish you'd never been born. If you don't already, that is.*

Not every man can save the world, so what the hell? You play the hand you're dealt. And it's not as if life was easy for the men who stayed behind. The staff shortage caused by their comrades marching off to war meant the remaining guards had to work longer hours and were forbidden to take leave. It also meant they still had to make use of the senior boys for a second level of discipline: it was the older lads who first pursued the dingoes.

Before the age of fifteen, Jack the Hat was committed to Gosford Farm Home, but he wasn't going to stay there. It had never been hard to escape from Gosford. Most boys could simply walk out the gate.

One hundred and thirty boys absconded in 1940, and about 30 were still at large the following year. Seventeen boys, aged between fourteen and eighteen, walked out on Saturday, 11 January 1941, a record number for a single day. A superintendent who came later to Gosford claimed, 'The system led to Seniors coercing inmates to abscond and being rewarded by pursuing and capturing the absconders. How ludicrous the position became could be illustrated how, by collaboration, seventeen inmates absconded in a group. They were pursued spontaneously by a number of Seniors whilst another inmate "broadcast the race" from a water tower.'

And maybe that *was* the way it happened. Maybe.

Officers from Gosford tracked down four boys to Strathfield. Two more boys walked out on Thursday, 30 January, by which time twelve of the original seventeen had been found and eleven had been returned to the home. But one of the boys out there—from one escape or another—was Jack Denning. He wasn't yet Jack the Hat, but he was nearly there.

In May 1941, Jack appeared in the Children's Court alongside three sixteen-year-olds—Sidney Bloomfield, Patrick O'Mullane and Joseph Griffin—charged with entering a house and stealing a cash box, stamps, money and a rifle. Bloomfield was another escapee from Gosford, described as 'an inveterate car and cycle thief'. Even the authorities at Gosford said they could not control him. His mother told the judge her husband was dead and her elder son punished Sidney too strictly, and she vowed to take him out of Sydney if he were given another chance.

Griffin, the court was told, had said he could easily get hold of a revolver and wouldn't hesitate to shoot. His mother promised she could get him a job if the court set him free.

Nobody spoke for Jack Denning, who had lost his mother at eight years old. He offered his own assurance that, if he were sent back to Gosford, he wouldn't abscond again. Unlike his friends, who lived in Glebe, he appeared to have no address.

The boys had pleaded guilty, for all the good it did them.

Since they were all still too young to go to jail, said the judge, all he could do was commit them to an institution for the maximum term of three years. The institutions did not want them because of the trouble they had caused, but they would have to take them.

Conditions at Gosford Farm Home deteriorated during the war. The growing overcrowding became even worse. Kids were sent out to work on nearby farms, or as house-boys for families—including officers' families. They learned their place but they were no longer learning trades. By 1944, the boot-making shop at Gosford had closed, the pigs had worms, the farm machinery was down to a single plough and the boys were wearing rags.

When Jack finished his time at Gosford, he worked as a labourer. By August 1946, he was twenty years old and up before the magistrate at Paddington Court, charged with having an unlicensed loaded pistol and illegally using a car belonging to the Commonwealth Government.

He had been spotted by detectives driving down King Street, Newtown, with another man, in a car with government numberplates. The police chased the car into a lane where the two men jumped out and fled. A CIB detective said Denning had dropped a pair of gloves and a revolver as he ran and, once he'd been placed under arrest, he'd admitted borrowing the gun to hold up the Sydenham Theatre.

Jack swore the police had used the pistol to frame him. 'About a week previous to my arrest, Detective Jack told me that he would plant a gun on me,' he told the court.

The magistrate believed the police, and Jack was sentenced to eighteen months' jail and a £20 fine. 'I have not the slightest doubt you would have shot to kill had you been cornered,' he told Jack, even though Jack had never shot anyone, let alone killed them.

In 1950, Jack the Hat Denning married Patricia Massey in Annandale, when he was 24 and she was seventeen. Their son, Ray, was born in Port Kembla, where the smokestacks of the steelworks scorched the sky, on 8 April 1951. In August, two police cyclists patrolling in Tempe, Sydney, stopped a truck with a defective red light. It turned out to be driven by Jack the Hat. Earlier in the day, a sedan had been reported missing from a street in Camperdown and had later been found stripped of its wheels and radio, which the police found in Jack the Hat's truck. Denning, described variously as a motor driver and a labourer, got three more years in jail on November 7.

So Jack the Hat wasn't around while Ray was growing up with his younger sister, Charmaine. Patricia divorced Jack while he was inside and told the children he was dead. When Jack found out she had left, he wrote and threatened her. Patricia broke off contact and moved in with a drinker who beat her and had two sons of his own.

Jack the Hat did his jail time then, in November 1956, he and another labourer, Alfred Ernest Crawley, were charged with armed robbery. They had used an unloaded air pistol to steal the takings of housie games held at the Albert Palais dance hall as the cash was being delivered to the presbytery of the dour St Columba's Church on Elswick Street in Leichhardt.

There were four people accompanying the money to the church. As driver George O'Hare hauled from his car two heavy Gladstone bags holding more than £400, either Jack the Hat or Crawley tried to grab a bag and race away. O'Hare managed to keep a grip on the handle and his assailant kept on running, only to be tackled to the ground by eighteen-year-old Kevin Schneider, whose father, Ronald, was being held at (air-)gunpoint by the second robber.

As his mate rolled around with Kevin Schneider, the (air-)gunman ran to his aid.

'Shoot him!' called out the man on the ground—perhaps unaware that the airgun wasn't loaded.

The first man struggled to his feet and the two would-be robbers made their escape, but Jack the Hat and Crawley were caught by police within days.

The cops claimed they had confessed, which was extremely unlikely since Jack the Hat never pleaded guilty to anything. Both men gave long statements from the dock alleging they had been framed. When Jack the Hat was sentenced to another five years' jail, he yelled, 'This is the greatest miscarriage of justice that's ever been known!' A reporter from *The Sun* newspaper described Denning as 'red-faced and tearful' as he turned to the press box and shouted, 'I appeal to the papers to investigate this case!'

But the evidence at the crime scene was damning. When the two attackers fled, they left behind a gabardine overcoat and . . . a hat.

Jack the Hat led a largely luckless life. Detective Inspector Aarne Tees once told a court that his greatest claim to fame—'which he was very proud of'—was having once been arrested by Ray 'Gunner' Kelly, also known as 'Verbal Kelly', one of the best-known, toughest and most corrupt detectives of his era.

—

Ray Denning's aunty, Faye Kerk, said Ray was a 'normal little robust boy, getting into trouble and doing all the normal things that other little boys do. And he was very loving towards his sister and very loving towards his mother, had a good relationship with his father at that time.' As a young kid, he used to box with his dad.

While Jack the Hat was in and out of prison—but generally in—Ray, Charmaine and their mum moved short distances and got nowhere before they ended up with the kids' grandparents in Wollongong. Ray didn't go to school much. He often didn't even have the bus fare to get there. Charmaine had only ever seen her dad once, in jail, and she could not remember him.

'It was a very hectic life,' Charmaine later told the ABC. 'We were shifting a lot. We never lived in one permanent place, nothing we could call home, nothing we could call a family. We never stayed put, never made friends. We just had each other. We were quite used to getting dragged up in the middle of the night to say we'll be going to somewhere.

As long as me and Raymond were together, we didn't really care. As long as we had Mum.'

Patricia worked as a barmaid at a Wollongong pub and married a Walter Wright in December 1960. Like Patricia and Jack the Hat, Walter Wright was a drinker. The kids called him 'Mr Wright' and they moved with Mr and Mrs Wright to Fern Street, Windang, where Lake Illawarra meets the Tasman Sea beneath the Windang Bridge. They carted their stuff into a bungalow with a washing line and a genuine posted-and-painted white picket fence. Their new home's rendered walls, red-tiled roof and two long windows staring blankly into the street gave it the look of a cartoon house where a child had forgotten to draw the front door. The only entrance was at the side of the building, opening to the drive. It seemed like a stable place, but Ray and Charmaine knew Mr Wright didn't want them to live with him, because he and Patricia argued over them all the time.

Patricia heard Jack the Hat was about to get out of jail. On the night of 15 April 1961, when Ray was ten and his sister was six, Charmaine put her brother to bed then heard Patricia screaming from the kitchen. She and Ray rushed to help and found her 'totally in flames', with Mr Wright struggling to help. 'She was running through the house, setting the house on fire,' said Charmaine. 'Flames were coming up. Raymond grabbed me, pulled me away from the flames, and we just watched our mother. She ran into a bedroom, over the beds, trying to put herself out, under the bed. She was just a human torch. She was just fully alight. You couldn't see her features or anything. There was just one huge ball of flames. And my stepfather, he was trying to put her out.

But where she was walking and rolling, the house—the flat—come on fire.

'We always locked the doors and we only had the one way out,' said Charmaine. 'And Raymond was standing on a chair, trying to find the key. Of course, Walter was saying, "Find the key! Get out! Get out! Get out!" But I was just paralysed. I couldn't stop watching Mum. But Raymond seemed to be calm and he kept grabbing me away from the fire and saying, "Don't go near the fire. Don't get burnt."'

Ray once told the story to a court-appointed psychiatrist, who noted: 'The neighbours broke in to the house, which she had locked, and she was taken to hospital where she died.' As for Ray, 'He did not cry.'

—

The attempted theft of two bags of bingo money with a child's weapon was the peak of Jack the Hat's unsuccessful criminal career, but Jack the Hat was an Australian John Gotti compared with Conrad Colin Paul Schnitzerling, the father of Russell Cox.

In contrast with Jack the Hat, who was born into poverty and misery, 'Con' Schnitzerling was the son of an illustrious Queensland family—but the Schnitzerlings, well known around the western slopes of the Great Dividing Range, had their own shadows in the past. Con's pioneer great-grandfather, Martin Schnitzerling, had emigrated from Germany with his family in the mid-nineteenth century and settled on the Darling Downs. In May 1859, his eldest son—Con's grandfather, Conrad—was sentenced to six months' hard labour for stealing items including a shirt at Warwick, a Queensland town on the Condamine River. In March 1861,

Conrad was given a further two years with hard labour for unlawfully killing and maliciously wounding another man's horses. In 1879, Conrad was summoned to Warwick Police Court by his wife, Christiana, for 'illegal usage'—but neither party turned up, so the case was struck off.

Con's father—we'll call him Conrad II—was born in South Warwick, in a timber-framed brick cottage on Rosenthal Creek, which flows into the Condamine River from the hills that border NSW. Conrad II was a stonemason and his hands helped shape Warwick's most imposing public buildings—the sandstone courthouse and town hall, the Sisters of Mercy's convent and the railway station. Conrad II also quarried the granite from Greymare in the Southern Downs that was used to build the imposing Taxation Office in Brisbane, and ran brickyards then a store in Warwick. His brick dust and kiln smoke was part of the air breathed by the people of Warwick, and Conrad II was a part of the town, the last survivor of the tug-of-war team that had beaten an all-Irish side at the local Hibernian Games in 1893.

Conrad II was a hard worker and a businessman who did not marry until he was 34 years old, when he wed 21-year-old Emily May Hughes in September 1902. Emily May gave birth to Con in May 1917, and the family moved to Brisbane in about 1929, after a dispute over Con's grandfather's will: the Warwick brickworks went to one side of the family, some Brisbane properties to Conrad II.

Conrad II had been too old for the First World War, but Con joined the Australian Army in July 1940. He was 23 years old, working as a labourer and living with his wife in Red Hill. The army medical examiner noted his brown hair and grey eyes, and the tattoos on his upper arms. Conrad signed up as an engineer and became a sapper then a driver with the 1st Field Survey Company, a mapmaking unit. His military career was brief and ended when he was discharged for discreditable conduct in April 1941.

Late one evening in November 1948, Con, now living in the insalubrious Wacol Housing Commission Camp, was driving through Rocklea when his tourer collided with another car. Most of the body of Con's vehicle was torn from its steel framework, and Con was taken to hospital with extensive cuts, concussion and suspected internal injuries. He already had three children—Karl, Russell and Ashley—when his youngest son, Melville Peter was born, tiny and premature, on 15 September 1949. The family gave Melville the nickname 'Timmy' (as in 'Tiny Tim') but he would grow up to rename himself 'Russell Cox'.

Timmy's father was an unstable character and his offences were sometimes strange and rare. In 1950, he received a stolen cheque, which was a common enough crime. But that same year, at the age of 33, he was found guilty of raffling a dozen beer bottles in aid of himself in the saloon bar of a pub opposite Roma Street station. Con offloaded one ticket for a shilling and was fined five pounds with six shillings costs for selling illegal lottery tickets. His lawyer told the Police Court that Con became 'very foolish when he had a few drinks'. Four years later, Con faced the Court of Petty Sessions on a charge of stealing a sausage worth four shillings and sixpence. Con—who, in contrast to Jack the Hat, always pleaded guilty—was sentenced to repay the cost of the sausage along with a fine of one pound, four shillings and sixpence.

—

It took Patricia Denning three days to die. After she passed away, Jack the Hat went to Wollongong Hospital to see Walter Wright, who was also badly burned. Jack the Hat felt guilty, as if what had happened to his ex-wife was his fault. She had burned herself, it seemed, because she knew he was coming out and thought he was coming after her. He had made certain threats.

Ray and Charmaine Denning were separated. Each child went to live with a different aunt. Charmaine stayed in Wollongong with Aunty Faye. Ray moved to Nowra with his Aunty Dot, her sick husband and their three boys. Walter Wright ended up in jail. Jack the Hat tried to get custody of his son—'not my daughter,' he said, 'because I knew she was in good hands'—but the magistrate at Nowra ruled against him.

In Nowra, Ray attended school regularly. He was an average student, swimming in the middle streams at Nowra Public School then at Nowra High. His best subject was maths, but he struggled with English. He couldn't read easily and he never learned to spell. And he didn't get on with his new family.

In a poem he later composed in prison, Ray wrote:

I went to relations
Who took me in as a slave
And would not let me see my mother's grave

When Ray was about twelve years old, he was accused of stealing a small sum from one of his cousins. He ran away, was caught, and spent a week on remand at the dismal shelter attached to Yasmar Children's Court in Haberfield.

He stayed at Yasmar for such a long time, he later claimed, because his relatives were in no hurry to pick him up.

Ray was about thirteen-and-a-half when he got 'the wanders', said Charmaine later. 'He didn't know what to do with himself and he took off. He was by himself, and he's been by himself ever since.'

He hitched a ride from Nowra to Sydney and ended up in Central Station, with a schoolbag full of clothes. He slept two nights at the station, breathing in brake oil, then slept rough in nearby parks, stole food from markets and lived on his wits until he found a job as a bellboy at the Australia Hotel. He met his first real girlfriend, Rosalyn Lawson, at a coffee lounge in Kings Cross. He grew street-wise to survive and moved in with a pair of working girls.

He was a good-looking boy—dark-haired, hard but huggable; puzzled and hurt. He earned a wage in the pharmacy of St Vincent's Hospital but took his fun shoplifting and riding around in other people's cars. He later claimed to have worked in a garage and a factory.

Jack the Hat was not uncaring, he was just useless. When he lost track of his boy, he placed an advertisement in *The Daily Telegraph* asking for information on his whereabouts. An anonymous caller sent him to a billiard hall in George Street, where father was reunited with son. Jack the Hat took Ray back home with him to Earlwood and his second wife. Ray saw a chance: the hint of a hope that there might be a real family for him. He asked Charmaine to come and live with them—brother and sister reunited with their dad—but Charmaine was content with Aunty Faye and she blamed Jack the Hat for the death of her mum. And it didn't work out, anyway. After a few months, Jack the Hat and his wife moved to Armidale and left Ray to 'fend for himself', as Jack put it.

In June 1966, Ray was found guilty of stealing cars and driving without a licence. He was released on probation but, less than two weeks later, he was charged with receiving a stolen watch. Ray was only fifteen but he told the cops he was older, so he served his time on remand at the Central Industrial Prison (CIP) at Long Bay. In November 1966, Ray was up in court for the third time. Once again, he'd been caught taking and driving cars. Jack the Hat turned up at the children's court and advised the magistrate to send Ray to Gosford. Jack the Hat, who knew all about Gosford—the dingoes and the holystones and the bedsheets soaked in piss—thought a bit of time on the mountain might do his son some good.

I mean, look at me. I'm Jack the fucking Hat, aren't I? It never did me any harm.

2

The Sins of the Brothers

Billy Stokes, in his memoir, *Westbrook*, claimed to remember Timmy Schnitzerling's arrival at Westbrook Farm Home for Boys, near Toowoomba, in about 1959. Stokes called Timmy 'Merv' and described him as a very small ten-year-old who had been up before a Warwick magistrate on a charge of stealing a pushbike. According to Stokes, the court heard Timmy was neglected by his mother, 'a young migrant woman from Europe', so the judge sent Timmy to Westbrook. 'Not the slightest notice was taken of her pleas and worried concern as her tiny son was escorted off,' wrote Stokes.

At Westbrook, the authorities hardly had the clothes to fit the 'kindergarten kid'. Deputy Superintendent Kolberg dressed Timmy in the home's smallest gear. 'The hat smothered his ears,' wrote Stokes. 'His boots were too large.'

A mate of Stokes's looked at Timmy's hairless body in the shower and made a joke about Timmy dropping the soap.

But he was tougher than he looked, this Merv Schnitzerling. There was something about him.

It is an intensely detailed picture, but not factually accurate.

Schnitzerling was Timmy, not Merv. He was at least fourteen when he arrived in Westbrook, not ten. His most recent theft had been a car, not a bike. And Timmy's mother, Patricia Beryl Pollard—known as Beryl—was born in Bellingen, New South Wales, in 1918, to David William Pollard and Elsie May Graham, who married in Grafton, NSW, in 1913.

Billy Stokes and Timmy Schnitzerling were not even at Westbrook at the same time. Stokes, whose book was published in 2010, was probably drawing on an account written in 1991 by the late Mark 'Chopper' Read, who holds an unusual place in Australian criminal history as perhaps our only confessed multiple murderer who had never been accused—let alone convicted—of multiple murders.

Chopper wrote that he'd known Russell Cox in Pentridge Prison, and the turning point in Timmy's life had come at ten years old, on the day he'd bought the winning raffle ticket for a 'brand new beautiful bike'. Timmy missed the draw and when—'filled with boyish excitement,' according to Chopper—he arrived to collect his prize, he was told the bike had been raffled again and given to somebody else. So Timmy stole a new bike and said it had come from the raffle.

Chopper also wrote Cox had later won—and collected—$15,000 on TattsLotto while on the run from the police.

'I've shot people for less,' wrote Chopper, who hadn't.

Chopper liked to mix and match a couple of vaguely related ideas and use them as the starting points for a long and unlikely story. In this case, one of the facts might have been that Timmy spent some time in a Boys Town home, an institution known for raising funds by selling raffle tickets.

In any event, the extent Cox confided in Chopper is probably shown in the opening lines of Chopper's poem, 'Russell':

There was a wild Australian boy
Russell was his name
He was born in Sydney town
Five miles from Balmain

—

Timmy Schnitzerling was born in Brisbane, about 920 kilometres from Balmain—a Queenslander like his father, his grandfather, his great-grandfather and his great-great grandfather. In 2008, the very fine Queensland journalist Frank Robson spent several weeks trying to track down a member of the Schnitzerling family who could shed some light on Timmy's early years. Robson finally found a mother and son who would only speak to him on condition of anonymity, and—consciously or not—they sold him a whole litter of pups.

They told Robson that Timmy's dad, Con, had joined the army when Timmy was young, when in fact he had been drummed out eight years before Timmy was born. They said he'd reached the rank of sergeant, when he'd never been promoted beyond sapper. They said he'd died of cirrhosis of the liver when Timmy was five years old, but his tombstone says he lived until 1964, when his youngest son had turned fourteen. They said Beryl—they called her Patricia—had died of cancer in about 1970, when she seems to have passed away on 6 December 1979. They said that when Timmy was five he had moved in with his grandparents in Spring Hill, but his grandfather—who had retired to Brisbane 25 years previously—went back to live in Warwick when Timmy was five.

So what do we know about what really happened to little Timmy Schnitzerling?

We know his parents split up in about 1954, though his father didn't die. We know his brother Karl played representative football for Queensland schoolboys in 1952, and his brother Russell became an internationally known sportsman under an assumed surname, appeared in three movies, and never made it public that he was related to Russell 'Mad Dog' Cox. We know Karl began his three months' national-service training at the 11th National Service Training Battalion in Waco in 1957 and we know he was an unemployed shearer who had done a few days' casual work as a member of the Federated Ship Painters and Dockers Union, an uneasy hybrid of trade union and criminal gang. We know Karl had a couple of minor convictions: for stealing and for using obscene language. We know he was court martialled within two weeks of his induction into the military and charged with a cocktail of offences including using offensive language to a superior officer and attempting to escape from military custody. And we know his co-defendant, Private (Recruit Minor) Raymond Patrick O'Connor, went on to become an infamous Sydney gangster, who met his death ten years later in the Latin Quarter nightclub while trying to kill the notorious gang boss Lenny McPherson.

We know Timmy spent time in the care of the Sisters of Mercy at the imposing St Vincent's Home for Children in Nudgee, a Brisbane suburb dominated by a Catholic cemetery and bordered by a seminary, a Catholic junior school and 3500 square metres of church land that was the site of institutions including a convent and the orphanage. We know Timmy felt safe at St Vincent's, and nurtured. We know he wasn't sent there for committing an offence and we know he was not an orphan.

We know Timmy was living at 30 Toxteth Road, Glebe, New South Wales when he first came to the attention of the police in 1958. We know he gave them his name as Timothy Melville Hughes, and that he was nine years old. South Glebe in the 1950s was as rough as wrestling, an address often given by criminals, and Timmy's home was in a big old house with an iron balustrading shielding the balcony like a mouthguard. It sat across from a sandstone Anglican church, in a street where frangipanis bloomed in summer.

We know Timmy appeared in Ashfield Children's Court on three counts of stealing on 12 December 1958 and was given eighteen months' probation.

We know that Timmy's older brother Russell turned up in Sydney's Northern Beaches, announcing that he'd come to surf. We know that he, like Timmy, had taken the surname Hughes. We know Timmy spent most of his probation committing crimes: he went back to Brisbane and, between March 1959 and November 1960, he appeared five times in the children's court for stealing and destruction of property—and being a neglected and uncontrollable child.

We know that the legal definition of 'uncontrollable' did not apply wholly—or even mainly—to children who were wild, recalcitrant, unmanageable or disobedient. Different states developed their own criteria, but an 'uncontrollable' child in NSW, for example, might be a youth who had no visible means of support and nowhere to live, or who had no food or clothing, or whose parents were drunk or 'insane, unknown, undergoing imprisonment, or not exercising proper care of the child'. It wasn't a crime for a child to be uncontrollable, it was a crime against the child.

We know that uncontrollable Timmy was placed in the care of Queensland Children's Department on 3 February 1961, at the age of eleven, after a further four counts of stealing. We know he was convicted in Brisbane Children's Court on eight more counts of stealing less than three weeks later. We know that after another fourteen counts of stealing, he was put under 'strict security' in the care of the Children's Department. We know he appeared in Brisbane Children's Court for the last time on 6 October 1961. And we know that the next year, as a ward of the state, he was admitted to the newly opened Boys Town in Beaudesert, a dairy, cattle and timber town about 70 kilometres south of Brisbane.

We know a lot about Timmy's time at Boys Town, because the institution published a fundraising newspaper, *Boys Town Calling*, which regularly printed photographs of Timmy Schnitzerling.

Boys Town was built on 40 hectares off the Mount Lindesay Highway on the southern outskirts of Beaudesert, on land that had previously been used as a dairy farm and a horse stud. And if the founders of Gosford Farm Home had glowed with good intentions, then the men behind Boys Town Beaudesert were saints. They even took the names of saints. The Director of Boys Town, Brother Alban, was named for the martyred St Alban, the patron saint of converts. Like the other Brothers at Boys Town, Brother Alban was a member of the Catholic De La Salle order.

Boys Town wanted to be a real town. Its resident boys—'the homeless, neglected, abandoned and wayward'—were called 'citizens'. They lived twelve to a 'cottage' in spacious, modern dormitories. There were no locks or bars, and there was supposed to be no corporal punishment.

The boys received normal schooling, earned decent pocket money, and were taken on regular excursions. For chores, they made the beds, cleaned the kitchen, set up the dining room and swept the dormitories and classrooms.

In its earliest days, Boys Town was visited by the well-known Queensland journalist and former war correspondent, Merv Warren, who wrote that the pupils received 'love and affection' instead of 'buffs and knocks'. A day at Boys Town began with wake-up at 6.45 a.m., then prayers in the chapel at 7.45 a.m. Breakfast was at 8 a.m. Classes began at 8.50 a.m. and ran through until gymnastics at 4.15 p.m., followed by swimming at 4.45 p.m., dinner at 6 p.m., ten minutes of night prayer, half an hour of 'Christian doctrine', then an hour or two for games, TV or homework, before lights-out at 8.30 p.m. or 9.30 p.m. Brother Alban noticed the daily regime of moral and religious instruction eventually cured boys of their fondness for 'low, filthy, gutter language'.

The citizens of Boys Town even had their own elected government, comprising a mayor and four aldermen. The first election, held in May 1962, was a big day for the good people of south-east Queensland. About 2000 supporters turned up to cheer on the poll, which was conducted with the oversight of the Commonwealth Returning Officer. The electorate of 36 included Timmy Schnitzerling, who had recently finished runner-up among the under-13s in the swimming championship.

The winner of the mayoral seat—announced by the Lord Mayor of Brisbane—was an older boy, a burly, handsome athlete named John Wlodarczyk, who was keen on cattle and horses, and posed for photographs with a bull. John was congratulated on his historic victory by Queensland Police Commissioner Frank Bischof.

The first picture of Timmy published in *Boys Town Calling* showed him dressed as an altar boy in alb, amice and cincture. He doesn't look smaller than the other boys, but less placable, less impressed. The caption reads, 'The old saying is that altar-boys grow up to be angels or devils. Ask us for information in ten years time.' And we'll get back to that.

After an intramural swimming championship, the Boys Town champions went into a triangular tournament with Marists Brothers College at Eagle Heights and St Mary's of Beaudesert. Timmy won the B grade 25-yards competition for the under-13s, came second in the under-13s A Grade 50 yards, and second again in the under-13s dives.

The Brothers had a complicated attitude towards the boys. As Brother Anacletus told a visitor, 'If they were good boys, they wouldn't be here.' The Brothers blamed the boys' delinquency largely on feckless parenting and broken homes. However, *Boys Town Calling* regularly ran stories from distinguished local contributors, including a piece by Judge DG Andrews of Queensland District Court, who pointed out a truth that the Brothers preferred to ignore. 'No doubt,' wrote Andrews, 'there is domestic unhappiness in many homes of financially secure people in say Ascot, Hamilton,

Clayfield and St Lucia'—all middle-class suburbs—'but the fact is that almost never does a boy appear before the courts who comes from such areas. There are districts in Brisbane which seem to provide rather more boys in trouble than others . . . They are "poor" areas.'

Towards the end of 1962, the Brothers investigated the idea of allowing the better behaved boys to go home for Christmas. Timmy was one of the lucky ones who earned a break and returned to his family. In the new year, the staff at Boys Town was joined by Brother Raymund, named for the patron saint of children and the wrongly accused.

Brother Raymund had neatly parted black hair and ears like mug handles, and had taught at various primary schools in New South Wales and New Zealand. When the boys came back to Boys Town after Christmas, Brother Raymund had them compose an essay entitled 'How I Spent Christmas Holidays'.

'I went to Midnight Mass with my mother,' wrote Timmy. 'When I arrived home, I opened all my wonderful Christmas presents with which I was pleased. We had a very tasty and appetising Christmas Dinner.'

Even Police Commissioner Bischof wrote an article for *Boys Town Calling*, explaining 'the men who become policemen are those in whom the boy in them is seeking action, but in whom the boy's conscience demands the right action'. As well as a policeman, Bischof was a philosopher. 'When we are accepted and welcomed by others,' he wrote, 'and when each of us knows that what he is doing is right, and that he is doing it in the best manner he can, then, it may be said, he is a man.' As well as a policeman and philosopher, Frank Bischof was probably a paedophile.

Let's get back to things we know: we know Frank Bischof took bribes to protect brothel keepers and abortionists. We know he was named Queensland's first Father of the Year, even though he had no children. We know that he and his wife, Dorothy, operated a 'Saturday morning child clinic' to aid and advise unruly boys and girls. We know that Bischof also kept a lover, Mary Fels, and that two of Fels' sons claimed to have been sexually assaulted by him.

In 1963, a new council was chosen by the citizens of Boys Town. Al Marini replaced John Wlodarczyk as mayor, and Timmy was elected as an alderman. The first council meeting was held on May 28. Brother Alban was on hand to advise on procedure, because the brothers believed in rules and ritual and doing the right thing in the right way. There's a photograph of Timmy sitting beside Brother Alban at the council table. Timmy looks handsome and hesitant. Brother Alban looks bulbous and bald, like a washed potato.

The boys were given an assignment to write about a day they would always remember. 'Joe (16)' wrote about the night he 'borrowed' a car, started it with silver paper from his cigarette packet, and drove it to the edge of a cliff. 'Peter (aged 15)' remembered the time he got into a race meeting at Clifford Park, Toowoomba, and backed a string of winners. The stories were printed in *Boys Town Calling*. Each of the brief essays was appended with a comment from Brother Alban, the washed potato.

It seemed like there weren't many days that stood out in Timmy's life, so Timmy told the story of the night he came home from the cabaret at ten o'clock and his father asked him if he would like to fly in a Tiger Moth, a 1930s biplane, a Second World War heroes' training aircraft. 'The next day we went out to the aerodrome,' wrote Timmy. 'I was given a helmet and goggles to put on. After the plane took off, the pilot asked me if I would like to take the joystick for a while, so I took control of the Tiger Moth.'

But Timmy wasn't fooling Brother Alban. 'After reading this essay,' he wrote, 'I was quite convinced that Tim, aged 13, had never been to a cabaret and had not been up in an aeroplane.'

So fuck you, Timmy Schnitzerling. You're not pulling the wool over anybody's eyes.

His story was headed 'Talker Tim', to show that Timmy was big-noting himself. Talking. Telling stories.

Later that year, Timmy was pictured as one of the stars of the cup-and-pennant-winning athletics team. At the end of 1963, Brothers from the southern states took over the teaching at Beaudesert while the regular staff enjoyed a break in Sydney for their annual retreat. Some chose to 'catch a change of scenery at a popular beach resort'. They returned after Christmas, relaxed but horrified.

Brother Alban was later to address the Beaudesert Apex Club about the appalling lack of morals among teenagers on Australian surf beaches. He said, 'I have seen with my own eyes, young people indulging in sexual activities on these various beaches. Some of them are only of High School age.' Furthermore, he said, drive-in theatres were fine for family entertainment, but teenagers left to their own devices turned them into 'passion pits'. Between 400 and 600 girls at high school in Queensland could not sit for their examinations because they were heavily pregnant. Brother Alban blamed drunkenness, gambling and family separation, and claimed 98 per cent of children appearing before courts were not churchgoers and said that parents should give practical religious education to their children after they had left school. As well as a holy man, an educator and a keen social commentator, Brother Alban was probably a paedophile.

In 2008, Frank Robson spoke about Timmy with Brother Anacletus, born Brian Cunningham. The Brother described Timmy as an ordinary, well-behaved student who was good at woodwork, metalwork and technical drawing, and an active participant in Boys Town's sports program. 'I would have expected looking at the boy that he would have had a better future,' said Brother Anacletus. When Robson suggested Timmy might have been clever, the Brother replied, 'I would have said he was more cunning than clever, in that he didn't strike me as highly intelligent in the sense of having a high IQ.'

In about September 1963, Timmy absconded from Boys Town. According to Brother Anacletus, he stole a car and drove to Sydney. On September 30, Timmy appeared at Ashfield Children's Court on a charge of stealing, for which he was placed on twelve months' probation and returned to Boys Town. Less than two weeks later, he was convicted in Brisbane Police Court on four charges of stealing and three charges of wilful destruction. His mother was ordered to make restitution, and Timmy was sent to Westbrook Farm Home for Boys.

In 2011, the De La Salle Brothers paid a lump sum 'inclusive of costs and disbursements' on 'an ex-gratia basis and without any admission of liability on the part of any party' to a former pupil at Boys Town in the 1960s who said he had been assaulted by Brother Alban. In accepting the money, the man agreed he was not entitled to approach the order for any further financial assistance, including to pay for medical advice or damages, and that he would take no further legal action against the Brothers.

Brother Alban, born John Alphonsus Dwyer, came from a good family. His biological older brother, Louis Victor Dwyer, was the vocations director for the De La Salle order, where he took the name Brother Fintan. According to a man named 'Alan'—who was seven years old when his father died and he was given to the care of the De La Salle Brothers at St Bede's College, Melbourne—on the night he arrived at St Bede's in February 1942 'I burst into tears. Brother Fintan ordered me to stop crying. While I was half undressed, he dragged me to a bathroom, where he clumsily interfered with my genitals, while I cried and struggled ... Finally, giving up on me, he ordered me back to bed, while I was still sobbing. Just then, another Brother came to the bedroom and asked Brother Fintan why I was crying. Fintan replied that I was a naughty boy and had been punished.'

But you can't hold Brother Alban responsible for the sins of Brother Fintan. That wouldn't be just, or fair. I spoke to 'Alan', and he still burns with fury against the De La Salle order. He told me they only ever picked on the most vulnerable boys whose parents didn't visit. He told me the size of the other man's settlement against Brother Alban was not enough to buy a new car.

In August 2017, an 87-year-old man named Francis Brophy (Brother Cormac) was sentenced at Brisbane District Court for crimes committed at Boys Town Beaudesert between 1978 and 1983, long after Timmy had moved on. The court heard how Brother Cormac 'viciously' strapped a boy for smoking, and punched another in the stomach then walked away laughing as he told him, 'You're not as tough as you make out to be.'

After he beat the homeless, neglected, abandoned or wayward boys, Francis Brophy sodomised them. A journalist reported 'tears in the public gallery' when the court heard how one of Brophy's victims froze and suffered 'significant pain' when the Brother pushed his penis into the boy's anus.

At the age of 87, Brother Cormac was found guilty of five offences and sentenced for more than 30 counts of sexual abuse against children. He was judged 'a cowardly, evil paedophile' who had inflicted 'sheer terror' on vulnerable boys.

Brother Cormac was sentenced to eight years in jail, although he would be eligible for parole in two. It might be worth mentioning that on 22 April 1971, Timmy Schnitzerling—by then Russell Cox—was sentenced to two years' hard labour for breaking, entering and stealing.

—

So now is as good a time as any to accept the invitation made under the photograph of Timmy and the other altar boys in 1962 and look at where some of our characters found themselves ten years later. In 1972, Cox was still in jail. But why stop at ten? Let's make it twelve years. On 20 February 1974, the first mayor of Boys Town, John Wlodarczyk, then a Painter and Docker, was found floating in the Brisbane River with a bullet in his head and his throat cut from ear to ear. On July 12, retired police commissioner Frank Bischof was arrested for shoplifting from the Barry and Roberts department store in Queen Street, Brisbane.

How about we make it thirteen years?

On 1 January 1975, Brother Alban was awarded the Order of the British Empire.

Or 55 years.

The Royal Commission into Institutional Responses to Child Sexual Abuse, which reported in December 2017, found 219 claims of historic child abuse levelled against the staff at Boys Town Beaudesert—more than any other Catholic institution.

But that's all to come. After all, it wasn't rapist Brothers or corrupt cops who were punished at Westbrook Farm in 1964. It was the 'uncontrollable' ersatz orphan, Melville Peter 'Timmy' Schnitzerling.

3

The Sins of Roy Golledge

Boys raised in Australia in the 1950s grew up accustomed to violence. Teachers caned them and strapped them. Parents spanked them and slapped them. They had sense knocked into them with uppercuts and rips.

Hundreds of thousands of children lived with fathers who had fought in the world wars, when generations of men had suffered the calculated brutality of basic military training and survived the battlefield with lessons learned on the parade ground, drummed in with a belt, a kick, or a slap around the head.

And what fathers had been given, they would often pass on to their children, in drunken anger that simmered over schooners at the RSL then flared up across the dinner table. And the wife might cop a serve too, if she showed ideas above her station, if she shrewed and bitched and nagged, if she needed to be taught who was boss.

And at some Catholic colleges in particular—but in other independent schools, as well—the teachers punished boys with greater enthusiasm and experience than any sallow unimaginative corporal. So don't go crying to a returned man if you got a clip around the ear after you'd broken into some poor bugger's home and scarpered with his television or the wages he kept coiled up in a cake tin. Weak little hoons could moan all they liked about Gosford, but how was it any different from a big boys' boarding school?

A TV presenter once put this question to former Gosford inmate and armed robber Kevin Storey, who replied, 'Well, I don't think putting a rock pick in your hand and a hammer and gad, and getting out and digging a football oval out of the middle of a mountain is actually what'd happen in a boarding school. Or I don't think carrying a stone outside the governor's office all day would happen in a boarding school. I don't think you'd have to be made to stand up for eight hours a day in the one spot in a boarding school.'

But worse things happened at war, and in 1962 Australia quietly began to provide small-scale assistance to the government of South Vietnam in its battle to quell a Communist-led insurgency. Two years later, the Menzies government announced that every Australian male (with some initial exceptions, such as foreign-born residents) was obliged to register for national service in the year he turned twenty. 'Marbles' marked with birthdates were poured into a TattsLotto barrel, then a fluctuating number were plucked out by an official in the company of some mundane patriotic dignitary. Owners of the winning birthdates were then liable for two years' service in the Australian Army. If they got through the medical and psychiatric tests, and the criminal and security checks, they could be sent to a recruit training battalion at Puckapunyal, Kapooka or, later, Singleton, then on to a regular army unit for further instruction. Upon completion of their training, they had about a one-in-four chance of being sent to Vietnam.

And so, once again, masses of young men were marching across drill squares, short-haired and clean-shaven, high-spirited and cowed, ready to be broken down as individuals and rebuilt as soldiers. In the barracks, the better recruits learned to bash the bludgers and ratbags into line—drag them into the showers, tear down their pants and blacken their balls with boot polish.

And those poor buggers had committed no crime at all. The first national serviceman killed in Vietnam, Errol Noack, was accidentally shot dead by his own side on 26 May 1966. Eleven young conscripts were cut down by the Vietcong at the Battle of Long Tan on August 18. So if you were whining about an icy winter in Gosford, how would you like to spend a sweltering summer in the jungles around Nui Dat, eh, boy?

Life wasn't meant to be easy.

Although it was easier for some than others.

In Australia in the early 1960s, authority was respected. Abuse was invisible. Mores and expectations were different. So it was important that the Commission of Inquiry into Abuse of Children in Queensland Institutions reported in 1999 that the 'gross excesses in physical abuse' at Westbrook Farm Home for Boys were 'beyond any acceptable boundary in any period'.

When little Timmy Schnitzerling arrived at Westbrook, the facility was the most feared in the state's alarming system of juvenile care. If kids in other institutions played up, they might be pulled back in line by the threat of being sent to Westbrook.

It was just a dairy farm in the granite belt, a compound of low white-skinned buildings—part barracks, part homestead, part training school. Boys could grow their own vegetables in small private plots and acquire agricultural skills that might have been useful to them in days gone by, had they been farmers' sons and not the children of desperately drinking factory workers in the industrial suburbs of Brisbane. But farm labour—like military training—was thought of as a medicine in itself. At Westbrook, boys had the best of both worlds. They rose with the sun to begin an honest day of hard work interspersed with tough, repetitive military drills. Sure, they were prohibited from wearing underwear at any time, beaten for the sexual satisfaction of the administration and perhaps buggered by the same older, bigger boys—'sergeants' at Westbrook—who would chase them down as dingoes and drag them back to face their punishment if they tried to escape. But at least they learned how to march around and milk cows.

Westbrook's very worst days were over by the time Timmy turned up to get what was coming to him. The villainously cruel Superintendent Ray Golledge had moved on in 1961, after a tribunal that became known as the Schwarten Inquiry had found that boys at Westbrook had recently earned slices of the cane across their bare buttocks for reading in bed, dropping marbles on the floor, making a *pop* noise with the tongue, eating carrots, talking in the bathroom, taking a piece of bread out of the dining room, making faces and causing laughter, and not playing football.

The boy punished for not playing football was a seventeen-year-old with the IQ of an eight-year-old, who had been transferred to Westbrook from an orphanage. He was born with two deformed feet. On his way back from the football field, he said, Golledge beat him with a pipe or a hose for not keeping up with the other boys. 'I think I tripped over something and he started hitting into me,' he said. 'He kept hitting me across the neck with a hunk of hose and then I pulled myself up. It was a fairly hard hit. It made all my neck swell up.'

Golledge offered a milder account of the incident, in which he only hit the disabled boy on the buttocks with a piece of hose then caned him on the buttocks in his office. Commissioner Schwarten found the boy's evidence more credible than the superintendent's, even though Schwarten had been careful to note that the inmates were 'not such whom a court would give unhesitating credence' since most 'had one or more criminal convictions'. Westbrook provided a perfect playground for a man of Golledge's inclinations, because who could believe his victims when many of them were only in his care because they had proven to be dishonest?

—

The Schwarten Inquiry found clues to Golledge's character in an entry he made in the Westbrook punishment book where he described confronting a boy about tearing his own clothes. The boy 'got impudent' when accused and 'I smacked him across the ears,' wrote Golledge. 'I then said, "Put your trousers down. I will not take cheek from you." He refused. I slapped across the lower part of his back with a belt—1 stroke. He got impudent again, and I saw he was out to defy me, when I again put him on the floor and showed him he was not going to defy me, something which I will not take from any of them. His trousers were taken down and I gave him six across the seat.' Golledge told *The Courier-Mail*, 'If a boy gives trouble I make him drop his trousers and I give him the strap until he submits.'

No matter how many times Schwarten heard the words 'buttocks' and 'flogging', and irrespective of the number of stories he was told about domination and submission, he had a less sophisticated understanding of Golledge than the dimmest Westbrook boy. Schwarten wrote, 'I do not for one moment believe that the custodial staff were the "sadists" that some of the inmates termed them, with no understanding of what that word really meant.'

But the boys knew exactly what sadists were. It was Schwarten who couldn't recognise the laughing spectre standing naked before him—the same Schwarten who was disturbed by 'homosexuality practices' at Westbrook. 'These practices may be difficult to detect,' he wrote, 'but I suggest that the warders pay more attention to the bath-house on Saturdays and Sundays.' A former inmate later described Golledge as 'a voyeur inevitably present in the bathhouse'.

Westbrook changed with the departure of Golledge, but the same staff stayed on under the new boss. Guards who had enjoyed working under Golledge still exercised physically an authority they had lost morally long ago. The system of corporal punishment was officially reformed, but fists and straps were still said to be used against boys when no witnesses were around. Warders made unwilling inmates lace up boxing gloves and 'fight', as a punishment for the weaker lad and theatre for themselves. Disobedient boys were drilled until they were ready to drop. Dingoes were beaten and kicked. Rape remained an entertainment for the stronger senior boys. The actions of certain warders continued in the style of Golledge. One former inmate told a 1999 inquiry, 'They used to make you climb this tree back to front in the raw ... and when you were up there they used to feel your bum. Everything they made you do they'd make you strip.'

These were the people in whose care Timmy Schnitzerling found himself, after the kindness of the nuns of Nudgee and the suspect ministrations of the Brothers of Boys Town. Westbrook was run on violence, and prolonged exposure to violence offers lessons a boy can take away for the rest of his life. It trains you to be circumspect, to keep your intentions hidden. It teaches you to duck and roll and bob, but also to feint before you throw. Any fighter is a liar. A great fighter is a charmer who uses his wiles to lull his opponent into dropping his guard, then steams in and knocks his fucking head off.

Al 'Crow' Fletcher, a Westbrook inmate in the Golledge days, said, 'You came out of there very sick ... You then became two people.'

The man who became Russell Cox never spoke publicly about what happened to him in Beaudesert or at Westbrook, although dark hints occasionally dripped from the lips of his lawyers. And when Cox escaped prison, the *Police Gazette* described him as bearing a 'one-inch scar' inside his left wrist.

That's not the kind of wound you get from fighting.

—

Timmy Schnitzerling was out of Westbrook by 1966, when he copped a three-month jail sentence for stealing a car. His brother, Russell Hughes, was surfing up in Noosa, Queensland, and soon became a faintly mysterious identity around Byron Bay on the north coast of New South Wales. Hughes was a gun boardrider, a spiritual and instinctive soul surfer. In May 1966, he won third place in the Australian Surfboard Championships at Coolangatta, where first place was taken by the great Nat Young, who won the world title in California later that year. Hughes went on to win the Queensland championship in 1967 and finish third in the world in Hawaii in 1968. He was good looking and well liked, a smooth talker who told friends he had grown up in a circus. Hughes worked as a board sander and didn't speak much about what else he did when he was out of the waves, but many people had their suspicions. In later years, Hughes became close friends with the tough Californian Miki Dora, a colourful surfer with no visible means of support.

Even before the first national servicemen had set boot in Vietnam, the nation strode confidently into the 'new decimal era' when the dollar replaced the pound sterling on Monday, 14 February 1966. An announcement was made that all £1, £5 and £10 notes would be withdrawn from circulation as soon as they reached a bank. The day of the changeover was christened 'C-Day'. The Chairman of the Decimal Currency Board appealed for patience and consideration. 'We will be looking for helpful understanding from bank staff, shop assistants and Government employees,' he said. 'And to us, as much as to them, simple courtesy should be the password on C-Day—Courtesy Day.'

Twenty-four-year-old John Killick marked C-Day by driving a newly acquired Holden from Parramatta to Cabramatta. He found a parking space on busy John Street and left the Holden's motor running while he prepared to duck into the ANZ Bank about 30 metres up the road. A concerned passer-by caught up with him, tapped him on the shoulder, and reminded him to turn the engine off when he wasn't in the car. This was a challenge for Killick to manage discreetly, since there were no keys in the ignition as he had started the Holden with rolled-up silver paper.

Killick followed a butcher into the bank. While the teller counted the butcher's takings, Killick—described by witnesses as 'young and well dressed . . . calm and fast talking'—pulled out an automatic pistol and told the teller, 'I'll take that—and the money in the drawer as well.'

Chased by the bank manager and another man, Killick ran across John Street to the stolen Holden. He struggled to restart the car with silver paper while holding his pistol in his gun hand. The two men from the bank climbed into a car behind him and followed him through the streets for about seven kilometres before Killick lost them, abandoned the car and ran through a paddock to Warwick Farm railway station, where he jumped on a train.

Killick, Australia's first decimal currency bandit, didn't get away with much decimal currency. Almost all his haul was in pounds, shillings and pence. 'I thought, *C-Day*, there'd be heaps of money,' Killick told me. 'Well, I was wrong. By the time I got there, everyone had taken money out of the bank.'

Killick was the adopted son of a drunken father and a mother who died when he was seventeen. He was also something of a pioneer of armed hold-ups in Australia. 'Robbing banks in the sixties, the only ones I knew about were Darcy Dugan and Kevin Simmonds,' he said. 'There weren't any other bankrobbers.'

Killick was bodgie handsome, with a leading man's jaw and lightning eyes. He was a singer and a boxer, a deft writer and a compulsive gambler. He had talent to spare, chances to waste, and briefly dreamed of becoming an Australian rock'n'roller like Johnny O'Keefe, but by 1966 he'd already done time in Long Bay, Goulburn and Bathurst jails.

'I didn't like robbing banks,' he told me. 'The trouble is, I always did it when I was desperate. I didn't plan months ahead. I'd get in trouble gambling, or something like that, and rob a bank. I'd worry about it the night before: *This could be it. It could be the end of your life, or you're going to jail for fifteen years.*

'Which is what happened.'

Ray Denning spent the last days of 1966 in Gosford. Authorities of all kinds have always felt that the best way to change an institution that has acquired a bad name is to give it a new name, so in 1946 Gosford Farm Home had become Mount Penang Training School for Boys. It opened up to new ways of thinking, such as the more liberal post-war ideas about child welfare, and boys could only be caned on the hand.

But the inmates were still organised into companies and ordered to drill and march like sailors. At the most junior levels, the youngest and most frightened boys were not allowed to speak from 6 p.m. until lights out at 8.30 p.m., and had to spend their evenings folding their clothes and pressing them with a board. They were still only allowed visitors once a month, and only permitted to write home one (censored) letter per week. Dingoes were still hunted and caught by senior boys, who rode in the officers' cars to track them down.

Denning once said that Mount Penang was the start of his downfall: 'It was one of the worst experiences I have ever had in my life. I was put in a dormitory with 60 other boys and there was no fruit or mirrors or private toilets or no privacy at all. Nothing but hard work and sadistic treatment from the officers. It was the beginning of my career of crime as all we had to talk about was the hate we had for the people who made us suffer in this way and all my mates were only talking about past crimes and the good time they had when they were out. On my release, I found that the only people I knew of my own age were the boys I knew at the home.'

Mount Penang was a trade school for criminals, a thugs' TAFE with a stellar graduate employment rate. Denning later reckoned he had seen three quarters of the 500 boys he'd first met in Gosford in other jails since. But one man's hell is another man's hard work, and a former inmate named Bernard Thomas Matthews thought Mount Penang could've been worse. 'I'm a runner,' he told me, later. 'I didn't think about running away from there, but it was easy to run away from.'

Matthews, whose destiny danced with both Denning and Cox, was a tough kid, part-wharfie, part-Maori. His parents had split up when he was three years old and his mum had taken him from Sydney to grow up in the country, where he ended up in Wagga Wagga then Griffith. They were hard-drinking shearers' towns, but Matthews was built for the life. He learned to box and enjoyed his childhood—except for Friday and Saturday nights, when his mum and stepdad tore into their pay packets at the hotel then ripped into each other when they came home.

Knockabout lads were as ordinary as wool in western New South Wales, but at least one thing made Matthews stand out from the other wiry kids with their closed fists and sun squints: among laconic, unquestioning farmers' boys, Matthews was furiously intelligent and starving for adventure, with grey-blue eyes, the colours of mountains and skies. He started doing break and enters in Wagga, left home at fifteen, came to Sydney, and found a job in an auction house near the city. He and a mate, Gordon Thomas, botched a robbery of their workplace, then tried to burn it down to erase their fingerprints. Matthews was sent to Yasmar, where Thomas later joined him to front court. 'So he come over,' said Matthews, 'we belt the fucking screw and that was my first escape. I go over the back fence and he goes out the front fence. I lasted two weeks or three weeks. He lasted a couple of months.'

They were both picked up and held at the boys' shelter at Albion Street Children's Court in Surry Hills. As escapees, they seemed bound for Tamworth, the toughest juvenile facility in NSW, which rapist and gangster Neddy Smith later described as a 'concentration camp' where young boys were treated like animals and bashed every day.

'I tried to escape from Albion Street and it fell on its arse,' said Matthews, 'so I thought *I'm on an A-class special for Tamworth*. But, by some grace of God, I got myself through the break and I went to Mount Penang.'

Matthews had a 'general committal' of six months to three years, and ended up doing twelve months in 1965, the year before Denning arrived. 'I was digging out the oval, cutting the sandstone rock with edges. You'd come home with fucking blisters all over you. On a Saturday morning, you'd dig up a field—you'd have about a hundred kids in a line, and you'd shovel-bang move on, shovel-bang move on. It was a backbreaking bastard of a job.'

But Matthews knew Tamworth would have been far more terrible so he stuck it out until December, when he was released. He took work in a textile factory and lied about his juvenile criminal record to get into the Citizen Military Forces (CMF), the Australian Army's part-time reserve.

While Matthews settled down after Mount Penang, Denning couldn't stay still. He drifted all the way across the country. In January 1968, he appeared in court in Kadina, on the Yorke Peninsula, South Australia, charged with unlawful possession of a car and was given six weeks' imprisonment in Adelaide Gaol. He next faced court in June, for breaking into a swimming pool in Western Australia, apparently to steal his fare home to New South Wales. He was sent to Longmore Remand and Assessment Centre, a facility for boys and girls which, he later wrote, was the only place where the administrators tried to help the children.

Back in Sydney, Denning was arrested for swearing at police when they tried to eject him from a hotel at closing time. He copped a fine for dangerous driving in September and, two months later, he was arrested for trying to break into a garage in Brisbane. In December, he was caught in Adelaide with 'insufficient means' to support himself and was committed for two years to McNally Training Centre,

Magill. Denning called the place 'McNally Block House' and saw it as 'run on military lines': 'Limited talking. No books. No radio. No rehabilitation whatsoever. Just built to punish.' After eleven months, he was released into the custody of a teacher from McNally. Denning once again returned to Sydney and was once again arrested for swearing at a police officer.

'They put my father in jail for something he didn't do,' he said, 'made my mother commit suicide, so it's understandable I'm thinking they're the bloody enemy. I'd go past coppers directing traffic in the street and even abuse them.'

Meanwhile, Bernie Matthews had kept out of the courts and taken his thrills from his three years' part-time service with the reserve infantry regiment, 4RNSW. Matthews had been promoted to corporal and hoped to carry his military training, and NCO's rank, to the war in Vietnam, but was told he would have to get a discharge, resign and re-enlist as a private in the regular army. 'I'd come to a fork in the road,' he said. 'They wouldn't let me go that way, so I went the other way. I stole a couple of army submachine guns and done an armed robbery.'

4

The Sainthood of Michael Matteson

Like anyone else, when Bernie Matthews wanted money he went to the bank. 'The only difference is,' he told me, 'I employed a gun.' It's a clean line that has been polished over many years, stripped down and reassembled like a rifle in the dark. But it will never reach the notoriety of a statement Matthews made to a journalist in 2004: 'To be quite frank, robbing banks was better than sex.'

After Matthews stole his machine guns, he and a mate from Mount Penang stuck up an all-night garage near Guildford, New South Wales, then the pair took more than $30,000 from the payroll of a factory in Parramatta. That turned out to be the most luck they ever had. On 13 October 1969, Matthews was arrested and sent to Parramatta Gaol, a sandstone-and-slate relic of early Victorian days.

Some parts of jail life were familiar to a young fella who'd already been knocked around by his stepfather and drilled and punished in the Gosford hills. There were the usual puce-cheeked older men, yelling like drunks reeling for a grass fight, trying to force him into line with curses and threats. But Matthews was strong. His body had grown harder and was decorated now with a tattooist's promises: a skull and crossbones, a rose and heart, a swallow and a scroll—love and death.

He quickly began to plan his escape. He swallowed razor blades in the hope he would be transferred to the psychiatric section or a mental hospital, from where he could easily walk free. Instead, he was sent to the maximum-security Observation Centre (OBS) at Long Bay, an unforgiving prison complex that glowered over the waterside suburb of Malabar in south-east Sydney. At the OBS, he was given a windowless cell with a slit for light and attacked by two prison officers who beat him with their batons in a semi-official welcome known as a 'flogging'. They were trying to show him that if he stood up to authority, authority would knock him down. The screws hated a smart-arse, a crim who fought back or an escapee. Unfortunately for Matthews, he was all three.

Matthews was moved to Long Bay Metropolitan Reception Prison (MRP), where he had another crack at escaping and earned another beating and 28 days in solitary confinement. When he was driven to court for his scheduled sentencing on 19 June 1970, he king-hit his police escort, jumped out of the van and ran. He was caught and restrained by uncowed squareheads and eventually sentenced to ten years for the armed robberies with six months tacked on for the escape attempt.

This did not stop Matthews trying to escape.

'I just didn't like jail,' he told me.

Some regional prisons had neither heating nor plumbing. Inmates sweated through summer, froze in winter and slept with their noses to the shit tub. In nineteenth-century buildings they lived nineteenth-century lives, reading by candlelight. They were not permitted to sit down in the yards, where they mustered three times a day, hemmed in by high walls, razor wire and gun towers, fish in a barrel.

Food was poor, medical treatment often awful, and there was little for prisoners to do with their endless spare time. Debased old crims raped younger prisoners for fun. Men who arced up were flogged by warders until they gave in.

Many prisoners—innocent and otherwise—had been jailed largely on the evidence of unsigned confessions or 'verbals': uncreative writing by police officers, featuring stock characters such as the everything-by-the-book detective and the outfoxed, demoralised villain, guilty as sin and willing to admit everything but never to scribble a signature. There was no need for that, he said. It was a fair cop by fair cops. He'd told his story—which was that he'd done the crime for no particular reason with accomplices he couldn't name—and he wasn't going to waste his time sticking his initials on a statement.

If the police felt the verbal might not be enough to secure a conviction, they could load up or 'brick' a suspect with a weapon. Often the crim in the unsigned statement would express surprise—and, yes, admiration—at the thoroughness of the police work that had him snookered. This was only to be expected, as he was generally monosyllabic, stupid and devoid of any insight into—or, indeed, detailed memory of—anything he had done.

If it seemed a jury might be unconvinced by an unsigned statement that the accused person would invariably disavow, a judge might turn to the twelve just citizens in the box and ask who they would more readily believe—a man of bad character such as the defendant, or a respected officer of the law such as Roger Rogerson. Or Detective Inspector Aarne Tees.

So the prisoners had all kinds of grievances, but most inmates were poor men inclined to accept whatever was done to them because, in life, they had come to expect brutal treatment. All but the toughest knew that their best option was to salute the screws, call them 'sir', and make the best of a long lagging with prison homebrew, jailhouse durries and a bet on two cockroaches racing across the cell floor.

In 1970, something changed. *Maximum Security* author James Morton has written, 'Prisoners, who now included a number of Vietnam veterans, were not so keen on simply keeping their heads down and doing their time.' In fact it's unlikely there were any Vietnam veterans in NSW jails by 1970, and certainly there were none in the leadership of the prisoners' movement. But the Vietnam War—or, at least, the protests against it—did play a small part in prison unrest.

In Queensland, where policing was viciously corrupt under childless Father of the Year Frank Bischof and the rotten government of Joh Bjelke-Petersen, street marches were officially prohibited, as if protesters were the real criminals, rather than paedophiles, standover men and crooks. But throughout Australia, individual draft resisters attracted more sympathy than huge throngs of demonstrators, and certainly caused bigger headaches for the government.

One of NSW's more prominent anti-draft activists was the anarchist Michael Matteson, an American citizen who became eligible for the ballot in Australia in 1967 and who hammered out his position on conscription in long debates over spaghetti dinners with his friend and fellow anarchist, Geoff Mullen.

Under the *National Service Act*, men were liable to a two-year prison sentence if they refused to enter the army. Matteson decided to publicly break the law and pay the full penalty, so as to demonstrate the inhumanity of the legislation. But it was quite difficult to get the two years' jail. The first step was to serve 30 days for refusing to register. Matteson, then a student at Sydney University, announced himself as an 'Unconscriptable', and was finally handed his 30-day sentence in 1968. He was sent to Long Bay, where he expected to be raped or bashed and had decided he would protect himself from predators with a brick or bat, but never a knife. However, he was held in the complex's comparatively safe Metropolitan Remand Centre (MRC) and nothing happened to him.

In 1969, a disturbance at Parkhurst Prison in the United Kingdom began with a sit-down protest against beatings and ended with desperate prisoners—led by armed robber 'Mad' Frankie Fraser—fighting a losing battle against a riot squad. This proved to be a pattern for prison uprisings worldwide. In Bathurst, NSW, on Friday, 16 October 1970, a sit-down in the yard led to the wild, unrestrained bashing of almost every prisoner in the jail. When the prisoners' grievances were reported in the press, they were trivialised and condensed into a list of comical 'demands' for 'better food, more modern haircuts, longer radio listening time in their cells, better seats in the exercise yards and a better medical service'.

There was trouble at Goulburn, too. And, after a sit-down strike at Long Bay on October 16, when a Corrective Services riot squad gathered at the jail, prisoners barricaded themselves in C Block and tore the wing apart. They were persuaded to go back to the cells with the promise of no reprisals, then forced to run a gauntlet of warders who beat them bloody with metre-long rubber truncheons.

Michael Matteson was admitted to Long Bay the day after the riot, to serve another seven-day sentence for refusing to submit to an army medical. Matteson had missed the action, but he heard about it from another prisoner. When Matteson got out, he passed on a written statement to the state Labor politician George Petersen, retelling prisoners' stories of the mass bashing.

'The prison square was covered in unconscious bodies, blood, shoes and pieces of clothing,' he wrote. 'Many remand (unconvicted) prisoners had long hair and were dragged by the hair into the cells.' He described six broken noses, six broken legs, a broken kneecap, a broken collarbone, an injured back and one prisoner who had been 'virtually scalped'.

While the draft evaders were reviled as traitors and cowards in parts of Australian society, they were not generally considered criminally dishonest. Matteson's word was not worthless, like a crim's. On the other hand, he hadn't seen the gauntlet with his own eyes.

NSW Minister for Justice John Maddison dismissed Matteson's allegations as 'wicked and untrue' and designed to stimulate disorder and undermine the authority of the prison service. Only three prisoners had been treated in hospital, Maddison claimed, although he conceded one had stitches in his head and another had damaged his back. He later stated 70 prisoners had been treated, then modified the number to 20. He and the Robert Askin government angrily rebuffed calls for a public inquiry, but the truth about prisons was becoming clearer to any squarehead who cared—which was almost none, because if you can't do the time then don't do the crime, mate.

Matteson felt he wasn't hurting enough. He needed to suffer the full two years, in the terrible conditions experienced by ordinary criminals, to expose national service as modern-day slavery enforced by arbitrary and brutal imprisonment. He decided to go underground, with the goal of being chased and eventually getting caught and made to serve his time.

It was quite a complicated idea. Five decades on, he told me he had come to realise that the people who had sheltered draft resisters like him didn't really understand what they were doing—'because they think they were successfully keeping us out of jail: the goal was to get in jail'.

—

While Matteson was trying to get into jail, Bernie Matthews was still diligently attempting to escape. He eventually broke out of the Bay on 7 November 1970, hidden in a trolley load of pig slops. That night, a woman was snatched from the streets of Kings Cross, repeatedly raped and abandoned in Yagoona near Bankstown. A tabloid newspaper pinned the crime on Matthews. NSW Police Commissioner Norm Allan, who was later exposed as quite startlingly corrupt, described Matthews as 'very dangerous' and warned that the police were 'apprehensive for women, particularly young women' in the area Matthews was last seen.

Afraid that he was being set up as a monster to be shot by police, Matthews wrote to the press and a radio station denying the rape. His letters showed uncommon media nous and set an early example of how an escapee might try to get journalists onside. The real rapist—who turned out to be a parolee—was soon captured. As the heat on Matthews started to die down, he returned to robbing banks.

'Back then, I was working one-out,' he told me. 'Your weapons ranged from cut-down .22s to cut-down shotguns to Glocks. I used to look for banks on a main road. There's going to be very few people walking past—they're all driving past. So they're not going to be paying too much attention to a bank on a main drag.

'I used a street directory to find out where the nearest police station was and work out which route they were going to come, because they were going to come by a main road. So if you rob a bank on a highway or a main road, you just hit the backstreets when you're leaving. You don't even cross the cops. You're going the other way while they're still coming to the bank.

'I had a bit of army training, so you take the highest ground, which was the counter. So I'd jump on the counter, where you've got complete control over everybody on both sides of the counter. You force everyone onto the floor. Once they're on the floor, you get the bag, or the teller, you make him fill the bag, you close the bag and you go.'

Matthews loved robbing banks. 'The adrenalin was pumping,' he said. 'But there's collateral damage—that's called jail.'

John Killick felt differently. 'There was a high when you got away with it,' he told me, 'but this bullshit, to me, about going into a heist and you're on a fucking high . . . It's not a high to me. It's watching every second, knowing it could be your last. Somebody could walk up behind you and fucking kill you, and they'd get away with it.'

Matthews was recaptured on 18 December 1970 and sent to Parramatta. Matteson stayed on the run for fifteen months, but the only time the media was interested in his case was when he had a narrow escape, so he had to continually set up situations from which he could narrowly escape.

Meanwhile, his mate Geoff Mullen went to jail. From his cell, Mullen wrote a letter warning that Matteson would not be in physical danger when he finally got to serve his sentence: 'He will be protected most of all by the hypocrisy of his own captors,' predicted Mullen. 'To be sure, they will not recognise his dignity as a human being, nor will his principles be of any particular consequence. In their world of realpolitik, the essential consideration is to what degree his maltreatment would be a political liability.'

—

It was proving extremely difficult for draft-resisting butterflies to have themselves broken on the wheel of the inhuman machinery of the state. The government had never expected them and still had no idea what to do with them. They had successfully made a mockery of the law, and resisters and the authorities were now locked in a chess game that each was doing their best to lose.

In October 1971, Matteson and three other draft resisters set up a 'headquarters' in the University of Melbourne

Union building. More than 100 police smashed their way in and caused $6000 in damage to furniture and radio equipment, but the draft resisters escaped. Matteson, apparently, hid behind a false wall. In November, he made a live TV appearance on the ABC current affairs show *This Day Tonight*. The Attorney-General, who was interviewed in a different studio for the same show, suggested the producers should do their public duty and aid Commonwealth Police by detaining the fugitive, which they didn't.

In March 1972, Matteson addressed an anti-conscription forum from a roof of Sydney University. Meanwhile, Australia withdrew its last infantry troops from Vietnam. It was becoming a bit late for Matteson to make his last stand.

The draft resisters' underground was only loosely organised in NSW. At first, Matteson stayed with friends, who would contact a sympathetic friend from a non-overlapping friendship circle. 'And you wouldn't stay with that link person,' said Matteson. 'You'd jump from this circle to that circle.'

He would wake up at about 4.30 a.m. because he knew the police would most likely come for him in the pre-dawn light. He only gave interviews after he had pulled off a stunt, and then he might be in six or seven houses over the next 24 hours. He'd speak to a journalist over the phone and give the impression he was staying at a certain place, then leave immediately. Most of the time, the only people who knew his whereabouts were one family member or the driver who was to take him to the next safe house. He tended to stay in the city. 'Generally speaking, the country was a good thing to avoid,' he said. 'Everybody knows when anything is different.'

In the most spectacular triumph of his freedom, Matteson was arrested and handcuffed by Commonwealth Police on the grounds of Sydney University, only to be freed by a large crowd of students and a pair of boltcutters that some claim were operated by an official of the Builders Labourers' Federation (BLF), a trade union of which Matteson was a member.

Matteson hurried from the university to the home of Irina Dunn, a young anti-war campaigner who lived in Derwent Street, Glebe. 'I hid him for quite a while,' Dunn told me, 'and then I organised for him to go to various friends' places. We had an escape route for Mike through the shower and through a little window where you could hop out onto the roof, but it never came to that.'

In her time with Matteson in the house, she said: 'I learned everything I didn't want to know about the anarchist movement—about Bukharin and all the great anarchist leaders—and, I hate to say this about Mike, but he couldn't even make a piece of toast. So he was good on the politics, but really bad at looking after himself.

'And, of course, Mike did so look like Jesus Christ. And he dressed like Che Guevara. He had tight blue jeans, a tight black shirt, and he wore red mid-calf boots and he had long, glossy black hair, a long, droopy moustache and a beard, and the most sorrowful eyes you ever looked into. When he was telling you about Kropotkin.'

Matteson was finally—and quite deliberately, on his part—apprehended at a barbecue at his family's place in Enmore. He was only sentenced to eighteen months' imprisonment, since the period of national service had recently been reduced to eighteen months. He was jailed on November 10 but released on December 7 in one of the first acts of Gough Whitlam's incoming Labor government, which immediately abolished conscription.

Many steps in Matteson's strange and provocative journey through life in the underground were to be echoed by Ray Denning less than a decade later. It was a draft resister who set the terms for the armed robbers. Immediately upon his release, Matteson announced his next cause was prison reform. 'Jails like Grafton are nothing more than torture chambers,' he said.

Matteson was a rigorous intellectual, meticulous in his choice of words. And Grafton was the jail where Bernie Matthews had found himself in December 1971.

5

The Sin of Bonnie and Clyde

Like jumpsuits and flares, hotpants and big sunglasses, institutional corruption and spray-can radicalism, the armed hold-up trade flourished in Australia in the 1970s. To a soundtrack of AC/DC, Cold Chisel and Rose Tattoo, bank robbery, in particular, grew from a lucrative niche for a handful of desperate pioneers to a practical alternative to safe-breaking for professional criminals on the lookout for a regular earn.

In the 1960s, safe-breakers had been among the most respected men in the criminal milieu, as their calling required a steady hand, a cool head, and a bit more intelligence and dash than the average street thug. But the penalties were heavy and, in New South Wales, two cops—detectives Fred Krahe and Ray 'Gunner' Kelly—started to shoot at tank men. Knockabouts didn't have much to lose by turning to armed robbery. The rewards were often richer and the job demanded no technical skills.

Detective Inspector Paul Delianis, officer-in-charge of the Victorian Armed Robbery Squad, cited statistics to claim a 1000 per cent increase in 'major' armed robberies between 1965 and 1977. 'No one is immune,' he told a seminar in Canberra. 'We see bank officers gunned down; bank customers taken hostage and terrorised. We see chemists slashed by drug-crazed individuals, both male and female. We see taxi drivers robbed and then left to die. We see shopkeepers gunned down as they deliver their takings to the bank.'

He ended a conference address with a long list of 'causes' for the rise in armed robberies. Some of them were ludicrous, such as 'the greater emphasis on civil rights' and 'the overemphasis on rehabilitation as opposed to punishment' (which, as we have seen, was hardly the dominant idea in Australian prisons in the mid-1970s). Others were simply self-serving, such as 'the lack of police powers to effectively control the criminal element'. However, Delianis also hit on a couple of the real reasons behind the upsurge: the growth in drug use, and the availability of robbable cash.

Throughout Australia, there was a growing number of bank branches, handling an increasing amount of money—which was often in motion between one place and another, such as a night safe and a wallet. Banks were easy to reconnoitre—anyone posing as a customer could case a main-street branch, identify the risks, pinpoint the busy periods and form a plan. And an armed robber—unlike, for example, a drug dealer—needed no criminal connections, just a weapon, or the suggestion of a weapon, or something that looked like a weapon. An efficient operator could be in and out of a bank within 30 seconds. Even if they chose not to wear a disguise, there was little risk of identification, since 100 per cent of bank staff and customers would be looking at the gun barrel, not the gunman.

In the days before CCTV cameras, it was difficult for the police to gather evidence against an armed robber, since bandits tended to have no connection with the premises and leave nothing behind. And it wasn't just the banks. Commercial life in Australia was changing. There was more cash-handling after dark as service stations and pharmacists stayed open later into the night, offering isolated, undefended targets. As other entrepreneurial criminals noticed the hold-up men were not getting caught, they figured they might chance their hands too. And at the movies they'd seen *Butch Cassidy and the Sundance Kid* and *Bonnie and Clyde*, and in the dark they weren't Melville Peter Schnitzerling and Raymond John Denning, they were Robert Redford, Paul Newman and Warren Beatty, screeching off in a getaway car with Faye Dunaway. Okay, so they were torn apart by a storm of bullets in the final scene, but it had been worth it for the ride.

However, in Australia like everywhere else, there was a desperate shortage of Bonnies and an oversupply of Clydes.

The rise of the specialist armed robbers led to the formation of the specialised police armed robbery squads, which tended to recruit cops who were very smart, cops who were unflinchingly tough, cops who were wildly brave, cops who were dazzlingly corrupt, and a few, such as Roger Rogerson of the NSW Armed Hold-Up Squad, who were all of these things and more.

—

Not many 'professional' offenders began their criminal careers as armed robbers, although a career path was quickly established. They began by stealing bicycles, before they moved on to cars. They were then incarcerated in boys' homes, where they toughened up, built wide-ranging contacts, formed the cores of gangs and learned criminal ways. If their enthusiasm for the life did not die out in their early twenties, leaving them to shrink into mental illness or settle down behind a stubbie—the stocky, damp-eyed fella who hears an insult in every joke and takes a bottle into a blue—they might well pick up a gun and have a go at making more money in one minute than their fathers had scraped together in all their miserable, drunken, non-working lives.

Both Ray Denning and Russell Cox turned to armed robbery on the cusp of the 1970s. Denning came out of McNally with a new mate—Roy Anthony Pollitt, later known as 'the Red Rat'. Pollitt had ginger hair, but he wasn't a rat. He never talked to police. They called him 'rat' because he had a rat in his head. You only had to look into his eyes to see it tearing around its wheel, driving Pollitt crazy. Denning's association with Pollitt was to colour his whole life—but not yet. Not quite yet.

Denning was caught trying to break into a railway canteen in February 1970 and was given a five-year good-behaviour bond. A few months later, he was fined for possession of an unlicensed pistol. He was living near Central Station at the Sydney People's Palace, a large private hotel run by the Salvation Army. He went back to South Australia—even though things never did go well for him there—where he stole a car and paid a motel bill with a stolen cheque.

He earned three months at Yatala Labour Prison, overlooking Dry Creek in Northfield, where he was reunited with Pollitt.

In September 1971, two men wearing beanies held up the Narwee branch of the Bank of NSW in southern Sydney. One of the beanie bandits was armed with a submachine gun, believed to have been a Second World War model stolen from the Lancer Barracks Museum in Parramatta earlier in the week. The record is murky, but the boys under the beanies were probably Denning and Pollitt.

Ray worked with Jack the Hat for three months, digging for antimony at the Hillgrove mine near Armidale, NSW. Denning later wrote that he pulled off a few successful armed robberies then bought a sandwich bar in Botany. He liked the business because he was his own boss, but soon grew bored and returned to life by the gun.

Maybe.

But perhaps the takeaway was just a mundane fantasy of suburban life, with white sliced bread and fat tubs of marge. It wasn't mentioned in all the various statements he made over the years, reassembling his chaotic life into an acceptable order for a judge.

On Monday, 13 March 1972, Denning walked into the ANZ Bank in Flora Street, Sutherland, NSW, carrying a pistol in his hand. He grabbed a 26-year-old woman by her throat and announced, 'This is a hold-up!' He slammed a plastic bag on the counter and ordered a teller to 'fill it up or the woman gets it'. (This wasn't a police verbal cartoon-crim-playing-pantomime-villain; these were the words of witnesses). He then snatched a canvas bag full of money from customer John Daley, the licensee of the nearby

Como Hotel, ran out to his car and drove away. Denning got about $600 from the bank and $1400 from the publican and he used some of the money to bail out Pollitt, who had been arrested on another matter.

Denning later made his way to Western Australia, then hired a car to drive from Perth to Cloncurry, Queensland. He was arrested for not returning the car and allegedly assaulting police, and did a week in the cells at Mount Isa. Back in NSW on August 23, Denning was arrested in Campsie with Pollitt, and brought to court in March 1973 when he was sentenced to thirteen-and-a-half years for armed robbery.

Denning and Pollitt were apprehended by members of the Sydney Armed Hold-Up Squad, including Detective Sergeant Aarne Tees, a clever man who could be difficult to like. It wasn't always easy for Tees to be the smartest guy in a room full of cops, when the room squeezed its knuckles at the thought of bashing smarties. But the handsome, imposing Tees did himself few favours. They said he used to argue with his own reflection if he couldn't find anyone else to quarrel with. But maybe he just enjoyed looking in the mirror.

Tees later described Denning at the time of the arrest as 'semi-literate'.

'He was able to sign his name,' said Tees, 'but had difficulty in reading and practically no idea of spelling.'

If it could sometimes be difficult to figure out exactly what happened to Denning in the early 1970s, it was harder still to say anything definite about Cox. Many people who would talk about Cox didn't know what he had done, and many people who knew wouldn't talk about him. The ordinarily garrulous Bernie Matthews had nothing to say. There were court records and rumours, but few traces. In Queensland, Cox was close to a number of members of the Federated Ship Painters and Dockers Union. His brother Karl had worked with the Painters and Dockers; Cox knew John Wlodarczyk, a prominent Queensland Painter and Docker, from Boys Town; if he hadn't actually met Painter and Docker Billy Stokes at Westbrook, they both moved within the tight circle of tough men who did some of the hardest, dirtiest work on the Brisbane wharves, hidden in the hulls of ships, crawling through the bowels, cleaning out the bulges, hacking at the hulls—and sometimes fighting and stealing and settling their differences with knives and guns.

But Cox didn't stay in Queensland. In 1966, he was given three months in prison for offences related to a stolen car in Seymour, Victoria. It is thought that he then went to sea for two years as a merchant sailor. He was in Parramatta Gaol in 1969 and lived in NSW when he got out. In 1971, he was sentenced to two years for breaking and entering a house. He faced other charges for possession of a firearm and possession of housebreaking implements and had already begun to serve a sentence at Long Bay when he received another year, then two further years for breaking and entering a store. He was released in 1973.

Cox spent time around Balmain—not far from Glebe, where he had lived as a child—a dockside suburb with traditions of both organised labour and organised crime. Balmain was the birthplace of the Painters and Dockers and the practices that made the unskilled union powerful—including the insistence that employers hire casual workers from the union's own roster—grew up in the shipyards and drydocks of NSW.

In Balmain, Cox was again close to the Painters and Dockers. It's thought he worked with John Robert Dunks and his brother, both well-known local criminals. Cox seems to have done alright, although he was under pressure to look after corrupt cops: they wanted him to cough up 'rent'—that is, weekly payments.

Cox moved in with a knockabout Balmain 'earner', the ex-wife of a former official of the Federated Ironworkers Association (a union that competed for members with the Painters and Dockers). Her son by her first husband grew up to be a viciously incompetent crim. But she had a daughter, too, by the outlaw who had begun to call himself Russell John Cox and who came to refer to his child's mother as his wife. Cox was a striking man—with high cheekbones, a wide mouth and a solid jaw. He looked like a rodeo cowboy, strong, slim and silent, with ropes of muscle for riding bulls.

But in the years to come, he could look like anyone at all.

—

Cox also spent time in Victoria and had close ties with the dockies there. His first armed robbery crew, which operated out of the eastern suburbs of Sydney, included Peter Arthur Croft, a Melbourne Painter and Docker who had been shot during the long-running war for control of the union. 'I knew Peter a long time before I knew Russell,' Garry 'the Hand of Death' Page told me. 'Russell was a new kid on the scene. I was a petty criminal, living in the Ellis Motel in Bondi. I moved all the time. I was a shoplifter and robbing poker machines—being a thief, you've got to keep mobile.'

Croft and Cox ran with Greg Workman. In Cox's crew, said Page, 'Croft was number one, Workman was number two, Russell was number three.' Page knew a knockabout named Ronnie, who would go down the wharves and meet the ships. 'Any Yanks, you could buy a gun off them for $50,' said Page, 'and Ronnie was happy to sell them for $150. He told me he had six guns for sale, so I went to see Peter Croft. I said, "I can get you six guns."

'Russell had a hotted-up Torana,' said Page. 'It was brown with a white roof—Jesus, it could fly—and we went to Ronnie's place in Rose Bay. Russell didn't come in: he gave me $1500 and said, "Keep the change." Which meant it was a $600 earn for me. So I came back out with the guns, he threw them in the back seat, and he started speeding down to Double Bay. I said, "Russell, if the police pull us over for speeding, we've got the guns." He said, "Well, that's good. We'll find out whether they work or not."'

This seemed like a dangerous idea to Page.

'As soon as he had to stop, I jumped out of the car,' said Page. 'I said, "Thanks for the six hundred, mate. Enjoy the guns."'

At about 8.20 a.m. on Friday, 7 June 1974, an armoured van delivered two metal boxes containing $53,000 in cash to pay a thousand factory workers at Pye Industries in Marrickville. Ten minutes later, three men carrying automatic pistols burst into the pay office, ordered a dozen clerks into a corner and threatened to shoot them if they moved. The bandits picked up the cash tins and ran.

Cox was not yet experienced enough to know who to trust (that is, no one). He, Croft and Workman were arrested on July 24 by Detective Roger Caleb Rogerson of the Armed Hold-Up Squad who was working on a tip-off by an informer.

Now, *Roger* isn't much of a name for a hard man. *Roger Rogerson* is even worse. It's like your parents couldn't be arsed. It's like you're pretending to be your own dad. Throw in Caleb as your middle name—the one that gets read out in court when they finally pinch you for a tiny proportion of the things you've done—and it's odds-on you've got a boy who'll be bashed behind the bike sheds, not a standover man who'll grow up into a cold killer.

But 'Caleb' was often dropped from his title when they talked about Rogerson in the years to come. Because if you are going to dive into the world of fists and guns—if you're going to be *that* kind of Roger—then it's odds-on they'll call you 'the Dodger'. You don't even have to move out of the way of anything; it's all for the rhyme. As it turned out, of course, Rogerson did dodge a whole string of blues, and a good few men—and at least one woman—might have lived a while longer if they'd managed to dodge him and his mates. If they could just have stayed out of their way.

On 8 April 1975, on Rogerson's evidence, Cox copped fourteen years for two armed robberies with a couple of car thefts thrown in. With a non-parole period of seven-and-a-half years, backdated to the day of his arrest, Cox had little chance of getting out before January 1982.

Not legally, anyway.

You could argue that the 1960s—with its student power, dope culture and youth in revolt—finally came to Australia in the 1970s. But even then, Australian jails were still stuck in the 1930s. Prisoners were not allowed to talk to prison officers, except to receive orders.

In metropolitan jails, prison officers were generally sturdy, straightforward men who didn't mind a fight but didn't necessarily go looking for one. Many were veterans of the Australian Army and—particularly—the British Army, and they had learned their own lessons the hard way. They took the job because it paid better than most unskilled work, and they didn't look at themselves as teachers, priests or social workers. They were warders, turnkeys, screws, employed to keep order. And they'd like to see how the weak and gullible crim-loving civilian staff would cope when the crooks arced up and came at them swinging. They'd liked to see that, the screws would.

Some larger jails housed small maximum-security units, such as the Circle at Parramatta, where violent or rebellious prisoners could be kept under continuous surveillance from a central tower. The Parramatta Circle was used at first to receive 'men of particularly ungovernable and vicious temperaments where they can be temporarily detained until their mania had left them'. Prisoners were flogged in the circles, but not like they were in Grafton in northern NSW.

After a wave of attacks on prison officers in the 1940s, Grafton had become a punishment jail for 'intractable' inmates who refused to accept discipline, assaulted prison officers, rioted, fought their floggings, or escaped. Bernie Matthews was transferred to Grafton in December 1971 because, as usual, he had tried to get away. This time, Matthews and a mate had attacked prison officers in an attempt to get out of Parramatta Gaol, where they had already been classed as intractable and held in the Circle. Grafton was the next step up.

Matthews arrived at the prison with his hands chained at the wrists to a restraining belt tied around his waist. He and his mate were punched in the mouth and kicked in the stomach, then his mate was led away for a more private beating.

Matthews was uncuffed and ordered to strip.

'Bend over,' he was told, 'and spread the cheeks of your arse.'

Less than a decade later, Matthews tried to describe Grafton's jauntily named 'reception biff' on ABC Radio. 'It is a baton-whipping,' he said. 'They flog you from the neck to the ankles. You get it across your back, your shoulders, your guts, your ribs, your arse, the backs of your legs . . . When they started flogging me, I hit the deck . . . I ran out of the pound yard into the pound cell and the two screws followed me. They continued to flog me all the way into the pound. Blood started to flow from somewhere—I don't know whether it was my nose or my mouth . . . They eventually stopped and they left the pound cell. I was still in the nude, but I was covered in bruises from head to foot. The blood eventually caked on my face and on my guts, or wherever it dropped.

'They came back that afternoon and two different screws flogged us,' said Matthews. 'So we got two floggings in the one day, on arrival. We were to be flogged every time they opened that door of the pound cell for the next ten days. It works out to an average of about three times a day. If you looked at a screw, you got flogged. If you had a button undone, you got flogged. If you had anything in your pocket apart from a handkerchief, you got flogged. Any minor infraction, you got flogged.

'They wouldn't baton you on the head but they'd punch you in the head,' he said. 'You get it on the back and you smother and hope to Christ it's over. It feels like it's never going to end but it goes on for a couple of minutes, five minutes . . . You try and switch off to the pain and you don't yell out, don't scream out, because otherwise the other tracs will take the pissy out of you.'

Like a recurring nightmare, the floggers came back in the dark. 'After you'd been there for a while, if you were gonna get a flogging, you'd get it at night,' Matthews told me. 'They flogged me, and I was sore and all the rest of it, and I went to the door and you could hear them outside and they were talking about their fucking kids playing soccer on the weekend or something. And I thought, "You fucking maggots. You were just in here flogging blokes and now you're talking like a—" And that sort of changed my whole outlook on it. I thought, "These fucking pricks. They think they're doing everyone a favour by kicking the fuck out of us."'

The biffs and floggings were approved by the prison administration, and Matthews remembers only one prison officer who did not take part. 'That fucking place changed all of us,' Matthews told me, half a lifetime later. 'You get flogged, day in and day out: you've got five or six screws flogging the fuck out of you and there's nothing you can do about it—something's got to go up here.'

He pointed to his head.

—

Like miniskirts and topless sunbathing, gay activism and feminism, drug pushers and international terrorism, prisoner radicalism unsettled the world in the 1970s. In September 1971, inmates took control of the huge, overcrowded and desperately unhappy jail at Attica, New York. At least 43 people (including 33 prisoners) were killed in the rioting and the police attack that followed. In Australia, another riot shook Bathurst in February 1974, after an inmate threw a petrol bomb into the chapel during a movie screening. Prison officers opened fire indiscriminately in the yard. At least twenty men were hit. Some were shot in the back, others were fired upon while trying to surrender. One man, Dennis Bugg, was paralysed by a bullet in the spine. When the fighting was over, prisoners were forced to run a gauntlet of baton-swinging guards. A report into the Bathurst bashings and subsequent cover-up was written by the once-jailed draft-resister Geoff Mullen together with Tony Green from the prisoner-led Prisoners Action Group (PAG)—a sign that connections still existed between Vietnam-era radicals and the men left behind in the jails. Trouble was stirring, too, at Pentridge, Victoria. It was led by a man who was to become a good friend of Russell Cox, and an unsung hero of the Australian underworld, Stephen Donald Sellers, the much-verballed survivor of a police-instigated fall from a third-storey window and a public shooting by former Painter and Docker Graham 'the Munster' Kinniburgh.

6

The Sins of Steve Sellers

Steve Sellers wasn't an armed robber by trade. He may have seen himself as a mastermind of the big jobs, the brains behind the boys with the balaclavas and guns, but Sellers was no hopped-up hero jumping around the tellers' floor yelling that he'd shoot anyone who moved. But he had the guts for anything, and he would live to prove that—although he wouldn't live long.

Chopper Read told lies about Sellers and mocked him in death. Borrowing material from a news story in *The Age*, Chopper said Sellers was a safebreaker (he was) and a bank-robber (perhaps, at least in the planning) and a drug dealer (well, cannabis) and extortionist (not in the way Chopper meant it) and also a bad driver. The joke was that Sellers drove a car into a tree and was killed—except Sellers wasn't driving the car at all.

Chopper said he'd known Sellers in the 1970s but the time Chopper claimed to remember the best was a time that didn't happen, when Chopper came to stand over a St Kilda massage parlour only to find the management had hired Sellers as protection. The two men fought and fell into 'a large, soapy, hot bubble bath', where Chopper held Sellers' head under the water until he was almost drowned, and Sellers' life had to be saved by two women wearing 'high heels, worried looks and not much else'.

It was a scene from a Western movie, recut and recast with Chopper as the anti-hero, and nobody ever heard the story from anyone but Read. Chopper went on to call Sellers a 'poof rorter' (he wasn't) who worked blackmail schemes involving prostitutes and gay men (he didn't). He was, said Chopper, very close to a prominent Melbourne retailer who bankrolled Sellers' brothel ventures (there weren't any) and shot himself when Sellers ended their relationship (they didn't have one).

The germ—because there was often, but not always, a germ of truth in Chopper's stories—is that Sellers had a way of making friends with rich people. In Chopper's unhealthy mind, for Melbourne retailers you could perhaps read Jews, and Sellers knew some Jews and once loved and was loved by a Jewish woman. And he was friendly with a Jewish lawyer, Robert Richter, who came to think of Sellers as a 'black hole which tended to suck in all who came close to him'—but not, somehow, in a wholly bad way. Richter still liked him a lot.

And Vivien Altman loved him.

Clever, beautiful, petite Vivien was another protester from the Vietnam days. She'd been arrested at one of the big Moratorium demos, bundled into a van, carted off to the cop shop and released without charge. It was nothing dramatic, but she learned that the police took sides, that they were a side.

Vivien grew up in Hobart, the only Jewish pupil at a Quaker school. Her elder brother Dennis became an outspoken and angry activist in the young gay-liberation movement (there he is—a 'poof' for Chopper) as well as a campaigner against the Vietnam War. Vivien moved to Melbourne, studied criminology and helped out in the early days of the Fitzroy Legal Centre and then the Richmond Legal Centre, giving free advice to people who couldn't afford even the lowest fees. She was in her early twenties on the cusp of the 1970s, when she heard Steve Sellers was having a terrible time in jail and another prisoner asked if she could get a lawyer out to see him. 'He needed someone basically who'd come out and show the prison officers that he had some support outside,' said Altman.

Altman organised the lawyer and, months later, she received an unexpected phone call and then a slightly wild looking, sturdy, swarthy guy knocked on her door in Carlton. It was Sellers, come to thank her for her help. She found him warm and funny, confident and tough, and very bright. He was interested in ideas, but also a little mad: crazy brave, but crazy nonetheless. 'I was connected in various ways to the "prison movement",' said Altman, 'and here was Steve, who was the living, breathing epitome of the hero who took on the system. He became a very flawed hero, but he was a bit of a hero.'

They started a relationship and he told her about his life.

There was no Steve Sellers, of course. Sellers was born Steven Jorgic. He had come to Australia from Montenegro with his refugee parents when he was three years old. The family settled in Adelaide, where Sellers, olive-skinned and Italianate, was a rare wog among fair-haired playmates. His parents split up and he became estranged from his father. He moved around various states, living for a while in Tasmania and Victoria. He was up in a children's court for the first time at the age of eleven, charged—of course—with illegal use of a bicycle. He was sent to a boys' home, expelled from school, dispatched to reform school then returned to a boys' home. Wherever he was taken he would run away but whenever he was locked up he would find the same kids. They made friends by necessity, although Sellers was always gregarious. He may have been bashed but he never said he was raped. And he quickly grew too strong to be bullied. He picked up his first adult conviction at about the age of seventeen—and his mother died of cancer that same year—then he learned to pay off the police, and he didn't get arrested so much anymore. He was a creative, energetic criminal who made good money through break and enters, but when he tired of paying the bung, he found himself in Pentridge, the unforgiving nineteenth-century bluestone jail in Coburg, Victoria.

The compulsively uncooperative Sellers soon took his place in H Division, the punishment wing for troublemakers and stirrers, ratbags, rule-breakers and would-be escapees. H Division was the Grafton of the Victorian prison service, a story told to hardened crims to shock them into line. With Grafton, it shared the reception biff and the military-style rules. Prisoners were made to march everywhere, swinging their arms high in the air, as if they were permanently on parade. Prisoners were known by their numbers, prison officers were called 'sir' and saluted, and any man who violated any one of the division's arcane and complicated rules (according to John Killick, they had to hold their salute for three paces when marching past the governor's cat) was a candidate for an educative bashing. For 'work' in the late 1960s, H Division inmates had to break large rocks into smaller rocks with a hammer.

Killick, who had bashed a prison officer with an iron bar while trying to escape from E Division, was in H Division at the same time as Sellers. He later told an inquiry that Sellers refused to obey orders, refused to salute and refused to break rocks. He told me Sellers was the first man to fully rebel against the regimen in H Division. Killick admired him but, 'I thought he was mad,' he said. 'He had all these wild ideas.'

Ray Mooney, who was serving time for rape, met Sellers in Pentridge in about 1970. Mooney was in A Division, judged harmless to prison officers, though structurally H Division was also part of A Division. 'When we were in the A Division yard, of a morning or a night, if there was anything happening in H Division you could hear it,' Mooney told me. 'And the first person who I ever heard carrying on was Steve Sellers. He was screaming out all the time that he wasn't gonna take anything, and he wasn't gonna get bashed by anyone.'

Sellers was not in H Division for long. 'The more he played up, the more they wanted him out of the place,' said Mooney. 'Because no one had ever bucked the system like that before, ever.

'He was a very courageous person who had strong moral values,' said Mooney. 'I'm talking about strong criminal moral values.'

—

Vivien Altman agreed that Sellers had standards, stances, ethics. He campaigned against verbals, frame-ups, unsigned statements. And he was a decent human being. He loved animals, especially horses. He could've been a vet. But he was also a professional criminal and Altman didn't really know the world she was getting into.

Through Sellers, she met Marko Motric, another migrant from the nation that was then still Yugoslavia. Sellers and Motric trusted each other and obviously worked together, but Motric was a quiet man, difficult to read. Altman was never sure what to make of their friend Jimmy 'Jockey' Smith, who was on the run from Pentridge and dirty with the cops because he'd been fitted up. Smith played the enigma, kept himself to himself.

But Altman's friends loved Sellers. She introduced him to them all and they saw him as a genuine bloke, an eccentric wit. And he shared their interests, such as avant-garde theatre at the Pram Factory in Carlton. 'He liked that kind of cultural politics of Carlton and Fitzroy,' said Altman. 'And he liked to read poetry.'

The actor Gary Waddell met Sellers at a dance at the Pram Factory in the mid-1970s. Waddell was part of the Fitzroy anarchists, who ran a free store where nothing had a price. The anarchists had a notional affinity with criminals like Sellers, who rarely paid for anything anyway. 'Steve was a hard man,' Waddell told me. 'He made you do things that you didn't want to do—not illegal things, just . . . *things*. He scared me.'

Altman was living at a friend's home in Drummond Street, Carlton, when Sellers phoned and warned her, *Don't open the door! The Armed Hold-up Squad is just on their way around to your house. I'll come in the back way, over the back fence, because there's stuff under your bed that shouldn't be there.* Sellers had a habit of not telling her the whole story, of winning the confidence of women and having them store things for him.

The police came knocking moments after Altman put down the phone. She was angry and scared. She knew the cops were nasty and she didn't open the door. Once they had gone, Sellers sneaked in, bagged up a hoard of antique clocks and took them away.

—

John Killick got out of Pentridge in June 1973. He hadn't done a bank in eight years when Sellers turned up at his place in Sydney offering a .32 Beretta in exchange for his help in a robbery. The third man on the job was to be Laurie Prendergast. Killick, Sellers and Prendergast had been in H Division together, and Prendergast had fought back against the screws, but Killick didn't like him and Altman had little time for him either.

There wasn't much left that was good in Prendergast, another boys' home casualty from a criminal family (his antecedents stretched back to John 'Snowy' Prendergast, who was shot dead by brothelkeeper Kate Leigh in Darlinghurst in 1930). Prendergast's close mates included Christopher Dale Flannery, later known as 'Mr Rent-A-Kill', an alleged murderer for hire. In 1969, Prendergast and Flannery were convicted of the rape of an eighteen-year-old woman they both slightly knew. Flannery raped her first, then Prendergast. After he had taken his turn, Prendergast stole her handbag. Certain authors have tried to play down the seriousness of this attack, to pander to Flannery's and Prendergast's defence that they believed the woman had consented, although the victim seems to have been a virgin whose vagina was so badly damaged that a doctor could not even perform an examination. Sellers had introduced Prendergast to Altman, although not in the way he could have done: *Vivien the feminist meet Laurie the rapist.*

Sellers reckoned there could be an earn of up to $200,000 in a bank he'd been casing—and Killick liked the gun—so Killick and Sellers headed to Melbourne to join Prendergast. Sellers stole a getaway car then told the others he couldn't go into the bank because he had been seen while he was planning the job. He agreed to drive but on the day—Tuesday, 2 July 1974—he claimed he was too crook even for that.

Killick and Prendergast cased the bank but abandoned the job. Prendergast returned to Sellers. When Killick went to pick up the getaway car, he was pulled over by police and arrested. Armed police then smashed in the door of the tiny third-floor South Yarra apartment where Sellers and Prendergast were waiting for Killick. They burst into the flat and yelled at Prendergast to get down on the floor. Sellers rushed to the window to throw out a bag of grass. Senior Constable Garry Schipper—known as the biggest man on the Victorian force—chased after him, gun drawn. He pushed Sellers and hit him around the head with his gun hand. Sellers tried to protect himself as Schipper and another cop reached for him, when everything suddenly went terribly wrong.

Sellers flew backwards through the window and plunged ten metres to the concrete below.

He didn't scream when he landed. He wasn't even in pain. He felt numb.

A cop came over, laughing hysterically.

'Look at him!' he said. 'He has no nose!'

Sellers ran his fingers in his own blood and thought he might be better off dead. His nose had been split down the centre, leaving a centimetre-wide gap in the middle of his face. Police surrounded him. At first, it looked to Sellers like there were six cops but then they seemed like twenty. In fact, there were eleven, but all Sellers could see was legs. An officer with handcuffs picked up his right arm.

'Don't handcuff that arm,' said Sellers. 'It's broken.'

'Fuck you, Sellers,' said the cop, fastened on the cuffs and yanked at the arm.

Sellers started screaming. He kept on screaming and the cop kept on yanking. Sellers looked down the barrel of a police pistol that was pointed at his eye.

'Don't do it!' he shouted.

The cops half-dragged, half-carried him away, jarring and scraping his broken bones.

Sellers was in pain he later described as 'indescribable' when the lazy screenwriter who plotted Sellers' life introduced a stock character as an unimpeachable witness—the local vicar.

Two young passers-by—a mothercraft nurse and a preschool teacher—saw Sellers lying on the ground, injured and yelling, with a gun aimed at his head, and heard him beg not to be shot. They ran into the nearby manse of St Andrews Church, where the Reverend William Frederick Gilmour took them in then went outside to see what was going on. He grabbed a rug and cushion to help make

Sellers comfortable but the police would not let him near. Once the vicar arrived, the police realised they should put Sellers down and get an ambulance. The cop who had been amused by Sellers' nose was still laughing, and Sellers spat blood at him.

'I'll put a bullet where your nose used to be if a spot of that gets on me,' said the cop.

But an ambulance arrived and Sellers was carried inside. Wandering hands took his money and his address book—Sellers never saw them again. The cop with the handcuffs rode in the ambulance with him.

'I'd been to that apartment a few hours before and I'd left,' said Altman. 'I didn't expect to hear from Steve, but that evening I got a call from Laurie Prendergast. He said, *Oh, don't worry but Steve was thrown out of the window. He's in the Alfred Hospital.*'

7

No Escape from Parramatta

When he was 22 years old, Warwick Robert James had murdered a murderer. When *he* was 27 years old, John Edward Mills of Redfern had stabbed to death Lola Jean Godwin of Potts Point, with her own kitchen knife in her own car. Twenty months later, in October 1972, New Zealand–born James smashed Mills over the head with a stool in Goulburn Gaol, then strangled him with a cord, pushed his corpse under a bed and covered it with a blanket. James was given life for the murder. So, if you were looking for a prisoner with nothing to lose and willing to kill with the nearest objects to hand, you might be forgiven if your gaze rested on Warwick James.

On 18 July 1973, Ray Denning was transferred from Long Bay to Parramatta. He became captain of the prisoners' touch football team and got on alright with some of the prison officers, but other guards saw a baby-faced agitator, a smartie stirrer, a boy who needed to be taught a lesson. In October, Denning was given two weeks' solitary confinement for refusing to return to his cell. He was taken to the Circle, where he heard prison officers attacking Stan Emmanuel, an armed robber who had failed to pull off a recent escape. Denning called out to them to leave Emmanuel alone. A few days later, Denning was bashed in his cell by six or seven guards. It was the first time he had been flogged in jail.

At Parramatta, Denning shared a cell with Warwick James. Bernie Matthews, who always seemed to be just around the corner during moments of high drama in the NSW prison system, was in Parramatta at the same time. Matthews knew James. 'He wasn't a bad bloke,' he said. 'For a killer, he was alright.' On the morning of Saturday, 14 September 1974, James and Denning, along with armed robber John Bradley and a prisoner named John Manley, apparently set out to escape. James asked Matthews if he wanted to go with them but Matthews was not interested.

Denning was working the morning shift on a construction site inside the jail, supervised by Senior Overseer Willy Karl Faber, a bricklayer who had joined the prison service two years earlier and was employed to teach trade skills to prisoners. Later in court, the Crown's case was that Faber had walked into the storeroom where he had found the prisoners picking up a makeshift ladder, and he'd been repeatedly hit over the head with an iron bar and a hammer.

The four prisoners left Faber locked in the storeroom then ran towards the wall with the ladder. Two of them, armed with knives, were overpowered by prison officers, and a man with a club was also subdued. However, the knives were apparently dropped before the would-be escapees were apprehended, which must throw some doubt on whether they were carrying them at all.

The fourth man fled the scene.

Other prison officers found Faber unconscious on the storeroom floor. 'He was quite badly beaten,' one of them told the *Daily Mirror*. 'I felt quite sick and was still shaking an hour afterwards. He appeared to have pieces of his brain lying on the ground alongside his head and blood was everywhere.' They called for help from prisoner Neddy Smith, who was working in the jail clinic, despite having no aptitude or training for the job. Smith looked at Faber, saw his brains hanging out of his head and told the warders to phone an ambulance—advice that pushed Smith's medical competence to its furthest limit. But Smith collected bandages and a blanket and attempted to press the poor man's brains back into his skull and keep him warm until paramedics arrived.

All prisoners were ordered back to their cells. A guard pulled Denning out of the yard and hauled him to an office, where Denning was strip-searched then kicked, punched and pummelled to the Circle, still naked. James, Manley and Bradley were also stripped, flogged and driven like cattle. That afternoon, the four men were transferred to Long Bay's OBS, the observation section where the cell lights never turned off. They were bashed into the cells, and guards kicked all night at their doors.

Twenty per cent of Faber's blood had leaked from his body by the time he reached Parramatta Hospital, where he was joined by his wife and a priest. It seemed it might be too dangerous to operate, but he fell into a coma at 12.50 p.m. whereupon a neurosurgeon performed a three-and-a-half-hour lifesaving procedure. A queue of prison officers visited Faber in the intensive care ward. One man told a journalist, 'The mongrels. It was terrible. There was blood splattered everywhere . . . So much for rehabilitation. That's what happens when you take a soft line with some of those mongrels.'

A doctor later told a court Faber had suffered six or seven fractures to the skull—one of them about five centimetres in diameter—which had brought him permanent brain damage.

One hundred and twenty inmates were moved to other jails the day after the escape attempt, as Parramatta was drained of potential troublemakers and runners. Prisoners mounted an early morning demonstration but it was quickly broken up by guards.

The next day, police officers came to Long Bay to question Denning, but Denning refused to see them. He said he knew the cops would verbal him—'just to save themselves from a lot of extra work and investigation'—but he was dragged to an office in the OBS. He had nothing to say except that he wasn't involved. He was shown a signed record of interview from Bradley who, the night before he had given the statement, had slashed his throat with a razor blade. The police wouldn't allow Denning a phone call and they wouldn't let him leave, so he jumped up and yelled, 'Let me out of here!'

The prison officers opened the door and a cop said they'd see what Denning had to say when he returned from Grafton.

Then he'd learn how smarties got what was coming to them.

Early the next morning, the four would-be escapees were dressed in oversized overalls and slippers and chained by their wrists to security belts, so they couldn't raise their hands to defend themselves. They were bundled into the back of a van and driven all day without food or water until they reached Grafton.

When the van arrived at the jail, prison officers pulled out Denning, threw him onto his chest, dragged him up by the hair and told him, 'Don't look up or we'll smash your skull in!'

Just like you did to Willy Faber.

In the floggers' minds, they showed the crims exactly as much mercy as the crims had shown their own victims. It looked like Faber might die. So what kind of retribution should a prisoner get for necking a screw?

You'd have to go by precedent, search the records, see if you could find a similar case. You'd need to go back to the armed robber Kevin Simmonds—a graduate, of course, of Boys Town Engadine and Mount Penang—who'd escaped from the Bay in 1959 with his mate Les Newcombe. While on the run, Simmonds and Newcombe—Laurel and Hardy, more like; Dumb and fucking Dumber—broke into Emu Plains Prison Farm, *because it was a place they knew*, to steal a car, clothes and a gun. While they were at it, they beat a warder to death with a baseball bat and a cricket stump.

When Simmonds was recaptured, he was given life for manslaughter then bundled off to Grafton to receive his real punishment. Not life, but death.

The screws flogged Simmonds every day. They bashed him until his balls swelled up like oranges and bruised purple like eggplants. They beat him until his fingers trembled and he drooled from the side of his mouth. So many screws flogged him so hard and so often that they drove Kevin Simmonds mad. So they hit him some more. Somebody used his body as an ashtray, made holes in his skin stubbing out burning cigarettes on his flesh.

At 12.30 a.m. on 4 November 1966, Simmonds was 'found' hanging by his blanket from the window bars of his cell. Before he had strung himself up, he had taken the precaution of tying himself up. The police immediately confirmed that 'he appeared to have used a method known to them of tying his hands, putting his feet through his hands and then tying his feet'. It is not clear how this method had become 'known' to police as there don't appear to be any other examples in Australian history.

It was a strange way to choose to die. Like a junkie overdosing on heroin after injecting himself with a needle in his back.

You should remember that.

So there was a model for what was about to happen to Denning. There was case law. Maggots who murder screws have to be shown the consequences, otherwise prisons would be stacked with the dead bodies of screws, and there'd be maggots crawling out of their mouths and ears and eyes.

—

After Denning arrived at Grafton, and was torn from the prison van, 'I was then pulled to my feet,' he said, 'and my head pulled back and shown a screw standing above me only about ten feet away pointing a rifle at me and that screw said, "Make a move and I'll blow your fucking head off before you can blink an eye." A screw then said, "Blow his head off now." . . . I then had my handcuffs taken off and my overalls taken off. I was then completely nude and then I was pushed into a yard where there was about seven or eight screws who had batons . . . They bashed me all over the back, side and front as well as on the legs and head. One of the screws grabbed me by the hair and he was grabbing me around the head saying to his screw mates, "Bash him to death." And they kept bashing me for about five minutes when I was given two hits on the side of my head that sort of paralysed me . . . I heard another prisoner being bashed and the two screws left and they said, "We'll hang you tonight, you bastard."'

The four men were flogged to their cells, then flogged again the next morning—for incorrectly folding their blankets. In Grafton, you weren't told the rules: you learned them at the end of a baton. The flogging continued every day for about three weeks. 'We were flogged and flogged and flogged,' said Denning. 'I had a split lip, a bleeding nose, a black eye. I had lumps and bruises all over me.'

When Denning and James first arrived in Grafton, James copped the worst of it because the screws knew he was a killer—the murderer of a murderer—and the most likely among the would-be escapees to have tried to kill again. Denning was still the sweet-faced street kid, with an urchin's eager grin. When they decided it was Denning who'd bludgeoned Faber, they set out to wipe that smile off his pretty little face and beat him into pleading guilty. He refused.

Denning's Aunty Faye later told the ABC, 'He wrote to my daughter and said he was crying, screaming, hurting, and he was praying that the nightmare would end. And he actually used to look over my head when he spoke to me.

He used to laugh uncontrollably when I went to visit him, speak incoherently, and sometimes he was crying a lot.'

Twenty-eight days after the escape attempt, the four prisoners were charged. Denning, Bradley and James all pleaded not guilty to malicious wounding, and Denning and James denied even that they'd been trying to escape. When Denning was finally allowed to read his own record of interview, he discovered he had—in his own absence—admitted everything to the police: he'd taken part in the escape, helped build the ladder and helped bash Faber.

In court, Denning complained he'd been tortured mentally and physically and insisted he'd made no confession. He asked the judge to make an order to stop him being returned to Grafton. The judge refused and, a couple of days later, when the four were sent back to Grafton, they were treated to a repeat of the reception biff.

Denning and James went to court—and returned to Grafton—five times between September 1974 and September 1975, after which Denning was held in Long Bay for the trial. On 12 February 1976 at Darlinghurst District Criminal Court, Willy Karl Faber testified, 'Denning came right at me swinging a carpenter's hammer and said, "Take that, you bastard!" He hit me over the head and after the hammer struck me, I only saw a green blur.'

Denning maintained he had been nowhere near the building site when Faber was attacked, and he could produce a record of having signed in for the cigarette queue at the time of the escape. The Crown's case was that Denning could've left the queue and rushed through the yards to hit Faber. But the warder who identified Denning as running from the scene saw the fugitive from about 36 metres through two screen fences and a line of visitors.

James and Bradley were cleared of the malicious-wounding charge, Denning was found guilty. Denning and James were also found guilty of attempted escape, which Manley and Bradley had admitted. Denning was given two years for the escape attempt—and life for the hammer attack.

Denning later said Faber should not have been called to testify since he was clearly brain damaged. He said Faber had been coached by police to name him as the man with the hammer. He claimed the prison officers who had beaten him at Parramatta had always held a grudge against him and had persecuted him for speaking out against the flogging of Stan Emmanuel. In private, he blamed Warwick James for bashing Faber.

The judge ordered a psychiatric report on Denning. A psychiatrist named WL Metcalf spoke to the prisoner for 'over an hour' and pronounced him 'an articulate, reality oriented young man who revealed no evidence of any psychiatric disorder'. He assessed Denning's 'intelligence' at 'the below average to average level, any backwardness being due to lack of education rather than any genetic, emotional or organic dysfunction'. A pained Metcalf cantered through Denning's cheerless history of neglect and incarceration then his accounts of being tortured at Grafton. 'The effects of the ceaseless unexpected and expected physical punishment is to provoke violent anti-social feelings,' wrote Metcalf. Denning had told him, 'I can take it physically because I am young, but I do not think that I can take it mentally; I am just being turned off the world.' The psychiatrist concluded, 'His background of a disturbed childhood, poor parental nurturing and eventual institutional life has created a form of institutionalized psychopathy which is ill-suited to frustration tolerance in a competitive society and so he has fallen by the way-side. He does not appear to be irretrievable, but I can see no way that there could be any rehabilitation if he is subject to prolonged physical brutality.'

8

No Escape from Long Bay

In August 1975, Dave 'Emu' Farrell was a new prison officer whose uncle, Stan Stewart, already worked as a guard at Long Bay. Emu got his nickname, he told me, because he'd 'eat anything and wouldn't take a backward step from the prisoners'. He described Russell Cox as a 'tidal swimmer with the prison population' at the Metropolitan Reception Prison, where he was being held while he appealed against his fourteen-year sentence for armed robbery. 'He went along,' said Farrell, 'he blended in; there wasn't any abuse of prison officers or the stuff you usually got' but he was 'respected by a lot of the heavy crims'. Among prison officers, 'the sensible ones were cautious of him', said Farrell. 'Probably the other prisoners knew more about him than what we did.'

Cox's co-offenders, Workman and Croft, had been transferred to Parramatta, apparently for causing trouble at the MRP. But Cox kept his head down and his nose clean. He worked as a jail barber, which gave him some freedom to move around. His barber's chair was a prison-built wooden stool that could be carried from yard to yard along with a pair of scissors, hand clippers, a barber's comb and a sheet to wrap around his customers' shoulders. Under the stool, Cox hid a gun—or something that looked like one.

'I was 24 years old,' Cox later wrote in a statement, 'but my experience in the free world was only 5 years. I felt I didn't know what living was. I wanted to live, and want is the greatest motivation. So an escape attempt was inevitable, and it was to take place sooner than later. In fact it took place on 8th August 1975 and the result was to be disastrous, in more ways than one.'

Cox got on well with his cellmate, Victorian armed robber Allen Roy McDougall. 'Allen, like myself, was very keen on escaping,' wrote Cox. 'We had mulled over several ideas. We were continually looking for a way out. I was also talking to other guys keen to escape.' Contenders included Marko Motric—a mate of McDougall who had been arrested in September 1974, with professional criminals Jimmy 'Jockey' Smith and Brian O'Callaghan, for conspiring to hold up Redfern railway workshops and steal $175,000 in payroll. At the time they were picked up—by Detective Roger Rogerson—Smith and Motric were wanted on a hold-up charge in Victoria and O'Callaghan was on the run from a prison in the UK, but only Motric was refused bail and sent to the Bay.

Farrell said Cox had 'eyes everywhere. He was probably about four days smarter than the average crim of the day. He was very astute, very cagey. He watched everything that happened. Prisoners don't miss anything. They watch for routines. They watch the front gate of the jail. Everyone thinks it's just "Operation Snore" but they're watching prison officers, they're watching the times trucks come in and out.'

Cox and McDougall had discussed a simple escape plan, 'Every afternoon around 1.30 p.m. a bread van or stores truck would enter the MRP doing deliveries,' wrote Cox. 'Our plan was to hide in the back of one of these trucks and hopefully not be detected during the search between gates. On the day of our escape we agreed to let Mark know what was going on. Mark immediately said he wanted to be in on this escape but said he had a better plan. To our surprise Mark said he had a replica pistol and it fired blanks. "With your wooden gun and this it will be a sure thing to bluff our way out and we won't have to hide in the truck."'

The three prisoners waited near the gatehouse while a five-tonne stores delivery truck drove slowly towards the hulking 'birdcage'—a fortified checkpoint with an iron gate at either end, where vehicles were searched on their way in and out of the prison. As gatekeeper Sam Pavich and prison guard Paul Cafe opened the cage doors, Cox, Motric and McDougall dashed towards the truck, yelling and screaming. The driver, a prison officer, stopped halfway into the gatehouse, thinking he must have run somebody over.

This made it impossible to close the inner gate.

Motric, whose pistol turned out to be a loaded Beretta, fired a shot close to Pavich. Cox jammed his wooden gun into Cafe's head and shoved him along. The prisoners herded Pavich and Cafe into the office inside the gatehouse, where they also trapped two other unarmed guards, Steve Tandy and John Keogh.

Steve Tandy said later, in the careful language of a man well used to making statements, 'I was then forced to the floor in the gate-office area. A gun was eventually put at the back of my head. I was ordered to face the ground ... I was of the opinion that myself or other colleagues would be shot.'

He was 25 years old.

All the guards were bullied onto their bellies as Cox demanded the keys to the outer gate. Motric jumped on Cafe, threatening him with the Beretta and shouting, 'Will we take this one? Is he a dog?'

The prisoners yelled at Pavich to give up the key to the wall safe, which was used to store the weapons of visiting police and escorting officers. Pavich denied he had the key. Cox ran from the office and forced the driver out of the truck. While the prisoners seemed distracted, Pavich—who'd had the key all along—opened the gun safe to arm himself, but he was spotted by Motric who grabbed two Smith & Wesson .38s from the cache.

The prisoners stormed through the visitors' area, dragging Cafe along with them. A fanciful report in *The Daily Telegraph* imagined that 'several women fainted and others clutching young babies dropped to the floor screaming and weeping'. (Women were a lot more fragile in those days, while babies, apparently, were more robust.) The *Telegraph* spoke to Judith Holmes of Revesby, who was visiting a prisoner with her twelve-year-old son and her pregnant daughter. As Motric and McDougall burst in, said Holmes, 'One of them waved a gun at a warder who immediately darted across the room to hide behind my daughter Christine. Another guard crouched behind me as the prisoner fired his first shot—it missed us by inches.' Holmes grabbed her kids and dashed towards a door. 'I could tell the prisoners were desperate men who would stop at nothing,' she said—which, presumably, means she answered 'yes' to a reporter's question along the lines of *Did they seem like desperate men who would stop at nothing*?

Christine hid in the toilet. 'The prisoners were firing everywhere,' said Holmes, although they weren't. 'I saw one warder force his way into the toilet with Christine to escape the hail of bullets,' she said, although there was no hail of bullets. 'Children and women were screaming and men were huddled in the corner of the room when the prisoners demanded our car keys,' said Holmes. 'I think they went berserk because they were jumping around shooting at anything. I don't know why twenty people weren't killed,' she said, although this was probably because only two shots were fired. (In the prison officer's version of the story, he pushed visitors into the toilets for their own protection. He then confronted the escapees but they walked straight past him.)

Prison officer John Horton was working in the jail hospital. He said, 'An industrial officer rushed in and told me the prisoners had taken over a section of the prison. I asked the switchboard to call the police and I raced towards the main gate to see if I could help. I got within twenty feet of the gate when an officer outside told me not to come any closer. "They're armed," he yelled.

'I heard shots, keys, shouting and sounds of a violent struggle,' said Horton. 'I've never felt so useless.'

Farrell told me, 'As a junior officer, we're only one rung up from the prisoners in standing. I was on a fixed post up near the laundry. All we heard was the alarms going off. One of the officers up a tower rang up and said, "There's prisoners loose in the jail. They've got a gun. Look after yourself."

'*Hang on a fuck—We were told he was supposed to look after us! He's up the tower!*

'A bloke was down about 50 metres from me on an extension gate. We waved at each other and communicated. He had a broom and I had a mop. We looked like a couple of street sweepers. We worked it out between us. We said, "If the crims come this way, we'll go that way."'

Paul Cafe was pushed into the stores truck. McDougall, standing outside the truck, fired a pistol into the air. The bullet bounced off the gatehouse roof and back onto the truck, shattering the windscreen. The prisoners were, effectively, firing on themselves.

Cox jumped into the driver's seat. 'Everything seemed to take place in slow motion,' he offered later. 'So we drove out the gate and turned right; we are now outside the walls but still within jail property.'

Long Bay outside the gates was a citadel of workshops, offices, warehouses, the cafeteria, officers' accommodation and carparks, an outer ring of the ordinary world that surrounded the sadness of jails at its core. The route to freedom beyond the perimeter led down 'The Avenue', an internal road edged with tall palm trees. 'We still have to drive about 800 yards,' wrote Cox, 'past three armed guards to reach the Anzac Parade and freedom. Sirens are already wailing and in the next instant we are getting shot at from the nearest guard tower.'

Bernie Matthews was in the front yard at the Bay. 'I smelled cordite,' he told me. 'I thought, "What's that fucking smell?" Because it was a strange smell. I heard shots.

Then the screw in the corner tower aimed up and started firing.'

The escapees came under assault from the ground too, by prison officers who had taken guns from the armoury and raced through the jail. The prisoners pushed Cafe's head out of the window but the truck continued to draw fire.

Motric, Cox and McDougall all shot back at the prison officers, while the truck veered towards a parked prison ute. In an oddly constructive piece of escape criticism, a judge later told Cox, 'The plan, although it was well conceived, was poorly executed. You, Cox, drove at a very slow speed which permitted the truck in which you were to be rammed by a bread van and a truck loaded with sand.'

The vehicles were both driven by prison officers, who handled them like competitors in a demolition derby. In the earthmover was Farrell's uncle, Stan Stewart. The bread van hit the side of the truck and the earthmover crashed into the back. It jolted and buffeted the prisoners—and rocked and rattled Cafe.

'Uncle Stan thought it was me,' said Farrell, 'because I had a bit of a mo' like Paul Cafe at the time. He told me later, "That scared the shit out of me! How could I fucking tell my sister that I had you injured?"'

The prisoners dragged Cafe out of the truck, using him as a shield as they shuffled towards the boom gate. Cox held a gun to Cafe's head, screaming, 'If you come any closer, we'll kill the bastard!'

Prison officers took cover among The Avenue's palms. 'The local joke,' said Emu Farrell, 'was, "How many screws can you fit behind a palm tree?" The right answer was "fucking heaps". Because when the bullets were flowing, they reckon the prison officers were standing shoulder to shoulder to keep behind that tree.'

Cox fired a shot—allegedly at prison officer John 'Alex' Cook, who fired back, hitting Cox. 'All of a sudden there is a crazy volley of shots from the prison officers,' wrote Cox.

Cox fell, lost his grip on Cafe, and rolled down the sandstone embankment of the prison road. Cafe tumbled too, along with Motric, who had also been hit. Savagely, deliberately and pointlessly, Marko Motric stuck his pistol between Cafe's legs and fired twice, leaving the prison officer with a bullet in each thigh. The other prison officers advanced shooting, catching Motric in the right thigh, left forearm and scalp. The prisoners defeated, the guards piled on, restrained them and rescued Cafe.

Cafe was quickly transported to Prince Henry Hospital in nearby Little Bay, while Cox, Motric and McDougall, two of them bullet-holed and all of them bleeding, were hauled off to the Central Industrial Prison (CIP), a larger jail in the complex. Within the CIP, they were manhandled to the OBS, where McDougall, at least, copped a flogging. 'I was stripped and thrown into a bare cell,' wrote Cox in a later statement. 'I was left there bleeding noticeably for four hours.'

'It's fair to say no one was too concerned about our well being,' wrote Cox.

The jail was locked down. Every man was returned to his cell. Cox and Motric were eventually given cursory medical examinations but not taken to hospital. The other prisoners were still unsure what had happened. 'The next morning, they let us out,' said Matthews, 'and Stan Emmanuel—who was mixed up with the escape attempt a couple of years earlier—said, "They've got three blokes over there and they're gonna fucking die."'

Emmanuel was the head sweeper at the OBS, although he never swept anything much. His job was to organise the other sweepers, but there wasn't much sweeping for them either, since every prisoner had to sweep his own cell. Nevertheless, the position of head sweeper came with certain hazily defined responsibilities to keep order. When Emmanuel saw Cox and Motric were badly hurt, he sent word out to the rest of the jail and prisoners threatened to riot if they were denied medical attention. 'At 5 p.m.,' wrote Cox, 'ie 26 hours later, I was taken to hospital and had the arm operated on and stitched up.'

Prison officers shut down the whole jail for two days, armed robber Ray Brownlowe told me, 'and they tore the jail apart. They dug up the gardens, got on top of the roofs of the wings. They were opening up power points, pulling sinks to pieces, pulling toilets to pieces. They went through the complete jail with a fine-tooth comb, looking for more weapons.' No guns were found.

Paul Cafe carried on with his career despite his spitefully inflicted wounds. He and other prison officers were also left with deeper scars. 'It's always in your mind,' said Tandy, 29 years later, 'how easy your life could've been snuffed out.'

—

Cox was transferred to Grafton, where he was met with the bashing and the batons. Matthews had been returned to the tracs by then, and he heard Cox being flogged. 'We were never eyewitnesses to the reception biff,' said Matthews, 'but we could all hear it—batons hitting bare flesh have a distinctive sound. We all marched with eyes to the ground and not allowed to look up, but you could "sly-slew" out the corner of your eye and see things.'

Cox and Motric were held in the segregation ('segro') unit of the OBS between their various Sydney court appearances. At the hearings, the three would-be escapees were all described as 'labourers'. At first, they were handcuffed together but ultimately McDougall was tried separately. There was no real need for a trial anyway, as it turned out that detective Roger Rogerson, who had originally arrested and verballed all three men for their various armed-robbery offences, had already solved the case. In December, he told the Court of Petty Sessions that he had interviewed McDougall at Parramatta Gaol, shown him all the guns used in the escape attempt and discovered that McDougall had a hangman's noose, supplied by another prisoner 'to put over a screw's head'. McDougall objected to the guns and noose being admitted as evidence and told the magistrate he had not made the record of interview. The magistrate overruled his objections and accepted the verbal and the load-up. Because, after all, who would you believe—Allen McDougall or Roger Rogerson?

The noose was a trademark Rogerson bricking, fashioned to make the escapees appear more vicious, with murder on their minds from the very start. Criminals interviewed by Rogerson. They only wanted to cause chaos and kill.

It wasn't until many years later that the detective gave the game away. In October 1991, Rogerson appeared on *A Current Affair* and told reporter Peter Wilkinson that police in NSW regularly loaded up and verballed suspects and framed them for crimes they knew they hadn't committed. Men from the Armed Hold-Up Squad, among others, would plant drugs or guns on crims to 'keep them in line'. Wilkinson, playing the squarehead, asked, 'And everybody including yourself knew about this?' Rogerson said, 'Yes. Par for the course.'

As for verbals, Rogerson described them as 'a part of police culture'. Wilkinson asked him if he had verballed people himself. Rogerson said, 'I don't want to answer that in such a straightforward manner'—as if he ever said or did anything in a straightforward manner. 'Why are you telling us this now?' asked Wilkinson. 'Everyone knows,' said Rogerson, because everybody in Rogerson's world did know. But Wilkinson, on behalf of his viewers, sternly reminded him, 'No, Mr Rogerson, everyone doesn't know.'

'Everyone that is involved in the court system—lawyers, judges, police, solicitors and certainly the defendants—all know about verbals,' said Rogerson. *Certainly the defendants.* Rogerson was a funny guy.

Rogerson agreed that NSW police regularly lied under oath and that lying under oath was also a part of police culture. Once he was warmed up, Rogerson couldn't stop banging on about verbals. He told celebrity lawyer and *Sun-Herald* columnist Chris Murphy, 'Police would think you're weak if you didn't do it. And prisoners think a policeman who doesn't give him a verbal isn't worth his salt.' Real crims expected to be verballed—appreciated it, even. 'The hardest part for police was thinking up excuses to explain why people didn't sign up' to records of interview, said Rogerson, laughing.

—

Outside of the imaginations of various detectives, Cox rarely said anything to the authorities. There wasn't much point since he was generally guilty and, even when he did say something, the police said he'd said something else anyway. According to one prison officer, Cox and Motric tried to break out of the OBS, and the next day were transferred to Long Bay's new maximum-security prison, Katingal, which had recently opened between the outer wall and the perimeter fence of the jail.

The origins of Katingal were mysterious. The idea came from NSW Commissioner of Corrective Services Walter McGeechan, one of the stranger characters to occupy a position of power in the state prison system. Katingal was McGeechan's private project. Building began in secret in October 1972. The jail was to be effectively escape proof, a vault built above the ground, a hi-tech, hygienic concrete tomb for the living dead.

There were protests against the construction of Katingal by the growing prisoners' rights movement. At least one bomb was planted in the building site. The Builders Labourers' Federation (BLF)—the communist-led trade union whose 'green bans' secured the preservation of many grand old Sydney buildings—black-banned work on Katingal, until the ban was overturned by the Trades and Labour Council. NSW BLF branch secretary Joe Owens later said, 'I think probably some of the members found it easier to put a ban on Katingal than put a ban on historic houses, because there was more than one of them that'd been inside.'

From the outside, Katingal resembled a brutalist desert fortress—all angles, no prisoners' windows—eyeless in Gaza. The jail represented imprisonment in its purest sense.

Inmates lost their freedom to live among the natural world. All the light and air inside the jail was artificial, machine generated. Every prisoner spent twenty hours a day locked up alone in a windowless concrete four by two metre cell, with a concrete bed, a toilet with a concrete base and a concrete writing desk. There was no mess hall. Prisoners had their meals pushed into their cells through a serving hatch. Their lives were controlled remotely. Cell doors and wing doors were operated electronically, opening out onto a barred corridor with a workshop at one end. ('Workshop was a misnomer,' said Katingal prison officer Richard Osborne, 'because no work was done there. All they had in the workshop was a TV set. So they used to write letters or read books or watch TV.') At the other end of the corridor was a cramped six by ten metre exercise yard with a narrow, barred roof. The otherwise identical areas were painted to prevent prison officers becoming disoriented, and became known by their colours and levels—'Lower Yellow', 'Upper Green'.

Grafton tracs closed down in October 1975, on the eve of Justice Nagle's Royal Commission into NSW Prisons, which was about to expose to the nation the sanctioned savagery of the tracs' regime—although the nation was not much stirred and had heard it all from armed robber and escapee Darcy Dugan many years before. At the Nagle Commission, McGeechan offered several different explanations for Katingal. He said it was meant for the one per cent—high-risk prisoners or those who needed special protection, and it had been made escape proof to encourage them to think about things other than escaping. He later said the block was designed in part to hold terrorists. Then he said,

'The thing that motivated me was the difficulty of keeping prisoners safe in the prison community from people who were likely to attack them.'

The first prisoners into Katingal were the worthless former soldier Allan Baker and his mate Kevin Crump, who had randomly murdered a man who was sleeping in his car by the roadside. In the same week, they kidnapped Virginia Morse from a property near Collarenebri, NSW, where Baker had once worked as a farmhand. The two men staked her to trees, repeatedly raped her and sexually tortured her with branches and beer bottles.

According to a statement by Baker, read out at his trial in 1974, at the end of Morse's ordeal, 'She wasn't tied to the tree, her hands were tied in front of her with handkerchiefs, she wasn't crying because I think she was beyond that, she'd been crying most of the time she was gagged and blindfolded. I aimed at her with the .308 and Kevin had the .222 and it was going to be like a firing squad and Kevin pulled the trigger and she fell to the ground before I could pull the trigger of my gun. If he hadn't of shot her, I would because we both decided to kill her because we done those terrible things to her and she would have been able to identify me.'

Both men were alleged to have raped Morse again once she was dead, before they rolled her body into the Weir River. Baker and Crump couldn't get much of a run in a mainstream jail. A prisoner in the exercise yard at Goulburn smashed Baker around the head with a piece of wood, and Baker was taken back to his cell with six stitches in his face. Then he was shanghaied to Maitland tracs, which he felt was deeply unfair since he hadn't done anything wrong since he had raped, tortured and murdered Virginia Morse almost a year before—and it was hardly his fault if some maniac decided to bash him with a bit of timber.

About six months later, Baker was taken to Katingal as a prisoner on protection. He had been suffering from low self-esteem for a while, but he found his confidence improved in Katingal. He thought the guys in his wing were pretty good. There was Crump, who'd told the court that Baker had forced him to shoot Morse. Later there was John Lewthwaite, who'd stabbed to death a five-year-old girl—more or less by mistake, as he had broken into her home intending to rape her nine-year-old brother. In all, Baker felt, he was pretty lucky to have fallen in with such a decent crew in the colour-coded protection yard known as Lower Yellow.

After Baker and Crump, next into Katingal were two killers—including Earl Heatley, an armed robber who had tried to hijack a plane during a transfer between jails—and then came Bernie Matthews, who simply would not stop fighting prison officers and trying to escape. Cox, Motric and McDougall joined them in Katingal in mid-1976 when they arrived at Lower Green.

Matthews thought the sex-murderers were brought into Katingal to fix in the public mind an image of all the inmates as monsters—the 'Brutes of Katingal', as they were later labelled by *The Daily Telegraph*. While the rock spiders appreciated the security of Katingal—where their fellow prisoners only rarely had the chance to shower them with boiling water or pelt them with bags of shit—Cox hated the jail so much that he was moved to make a statement about it.

'Every day in this place is identical,' Cox told the Nagle Royal Commission. 'The only thing different is what is on the television ... As far as I am concerned, we could be on the moon.' Cox could never find silence in Katingal. He complained of the 'constant banging of the electric doors and of people walking up and down the corridor'.

Armed robber and gangland murderer Barry Levy was also tormented by the noise of Katingal. 'You could hear a series of doors open when the staff members would come on duty and you would hear it reverberate through the concrete and steel structure from a fair distance away,' he said later. 'When your door opened, automatically electronic switch BANG! It opened up a lever and then a second lever, it moved the door along then BANG! It ended, then it moved again then BANG! Then BANG home for the electronic lock to place. Each individual door had to be opened for the prisoner to step outside the cell onto the landing.'

Cox wrote, 'I find it hard to sleep and always lay awake until at least 1 a.m. and usually 2 a.m. Often at night there is noise such as officers laughing and joking and often the floor outside the cells is polished with an electric polisher or wiped over with something like ammonia around midnight to 1 a.m.' The toilets in the cells could be flushed from the outside, by prisoner officers, 'and about five times per week on average at a random time an officer will flush the toilet', wrote Cox. 'It has happened to me as late as midnight and once even when I was using it.

'No pictures are allowed,' he wrote. 'There is no ornamentation of any kind. There are no windows and all I can see from the shop is the landing. When we are given our newspapers or the clippers or nail scissors they are thrown down to us from the gallery . . . This makes me feel like an animal being thrown a bone.'

It made Cox feel like a dog.

In his first months in the jail, 'There were usually four or five of us in the yard and we got on each other's nerves all the time,' wrote Cox. 'There was not much room in the shop and it was very tense. I had to either go to my cell and hibernate or stay in the yard and put up with the tension. If one of us went to his cell the others used to speculate about why he had gone. The only place we were allowed to walk was in the yard and this seemed funny. If three were watching television and one wanted to walk it stood out and the person walking felt funny. It was not possible to relax and at times a physical clash was close.'

Allen McDougall 'gradually deteriorated until he refused to come out of his cell at all', said Cox. 'I went in and offered to help him but he did not answer, just lay on his bed staring at the ceiling with tears running down his face . . . One night at about 10 p.m., late in December 1976, when I was going to my cell I looked into his cell and saw him on the floor with his wrists slashed.'

McDougall was taken to Morisset Hospital, a psychiatric facility near Lake Macquarie.

In his statement, Cox offered rare clues to his personal life. 'I asked for permission to buy some books,' he wrote. 'This was granted but I was told that it would take three months to get them in from overseas. Shortly after I had a visit from an aunt who lived in Townsville and she was told that I could not have any books or indeed anything at all. I know that other prisoners have received books on visits and my wife has even brought books to me.'

This seems to have been the only time Cox publicly mentioned his wife.

At his trial, Cox reverted to his more taciturn self. He offered a brief, unsworn statement that made little sense. He said the escape was unplanned—in fact, he'd never even mentioned it to McDougall or Motric—but nonetheless he had been led to believe the crew could bluff their way out of jail with replica weapons. They only seized the Smith & Wessons because Pavich had taken the guns out of the cupboard and Cox never intended to shoot anybody with his pistol. 'I may have pointed it in the general direction of the prison officer and fired,' he admitted, 'but it was always in the air; if it wasn't in the air, it was definitely by accident.'

The judge delayed sentencing Cox and Motric to give them a chance to tell police how they'd got hold of the Beretta, but Cox and Motric kept their mouths shut. On 4 July 1977, the judge pronounced, 'Parliament has said that shooting at prison officers with intent to escape from lawful custody is an offence that carries life imprisonment. I have been informed that this has never happened before in respect of the Long Bay Penitentiary. This is the first time there has been an attempt by armed prisoners to, in effect, shoot their way out of the gaol.' The judge gave each man life for the Pavich shooting, fifteen years for shooting at Cook and another fifteen years for shooting another guard, fifteen years for maliciously wounding Cafe, ten years for kidnapping Cafe, ten years for armed robbery of the two .38s and four years for escaping from lawful custody. All up, Cox and Motric got life plus 69 years. If their sentences were to be taken literally, both men would still be in jail long after they were dead.

But Russell Cox was not a man to take a prison sentence literally. In fact, he stayed in jail for less than four months.

9

No Escape from Maitland

It's an iron rule of the underworld that any criminal whose parents name him 'William' will be known as 'Billy the Kid'. So it was with William Lewis Sutton, born in Cootamundra, New South Wales, on 12 May 1956, and raised in Jugiong, west of Yass. He was brought up largely by his mother—she was always the one at the court appearances and jail visits or waiting for him to come out of a children's home.

Thirteen-year-old Sutton was committed to an institution in October 1969 on his second appearance at Ashfield Children's Court. The first time he was in the dock, he got two years' probation for break and enter, the next time he was given two years' care at St Andrews Home for Boys in Leppington, 60-hectare farm home on the Hume Highway, run by the Presbyterian Church, with accommodation for a few dozen orphans. He absconded, carried out a break-in, got caught and returned to care under 'general terms'—which meant he was inside until the authorities decided he was fit to be let out. Sutton later did time at Mount Penang, where he was perhaps taught what boys had been made for.

In December 1971, he began to face adult charges in children's courts. At Ashfield, he was found guilty of 'assault female'. This might have been an unlawful carnal knowledge charge—just two juveniles messing around—but it could have been something worse. The next time he was up at Ashfield, it was for armed robbery and escape. Billy Sutton was a convicted armed robber and serial escapee by the time he was sixteen years old.

Next, Billy the Kid took part in a real gun fight. On 20 June 1973, at just seventeen, he was charged with shooting at police to resist lawful apprehension. He got ten years for that, and it made him Butch Cassidy compared to some of the other outlaws around. It made him Jugiong's Jesse James. And Sutton was a pioneer. He'd started using heroin at fifteen, while there were still US servicemen on R and R in Kings Cross. Now and then, he liked a smoke or a bit of something different but Sutton was a smackhead, a first-wave Australian junkie, and he was lucky to live as long as he did. In December 1976, he escaped from Emu Plains Training Centre, to be recaptured at Dee Why within two weeks and sent to Maitland Gaol.

Sutton got served up a bit in boys' homes, knocked around, but on the surface he wasn't twitchy about it. He had bones broken and some teeth kicked in but, to talk to him, you wouldn't twig that he carried a grudge. Boyish, attractive, sardonic Sutton—always ready with a joke—kept his darkness well hidden. You might never notice it, unless you'd known him a long time—or at the wrong time.

Not like Roy Pollitt, whose madness was clear to all who met him. On 31 March 1977, Pollitt had been driving around Newcastle, NSW, in a stolen panel van. In the passenger seat sat Kevin John Gallagher, cradling a sawn-off shotgun. Three police vehicles tailed the van to Newcastle Road. When a police van drew up alongside him, Pollitt leaned back and Gallagher bent forward, pointing at the cops with the barrel of his gun. The police van dropped back but Gallagher turned and fired three times.

Nobody was hit, but Pollitt was arrested later in the morning. In a typically hackneyed verbal, he was said to have admitted to police that he had told his passenger (who had escaped) to 'blast the pigs'. In case there was any doubt, a police officer testified that Pollitt had 'said he wanted to get away, and if the police got shot it was bad luck'. Gallagher was eventually captured and Pollitt received eighteen years on August 10. He, too, was locked in a cell at Maitland Gaol.

Ray Denning had served a little more than a year in Katingal before he was transferred to Maitland on 5 March 1977. The jail was the usual working relic of the days of the gibbet and the lash: proud, forbidding and clean on the outside; putrid, chaotic and primitive behind its sandstone walls. The cells were rat- and roach-ridden, with chipped bricks and peeling paint. The head of a prisoner's bed was an arm's stretch from the toilet. A waking man might almost roll off his pillow and into the bowl. Prisoners were mustered and counted three times a day in a yard overlooked by a gun tower, where officers—who themselves pissed in a bucket and drank water from a canvas bag—stood armed with .303 rifles.

If the jail was filthy, so were many of the inmates. 'Scabies, boils, psoriasis—all that sort of horrible skin disease—runs riot in a place like this,' said Keith Bush, then a prison officer. 'We used to get deros off the street who'd never bathed, who had cockroaches running over their clothes.'

A new shower building had been constructed in 1974. As a block, it had its own head sweeper and the sweeper ran a team. 'Their job was to come in and lock the two doors at eight o'clock,' said Bush, 'get big buckets of raw bleach, and they'd scrub this place from top to bottom to kill disease. Soon as it comes to nine o'clock, prisoners would be let in fifteen or twenty at a time.'

In 1977, the shower sweeper was Billy Sutton, and Sutton saw the shower block's bower was higher than the watchtower and faced away from it, so anyone on the roof of the showers would not be seen by guards either in the tower or on their catwalks.

On either side of the shower room were ventilation shafts, which allowed the heat to escape on summer days when the temperature inside could be ten degrees warmer than the yard. Sutton studied the shafts: they were painted bright red as if to make them stand out inside the dreary, colourless jail, to attract the attention of shrewdies and smarties like exit signs pointing the way.

It was Sutton's idea to follow them out. He did his job every morning—scrubbing away the dirt and grease, a sweeper who actually used a mop—but he and Denning also worked for ten minutes a day on one of the ventilation shafts, clambering up to saw at the mesh that covered its mouth. It took them seven weeks to cut a hole through the steel netting. Once they had finished, they masked it up, taped it and painted it red like the shaft casing.

'Everybody was anticipating that something was going to happen,' said George Eastham, a prison officer. 'I remember being up on One Tower and the Red Rat, Roy Pollitt, just staring up there for a long time. I just stared back at him.'

On September 1, a couple of days after the vent had been breached, a team of seven prisoners gathered to clean the showers: Sutton, Denning and Pollitt, who had only been at Maitland for 22 days, along with Frederick John Owens, who was doing ten years for armed hold-up; Terry Humphries, who had 25 years for armed hold-up and escaping custody; Steve Shipley, who was doing 28 years for armed hold-up; and Richard Lynott, who had 22 years for assault and robbery.

The prisoners persuaded the guard on shower duty to take a break at 8.30 a.m. Then they smuggled in bedsheets, knotted them together to make rope, shinned up the 30 by 60 centimetre ventilation shaft and used the bedsheets to lower themselves down the outside wall and into East Maitland, where they split into two groups and ran. Shipley, Humphries and Lynott went west; Sutton, Denning, Owens and Pollitt headed east.

Two prison officers who came to check the showers at 9 a.m. found the prisoners had left the hot water running and turned the closed chamber into a sauna, making a hazy, choking steam-screen for their escape.

Betty Sellers of nearby Day Street was driving a fruit truck near the jail with her cousin Wendy Watson, when she saw Shipley, Humphries and Lynott jogging down the road. They flagged Sellers down and she thought they wanted a piece of fruit. When she stopped, the men jumped on her truck and pulled Watson out.

'We're taking over now,' one of the prisoners said to Sellers.

'No, you're not,' she replied.

Sellers beeped her horn, grabbed her car keys and jumped out of her truck, leaving the prisoners without transport. The escapees jogged to Morpeth Road, which ran between the jail and the railway line, where Joan Lewis had loaded her two children into her car, then gone back into her house to answer the phone. Moments later, her nine-year-old daughter burst in, screaming the traditional schoolkids' fantasy that robbers were trying to steal the car. She told her mum three men had jumped in then run off when they couldn't start it. One of them had even hit her.

Shipley and his mates were caught hiding under a house in East Maitland, taken back to jail and bashed. They had been free for less than half an hour.

Fifty police from Newcastle and Hunter Valley stations, together with two RAAF Iroquois helicopters from Williamtown Air Base, joined the chase for the remaining escapees.

On Thompson Street, Denning, Pollitt, Sutton and Owens had pulled open the door of a brown Datsun driven by Rick Fry—a solicitor, of all things—and one of them waved a pair of pliers in Fry's face and said, 'Listen, mate, we've just escaped from Maitland Gaol. We don't want to hurt you, we only want your car.'

'Okay, no hassle,' said Fry. 'You take the car.'

They pulled him out and drove off.

The Datsun sped through Morpeth to Duckenfield, 13.5 kilometres away, where it was spotted at a police roadblock. A cop chased the car to the Hunter River, where it broadsided a patrol car and the boys jumped out and abandoned the vehicle. Pollitt sprinted along the riverbank, while Denning and the others dived into the river and swam across to the north side where they stole a Holden sedan from a Mount Kanwary farmer, Barry Walters, who chased after them in his tractor.

Denning was driving the Holden when it crashed into a police car at a roadblock in Raymond Terrace, 40 minutes' north of Newcastle. The men were captured after the traditional brief struggle.

The last man at large was Pollitt, who apparently couldn't swim. He was discovered under a grain shed, 250 metres from the jail. 'Had a little run, mate?' asked the police officer who caught him, as he escorted Pollitt to the station. 'You're a bit of a born loser, aren't you?'

For less than two hours of freedom, each escapee had seven years added on to his sentence.

Denning, Sutton, Pollitt and Owens were charged with escape and with assaulting Fry. Denning was also charged with dangerous driving. He was brought into court wearing only a pair of shorts. His face was bloodied, in the traditional way. Shipley, Humphries and Lynott told the court they had been beaten and asked for a medical examination, which they were granted.

Denning, Sutton, Pollitt and Owens were sent to Katingal.

The escape gave rise to some initial confusion. A curious story in Sydney's *Daily Telegraph* claimed, 'seven of the most violent criminals in the state' had 'used razor blades and forks to chip their way through concrete'. According to the

Maitland Mercury, one of the police officers in the chase had been shot at by Pollitt earlier in the year. The media at first believed Steve Shipley was the mastermind behind the plan. But it was all Billy 'the Kid' Sutton, the clever, cagey, junkie shower sweeper.

At the next court hearing, a Maitland detective said Sutton had confessed to everything but had refused to sign a record of interview because he said he 'might want to do a somersault or have a few days out and cost the taxpayer a bit of money'. It was the kind of 'motive' always verballed onto an offender—mischief for its own sake, breaking out just to inconvenience squareheads, prison officers and cops—offered by the accused with the kind of smirk that was just asking to be wiped off with a heavy glove.

On October 6, Denning and Pollitt appeared at Central Court with their heads shaved to the skull. Denning objected to being addressed as Raymond John Denning since, he said, 'A Tibetan spirit has taken me over and I am now to be called "Lobsang Rampa".' Pollitt said, 'I want the court to know that the Tibetan spirit is also in me and I'm one of his disciples.'

Lobsang Rampa was the author of a bestselling book, first published in 1956, entitled *The Third Eye: The autobiography of a Tibetan Lama*. Except it turned out he wasn't a Tibetan lama, he was a plumber from Plympton, Devon, born Cyril Henry Hoskin, who had never even been to Tibet. Rampa published a number of further books with Tibetan themes, including *Living with the Lama* which, he claimed, had been telepathically transmitted to him by his pet Siamese cat, Mrs Fifi Greywhiskers.

10

Escape from Katingal, the Escape-Proof Jail

The mid-1970s saw an unprecedented meeting of minds and bodies between squarehead political militants and the prisoner-led prison-reform movement. The alliance grew up in part because protesters were regularly arrested and often verballed, bricked and even imprisoned for actions in support of causes that barely seem radical—let alone criminal—today. The Australian movement against apartheid in South Africa attracted particularly enthusiastic policing.

'I was given a two-month jail sentence for running onto the Sydney Cricket Ground to stop the racially selected Springbok team in 1971,' former Labor Party politician Meredith Burgmann told me. 'It was considered almost normal to have spent some time in jail and then come out and be a committed activist.'

Demonstrators for extremist ideals such as women's rights, gay rights and Aboriginal rights regularly had to find legal representation. 'We'd all met a lot of bright, young lefty-leaning lawyers through the fact that they had appeared for us in our court cases,' said Burgmann. 'So, after I'd been arrested a dozen or so times, I knew most of the criminal Bar of Sydney.'

Many young lawyers were outraged by the levels of corruption they found in the courts. Accomplished and sophisticated judges regularly oversaw cases where any illiterate street crook would've known the defendants had been framed. The police unblinkingly fielded detailed allegations about shameless dishonesty and violence, and always offered the same explanations in much the same words. Some older barristers and solicitors were cynical about police behaviour, but they were rarely prepared to speak out as they were the more-or-less willing captives of a lucrative and conservative profession.

Few judges had significant criminal-law experience and even fewer had spent much time as criminal defence lawyers. Most had no firsthand contact with crims and seemed not to understand they were being lied to by police. The tremendous, almost comical gap between the Great Public Schools–educated judiciary and Boys Town and Mount Penang–educated defendants helped prolong the perversion of the criminal-justice system as much as widespread public indifference to the fate of people accused of breaking the law.

Not every judge was fooled, of course: 'I always suspect these confessions, which are supposed to be the offspring of penitence and remorse, and which nevertheless are repudiated by the prisoner at the trial. It is remarkable that it is of very rare occurrence for evidence of a confession to be given when the proof of the prisoner's guilt is otherwise clear and satisfactory; but, when it is not clear and satisfactory, the prisoner is not unfrequently alleged to have been seized with the desire born of penitence and remorse to supplement it with a confession;—a desire which vanishes as soon as he appears in a court of justice.' Those are the words of Justice Cave in the Queen's Bench Division of the Supreme Court of New South Wales, speaking in 1893.

A prominent Australian jurist—who asked not to have his name put to his analysis—told me Sydney's corruption problems were rooted in the days of the Rum Corps. More recently, 'For at least a couple of decades after the Second World War, and perhaps earlier, there had been police commissioners who had collected bribes from organised crime—sly-grog merchants and illegal gambling-joint operators—more or less literally in brown-paper bags, through bagmen who went out and collected the stuff, and it was distributed according to a formula or system.

'You couldn't say all commissioners were on the take, and you couldn't say every second one was, because the commissionership generally moved between a Catholic or a Mason. And if every second one was on the take, it would prove all the Catholics were doing it or all the Masons. So, occasionally, you'd have a couple of honest ones interposed, and they tended to not hold office for terribly long and be the sort of people who wouldn't know if the town clock fell on them. Whereas the commissioners who were involved in corrupt practices tended to be there for a fair while and be pretty wily customers.

'And police, like lawyers, are great gossips—if everyone knows the commissioner is on the take, then you're likely to be a bit on the saintly side if you're behaving perfectly all the time yourself.'

That doesn't mean most cops were dishonest. The great majority of crimes aren't committed by professional criminals—even murders tend to be the work of squareheads—but police corruption tends to occur when cops interact with full-time crooks. And, until the 1970s, nobody much cared what happened to professional criminals. But after the Vietnam War, radical lawyers and law students began to speak out. They built a reform association, founded the free Redfern Legal Centre, joined the Society of Labor Lawyers, published the *Alternative Law Journal* and linked up with activists in organisations such as Women Behind Bars—founded by law students Wendy Bacon and Liz Fell—and the PAG (Prisoners' Action Group).

The PAG worked both outside and inside the jails. Its leaders in the prisons were often armed robbers, said Burgmann. 'I think it's because the certain personality that's attracted to the excitement and fear of robbing a bank were also attracted to action against the authorities,' she said. 'Plus, they were probably also the most likely to have been verballed.

'And there was a sense in which they were seen as more . . . not exactly clean, but if they had done a few armed robs and hadn't actually hurt anyone they were seen as less . . . criminal, in a way, than the other people we were dealing with. And often they were more likely to be believable. When they told you stuff, it was often true. Because they certainly had their own code of conduct, which was very different to ours. But I think part of it was that they were better than the other people in the prison.'

The PAG and Sydney Women Behind Bars campaigned to close Katingal as soon as it opened. In March 1976,

Corrective Services allowed a TV crew into the jail to counteract the 'ridiculous and extreme propaganda about the place'. The boys from Channel 10 nabbed an interview with sex-torture-rape-murderers Baker and Crump. It turned out the true brutes of Katingal loved the place. There was nowhere better for them in the NSW prison system. When they saw the demonstrators on TV, they were furious—'a bunch of ratbags,' said Baker, later, 'saying them prisoners want it shut and we're representing them. If we'd have got hold of them they wouldn't have been representing, I can tell you.'

He'd have given those women what for, Allan Baker would have. He'd have shown them what they were representing. He'd have shown them who needed protection. If he'd have gotten hold of them.

Cox shared his wing in Lower Green with Motric, Denning and Warwick James. Sutton, Pollitt and the rest of the Maitland Crew were in Katingal too, awaiting trial on their own escape charges. 'I find that I am losing my memory,' wrote Cox. 'I repeat myself and can't concentrate, I can't read and I become short-tempered. My only outlet is exercise. It is the only way I feel I can get away from this rotten place.'

Cox jogged up and down his corridor, practised yoga and sweated through his daily routine in the yard. 'He used to do press-ups, sit-ups, squat thrusts, burpees,' said prison officer Richard Osborne. 'He'd hang off the bars and do all sorts of static strength-building exercises.

'He treated all the officers in Katingal with a degree of respect,' said Osborne, 'which was quite unlike most crims in the place. He was very polite. I had hours and hours of conversation with the guy, because we got on pretty well together. Most officers got on pretty well with Cox.

'I'd studied karate and judo in Japan,' said Osborne. 'He used to ask me a lot about it. He said, "How capable were you?"

'Cox was very, very fit,' said Osborne. 'In fact, I probably played a small part in that. He said, "Could you bring in one of your exercise books for me?" I spoke to the boss, and the boss said, "Yeah, sure. Bring it in. Make sure there's nothing in it he can use to further anything other than his exercises." So I did and I gave it to him, and he used to do a lot of these static exercises that were depicted in the book.'

Cox petitioned the governor for a vegetarian diet, with limited success. At first, he was given ordinary prison rations without the meat. But Cox was determined to change himself, to become a different man. It was the way he had always adapted to survive. And the next version of Melville Peter Schnitzerling had to be freakishly strong, sinewy and slim. This time, he was truly going to escape.

'Cox did things very methodically,' said Katingal superintendent Edgar Bowden, 'in so much as he planned that escape not for tomorrow, next week but for a long way in the future.'

Even as his physical condition improved, Cox felt he was mentally deteriorating. 'My loss of memory is getting worse,' he wrote. 'On a visit I tell my visitors the same things I told them the last time and they have to keep telling me that I've already told them . . . sometimes I can't even remember the names of the people in my shop and this is extraordinary because I am confined with these people every day.'

Despite all its ultra-modern security provisions and remote-locking doors, Katingal was still permeable to the most determined smugglers. A prisoner on a case visit outside the jail brought back a hacksaw blade hidden inside his belt. According to one story, Cox broke up the blade and stored the pieces in toothpaste tubes. Earl Heatley, who was locked up on the same side of the jail as Cox, claimed he kept the blade in a brush ('I'm doing a life sentence,' he said. 'There's fuck all they can do to me . . . so it was no skin off my nose if the blade was found in my cell'). Matthews, whose cell sat on the opposite side of the jail, said half the blade went to Cox and the other half to the Maitland Crew.

Cox watched, worked out and waited. The only natural light in the prison came in through the exercise yard, so Cox followed the light. The roof of the yard was four metres from the ground and caged in by narrowly spaced two-centimetre thick bars. But one wall was meshed with cyclone wire, which offered finger- and footholds: a route to the roof. And even though the yard was no bigger than a double garage, there was a security blind spot in one small area.

When the prison officer on duty needed to operate the doors to let people in and out to the exercise yard, he had to turn away to the control board. 'Cox had organised other prisoners out there,' said Bowden, 'that they would come into the toilet in sequence. He knew when this officer started opening the door, how long it was going to be before he was back at the observation window, and he could be slightly out of his sight and run up the cyclone wire thing and saw the bar a bit and come back down again.'

Cox sprinted up the wall and grabbed one bar while sawing away at another bar with the hacksaw blade. 'He did this bit by bit over a long period,' said Bowden, 'and he was allowed to have those models you put together, complicated planes et cetera, and he had some green paint which the bars were painted green and he used to just smear a tiny little bit of paint on it so it didn't show up.' (A rumour spread later that the bars were under-spec, but this seems to have been a jailhouse furphy.)

Heatley said more than half the prisoners in the jail knew about the escape plan, and several helped with the sawing. Matthews said, 'The official version is that Russell held himself up on one arm and cut through it. The unofficial version is blokes helped him up on their shoulders. But the fact is, they cut through that bar. And they did it with no ladders or nothing else, just with brute strength. But, if you had someone standing on someone's shoulders, you had to have someone to make sure the screw on the gallery didn't come down to the glass partition and see what you were doing in the yard. So you'd have one bloke positioned to watch the screw on the gallery and once he's up the other end you give him the nod and go, "Up you go." Because for all its mod cons, there was no CCTV in Katingal.'

Matthews said all the Maitland Crew took a turn with the hacksaw blade. The plan was for Denning, Sutton, Pollitt and their mates to squeeze through the bars with Cox, but on the eve of the intended escape—at the point when the bar was finally sawn through—most of them had to attend court in Maitland to face charges for their earlier escape.

'They were gonna have another go on the prison van on the way up,' said Matthews. 'If they escaped from the prison van, well then all was good and well. But if that didn't come off, they'd be back in Katingal that night and they could go from Katingal the next day. Well, they tried to escape from the van on the way up but the escorting car saw something was amiss and they pulled into one of the police stations, strip-searched everyone and they knew something was going on. Rather than bring them back straight away after court, they left them at Maitland Gaol overnight. Now, back in Katingal, no one knew where they were.'

It was 3 November 1977. The escape was ready but the escapees were not. 'The only one was Russell and there was a hole in the roof,' said Matthews.

Prison officers had procedures, routines for detecting a breach of security. 'Every night they went along and banged the bars,' said Heatley. 'There's every likelihood that it could, at the next bang, give off a tone that lets them know that the frigging thing's cut. So Coxy waited until about eight o'clock hoping that they'd come back from Maitland and that we'd be able to verbal them into letting us out of the common room to have a bit of exercise—them being at court all day and everything—and when they were getting ready to shut us in our cells for the night, he said, "Well, I'm off."'

Cox had deliberately left his running shoes in the yard. He asked warder George Johnson if he could go back out and get them. Johnson said, 'Yeah, that's no problem.' Cox ducked into the yard, lodged a ping-pong bat between the diamonds on the cyclone-wired wall to make a step, and scrambled up the wall. He bent back the weakened bar, jammed himself through the opening and onto the roof of the jail. There, he was faced with a seven-metre drop onto a concrete yard. He could've plummeted like Steve Sellers, broken his legs, sliced up his nose, but he dived like Spiderman—Timmy Schnitzerling superhero. 'Talker Tim' from Boys Town Beaudesert? Fucking look at him now.

Cox managed to touch down on a ledge only three metres from the ground, then drop again and land safely to sprint towards two five-metre-high fences. A prisoner shouted that Cox was gone and the warder sounded the alarm, but the same systems that kept the prisoners locked in—all the physical barriers and electronically controlled interlocking doors—slowed down the response time of prison officers.

Cox was spotted by Charlie Kelly, an armed guard on the watchtower at the MRC, who called out for him to stop then fired at him once with a .38 pistol. The bullet missed. Cox ducked, zigzagged—*Now I'm in a fucking war movie*—scaled one fence then the other, then jumped over the jail's two-and-a-half-metre brick wall and sprinted off into Malabar.

Prisoner Barry Levy was watching TV when, he said, the two warders leading the chase 'found themselves locked in'. 'Then they couldn't get through the fence line to get at Russell,' said Levy, 'and one of them fell in the ditch or something . . . and Russell'd just disappeared in a puff of smoke.'

Police apparently described Cox's escape as 'almost superhuman'.

'Mate, we were rapt!' said Matthews. 'The screws got dirty! They were filthy on us! They tried to do everything to upset us! And no matter what they did . . . *Weeeeigh-hay!* Russell got one over youse! Your escape-proof jail's not escape proof anymore! Youse've flogged us, youse've battered us, youse've gassed us, you've done everything to us—and we've still got over the top of you. It was like winning the Grand Final.'

Some prison officers saw the escape as a consequence of management practices. 'Discipline was being eroded in Katingal,' said Osborne. 'The more it got eroded, the greater lassitude prisoners had. When we first opened, they couldn't scratch their arse without our permission. The rules were not all that hard, they were just strict. And we adhered to them. And, of course, consequently they got away with nothing. But thereafter . . . we had a lot of troublemakers down there, and the media and the Prisoners' Action Group—anybody who had a soft spot for the crims—would make noises and, of course, the department would bend over and try and placate them. And who would suffer? We would, of course. We were servants of the government, and we had to do what we were told. We had a good group of blokes. Middle-management were arseholes, they were crim-lovers.'

Cox's departure had a 'salutary effect', said Levy. 'We ended up being locked in the cells for a week while they did some modifications. They've brought in loads of steel and they've welded up a little sort of a dark area in each of the exercise yards out there to stop people having access to the bars where the warder couldn't see them.' Osborne said, 'There was modifications done, but they were still grossly inadequate. The only way to make the exercise yard secure was to replace the entire grilling system and put in proper bars—the ones that they have on normal cells—both case-hardened and large, something they just could not possibly cut through.'

—

Once Cox had gone, investigators searched for clues among his complaints. Suddenly, it seemed everything he had asked for had been fuel for his escape. His vegetarian food was described as a 'high-protein diet', indulgently bought for him using prison petty cash. The books he'd requested (in one newspaper report, 'demanded') to read included *The Most Wanted Man: The story of Ronald Biggs* by Colin Mackenzie, *The Carlos Complex: A study in terror* by Christopher Dobson and Ronald Payne and *Crusaders, Criminals, Crazies: Terror and terrorism in our time* by FJ Hacker, all of which could surely help a man break out of a maximum-security prison, even if he just piled them on top of each other to stand on them.

Not everyone—and, perhaps, at first, not anyone—believed Cox had escaped unaided. A worker at Katingal shared with the press the theory that 'someone from the outside has got up on top of the yard and either cut through a bar or dropped some equipment for Cox'. The staff member said it wouldn't have been much trouble for an accomplice to climb the perimeter fence and the two five-metre fences unseen, as the two watchtowers closest to Katingal were unmanned between 4 p.m. and 7.30 a.m.—and the guards in the watchtowers deeper in the Long Bay complex couldn't even see the Anzac Parade side of Katingal. The jail would be much easier to break into than break out of.

Which was exactly what happened next.

11

No Way Back

At first, they called it the 'Great Bag Robbery', but that sounded like a bag snatch, or a shoplifting spree at a luxury goods store. Sure, most jobs were named after the place the mugs kept their money—bank robbery, train robbery, safe-breaking—but the point about the multimillion-dollar heist on 21 April 1976 wasn't where the cash came from, but who. They took between fourteen and sixteen million dollars from the bookies, for Christ's sake. The fucking bookies. So it became 'The Great Bookie Robbery'.

The six-man team that raided the Victorian Club in Queen Street, Melbourne, was led by Painter and Docker Raymond Patrick Bennett (we'll call him by a family name and ringname, Ray Chuck) and included Painter and Docker Ian Revell Carroll, as well as Laurie Prendergast and dim sum maker Norman Leung Lee. They stormed the bookies' club after the Easter races, burst into the strong-room, cracked open the strong-boxes, packed the takings into bags—*just like bookies*—and escaped with more money than any member of the milieu could illegitimately earn in a dozen lifetimes. They also wrote their own death warrants.

Because it wasn't really an underworld. It was more like an under-village, with a population of a few dozen intermarried families, watching each other with jealous eyes, waiting for their friends to become enemies and their enemies to slip up. Even when you were a criminal mastermind like Chuck, there was nothing too conspicuous you could do with your money—except, ironically, give it to the bookies. But some people grow suited to the kind of life where you hide who you are and what you've got and what you know. Some men learn it and become it.

But there was another kind of crook who wasn't afraid to have his voice heard beyond the dismal dockie bloodhouses and waterside social clubs. Whether Chuck's mate from Pentridge, Steve Sellers, had fallen, jumped or was pushed out of the third-floor window, he wouldn't have ended up lying bleeding on the pavement with his nose split in two if the Victorian cops hadn't burst into a unit swinging. Sellers wanted to hold someone to account for his injuries—and draw attention from the fact he'd been trying to organise a bank robbery.

There was also a kind of squarehead who didn't go along with the cops—an ordinary, law-abiding citizen who couldn't accept that corruption was the cleanest and most efficient way to keep criminality under control. There was Dr Bertram Barney Wainer, for example, a former army doctor who had once commanded a military hospital: 'Bert was the most heroic man I've ever met,' said one-time barrister Peter Livesey, 'in terms of just ticker.'

While abortion was illegal, backyard abortionists were effectively controlled by the police. In return for their share of the take, bent cops play-acted law enforcement, raiding legitimate, sterile surgeries to bully qualified medical practitioners out of the business and leave the field clear for the cowboys. Melbourne's abortion butchers included an ex-cop, and their protectors went as high as the top of the Homicide Squad. In 1969, Wainer began a campaign to expose the rackets and stop the prosecution of doctors. His revelations led to an inquiry that resulted in the jailing of several police—including Jack Ford, the head of Homicide.

Wainer 'just wasn't worried about what the cops could do', Livesey told me. In 1974, Wainer set out to expose broader corruption within the force. His allegations that Victorian police routinely took bribes and framed suspects brought about Barry Beach QC's Board of Inquiry into Allegations Against Members of the Victoria Police Force (widely known as the Beach Inquiry). Sellers played a vocal and enthusiastic part in the Beach Inquiry, represented by the young barrister Robert Richter. 'At that stage,' Richter told me, 'he was in prison facing charges—and, in a sense, it was a self-defence kind of thing to say, *Listen, this is what the police have done to me—and that's what they do*. It was an advance defence of trying to establish certain squads, like the Armed Robbery Squad, the Break-In Squad, the Consorting Squad, verbal and brick people. In a sense, it was trying to establish his own defence as to allegations that he might have confessed to this, to that or the other. People with a criminal record were sitting ducks to be framed.'

Richter liked Sellers. He enjoyed his sense of humour. He agreed Sellers had 'a certain code of honour and a certain sense of honesty among people that he liked'. He said, 'He was a very clever man. He would've probably become the CEO of some large company had he had a different chance in life.' Through Sellers, Richter met Vivien Altman, who continued to visit Sellers in jail and in hospital.

'I really, really liked Steve a lot,' said Altman, 'but I think I came around to realising that we lived in two different worlds. He was a very intelligent and capable person, but he'd been involved with too many things for too long for me to think I could probably settle down with him.' Altman eventually broke up with Sellers and left the country.

The Beach Inquiry drew a furious response from Victorian police, who in 1976 began a 'work to rule' campaign and teetered on the edge of threatening a strike. Beach eventually recommended the prosecution of 55 police officers but only 32 were charged and none were convicted. Thirteen officers faced disciplinary offences and none of the offences were found proven. In the face of pressure from the Police Association, none of Beach's recommendations were implemented. Beach may have changed nothing immediately, 'but it had a massive impact ultimately', said Richter, 'because it meant that Victoria became the first state in the nation to require tape recording of interviews, and that really put the kibosh on the classic verbal. The whole methodology had to change.' Charges against Sellers did not proceed, but his evidence at the inquiry was never forgotten—the police hated him. Which was fair enough, as Sellers hated them.

—

The night Russell Cox escaped from Katingal, he tried to flag down a taxi but the driver refused to pick him up. More than 200 police searched the nearby Anzac Rifle Range and the NSW Golf Club, poked around for Cox among the graves of Botany Cemetery, and made the customary round of backyards and chook sheds, in case Cox was hiding out like Roy Pollitt. Detective Sergeant Brian Harding of the Armed Hold-Up Squad said, 'When we do catch up with him, it's unlikely he will come easily. We feel certain he is armed, and he has nothing to lose.'

It sounded like Cox might not get much sympathy—or much of a warning—from the cops in New South Wales, and he headed down to Victoria to renew old friendships among the Painters and Dockers. He spent time at Kath Pettingill's place in Ross Street, Northcote, and Pettingill—the matriarch of Australia's most troublesome and troubled criminal family—has claimed him as a lover. According to Cox's police file, he also had an 'unconfirmed' relationship with a 'Patty Hill'—which may or may not be a mishearing of Pettingill. Cox teamed up with Painter and Docker Thomas Edward Wraith, who had been deported from England—where he had killed his de facto, Grace O'Connor, the ex-wife of the murdered Queensland criminal (and Cox's brother's one-time army mate) Raymond 'Ducky' O'Connor. Wraith was going out with Pettingill's daughter, Vicki. On New Year's Eve, Cox and Wraith drove around to Ross Street to pick up Vicki when police spotted Wraith's car and chased it into a wall. Shots were fired, Wraith was knocked out, but Cox escaped.

Cox always escaped—and some of the boys back in jail were a bit dark on him for leaving Katingal alone. Prison officer George Eastham told me he was outside Denning's cell in Maitland the morning after Cox's breakout when

Denning shouted to Shipley, 'Did you hear that fucking cunt's gone without us?'

One newspaper reported that the breakout wasn't even Cox's idea. The Maitland Crew had only let him join them because of his fitness. Now, said the *Daily Mirror*, there was a contract out on Cox. 'He fooled his mates by escaping a day earlier than the breakout was scheduled,' a senior police officer was quoted as saying. 'It was the perfect double-cross.'

But the rumour that Cox had abandoned his friends bubbled alongside murmurs that Cox would never leave behind Jockey Smith. Katingal superintendent Edgar Bowden was warned Cox was going to take a family hostage to exchange for Smith, so Bowden's house was put under constant police surveillance. The family of the judge in Smith's upcoming court case was also given 24-hour police protection.

The Maitland Crew made one last bid to escape together on November 17, when Denning, Pollitt and Sutton tried to saw through a mesh grille in the back of the van taking them from court to Katingal. They were discovered before they could harm anything but the grille—and they copped a charge for damaging Corrective Services' property.

Cox on the run moved between NSW and Victoria. It's said he worked for about six months as a storeman in NSW. He was elusive, but only when he didn't want to be found. He hooked up with a mate, Sydney boxing trainer Johnny Lewis, in Saratoga on the Central Coast, and Gary Waddell met Cox in a house in Rozelle that Cox was visiting with Sellers.

And it turned out the police were right: Cox wasn't going to give up on Jockey Smith. Early in the morning on

31 May 1978, Russell Cox and Steve Sellers attempted one of the most audacious stunts in Australian criminal history. They drove out to Long Bay in a vehicle loaded with guns and breaking gear. They cut a wire fence and used an extension ladder to scale a brick wall. And then Cox did it a-fucking-gain. He came back in by the way he'd left. Cox pulled himself up onto the roof of the exercise yard in Katingal, where two men then worked under an almost lightless fingernail moon: Australia's greatest break-out artist and its bravest break-in guy. They fired up an oxy-acetylene torch, cut through the roof bars in eight places, unrolled a rope ladder and one man climbed down into the exercise yard. Then, according to Sergeant Wayne Barry, a police prosecutor, they 'virtually cut off a door leading to the prison itself' and came 'within five feet of the master switch which operates the doors of each of the prisoners in Katingal'.

Cox and Sellers had a bag of loaded pistols—guns for everybody. But you can't plan for everything. You can't take into account the possibility that an elderly woman in Bilga Crescent will get up and look out of her bedroom window. Why would she even do that, for Christ's sake? What did she expect to see?

Sellers never talked to Altman about the break-in. 'The one thing he did say was it was just really bad luck,' she said. 'There was a woman who lived opposite the jail who'd gone to the bathroom in the middle of the night, and she'd seen something. On the basis of that, she must've alerted the police, and I think that was what brought them undone.'

What the neighbour saw was one man on the roof of Katingal and another inside the wire fence. She called the cops, who raced towards the jail, with sirens advertising they were on their way. Sellers and Cox had cut and now they ran, leaving a rifle, the pistols, sticks of gelignite, a detonator, a chisel and other breaking tools on the roof and by the fence.

The men inside Katingal had a different view of the action. Matthews was asleep in the cell next door to armed robber Jimmy Murray, who knocked on the wall to wake him. 'He says, "Look out in the yard,"' said Matthews. 'Now, from our cell windows we could look through the security glass into the yard, where the control panels were. I looked out, and all that I saw was this shower of sparks. I've gone, "Holy Jesus!" And then we've realised they're cutting through the bars with oxy. It was like bonfire night—all these stars just streaming into the yard. And then they came down and they started working on the door.'

Matthews thought the intruders—whom he will not name—made a noise that alerted a warder who sounded the alarm inside the jail. A story in *The Sydney Morning Herald* said the cops might have caught Cox and Sellers except that one officer tripped up in the dark and called out, 'Fuck!' His mates thought he'd cried 'Duck!' and threw themselves to the ground, giving Cox and Sellers the chance to get away.

The record shows that Constable Chris Jones fell into a metre-deep ditch and dislocated his shoulder.

A prison spokesman called the raid 'a commando-type operation, a full-scale attempt to get prisoners, or a prisoner, out of Katingal'. Livesey thought Sellers had most likely gone along with Cox to rescue Motric—'Steve cared deeply for Marko,' he said.

Back in Victoria, Cox went to work with Ray Chuck and the Bookie Robbery crew. Chuck was a popular, clever and personable character—some of the other Painters and Dockers were less so. Chuck's rivals in the Kane family had a stake in the robbery—or, at least, believed they were entitled to one. The Kanes were old-fashioned standover men who knew what everybody was doing and elbowed in for a piece of the action. Three brothers, Les, Brian and Ray, were all, at least nominally, Painters and Dockers. They dominated their territory as SP bookies, safecrackers and streetfighters. They would even take 'commissions' from barbershops. Brian had the brains, Les the explosive temper.

Gary Waddell had worked as a Painter and Docker. 'Ray Kane sort of latched on to me because I was doing *The Sullivans*,' he said. 'He liked the whole thing of knowing people that were in showbusiness.' Dour, vicious Laurie Prendergast was around, too. 'I was sitting at the Albion Hotel with Ray one night,' said Waddell, 'and I said to Ray, "Do you want a beer, whacker?" And he said, "Don't fucking call me 'whacker'." And Laurie said, "Let's cut his throat."'

Cox started seeing Helen Deane, the sister of Ray Chuck's wife, Gail. Deane was born in Beechworth, a Gold Rush town in north-east Victoria, and went to school at Prahran Technical. She picked up a couple of minor juvenile convictions but trained as a nurse's aide then married a bloke from Singapore. The couple had a daughter in 1970. When they divorced, their daughter went to live in Singapore with her dad. Deane later moved in with a Melbourne criminal. She was always described as 'mousy' but she was green-eyed and pretty like a cat.

The gang gathered by Chuck, and including Cox, was infiltrated by an undercover police officer posing as a corrupt Mayne Nickless security guard. The undercover suggested to Cox a payroll hold-up at the Country Roads Board's head office in Kew. The evening before the raid, Cox and the undercover met in North Melbourne to receive money owed to the undercover for his inside information. When the delivery was late, Cox said they should wait at the Queen Victoria Market, which would be empty at that time of night. At the markets, they were stopped by chance by a team of uniformed police. Cox pulled out a .38.

The undercover believed Cox would shoot, so he stepped in first, disabled the police car's radio, stole the officers' guns, forced the men to climb into a skip and covered them with pallets. Cox fled, and the payroll job—and the undercover operation—was abandoned.

Towards the end of 1978, Cox became keen to show the Bookie Robbers the sights of his home state of Queensland. On December 12, the day after an Armaguard van had delivered the Christmas payroll, a crew made up of Cox, Chuck, Carroll, Prendergast and another man, hit the Prince Charles Hospital in Chermside, north Brisbane. They arrived in a stolen VW Kombi at about 8.45 a.m. Hooded and armed with sawn-off shotguns, the team made their way to the hospital pay office. In a grey dustcoat, Cox delivered the immortal line, 'This is a hold-up . . . Don't anybody move!'—because the boys were all stars in the gangster movie looping in their own heads—and threatened to kill the staff if they didn't give up the money.

They carried away $16,618. It was the first of a string of highly lucrative, well-planned and pitilessly executed heists for the gang. But let's pause for a minute to consider what we're really talking about here: a bunch of blokes—including a killer and a rapist—who have barely done a day's work between them or paid a cent of tax in their lives, burst into a teaching hospital specialising in cardiac and respiratory medicine (that is, wards stuffed with heart-attack patients) dressed like death. They promise they will murder the workers in the pay office unless they hand over the *Christmas pay* earmarked for the honest and overworked doctors and nurses, cleaners, cooks and orderlies in the hospital. Our boys weren't the Kelly Gang, that's for sure. They weren't Robin fucking Hood. But then, neither were the Kelly Gang. Or Robin Hood.

The same team, dressed in the same hoods and dustcoats, hit the ANZ Bank on Gympie Road, Strathpine, armed with sawn-off shotguns and military rifles. Two of them jumped the counter and grabbed $5780 and two .38 revolvers from the tellers' drawers. Later, the crew cut the wires to telephone junction boxes outside the pay office at the Royal Women's Hospital, Brisbane, came through the doors armed with pistols at 9.45 a.m., and left with $62,446.30, freshly delivered by Armaguard. Let's just go through that again—they cut the phone lines to a hospital.

Cox later said he sailed a yacht from Australia to England in 1978 and worked as a seaman for two years. He visited Germany then returned to Australia, again by yacht—and perhaps he did, at some time: he had a passport issued under the name Gary Nevin, of Williams Road, Toorak, and he was born with ocean waves in his hair.

Coincidentally, a Queensland Painter and Docker also named Gary Nevin lived in a property in Petrie Terrace,

Brisbane, owned by Cox's brother Karl. Upstairs in the house lived Cox's mother's long-term partner, sometime seaman Andrew Keane.

It was comparatively easy to obtain a false (rather than forged) passport, and the Painters and Dockers ran ratlines for members who needed to get out of the country. Applications were lodged with the Passport Office on behalf of men who had never left Australia, with photographs of a lightly disguised fugitive—wearing glasses, make-up, or a new hairstyle—in their place.

The year 1978 would have been a good time to disappear. On October 19, Chuck, Prendergast and another man visited Les Kane at home, pushed Kane's family aside, shot him dead and took away the body. On 12 November 1979, Chuck was shot dead outside Melbourne Magistrates' Court, only metres from his wife, Helen Deane's sister Gail.

Underworld opinion pinned Chuck's murder on a corrupt cop or Brian Kane or both.

In July 1980, Cox, Prendergast and another man, two of them balaclavad and dustcoated, fronted up with pistols to collect the payroll at Boral Cyclone in Geebung, Queensland, only a few minutes after the money had been delivered by Armaguard. They cut the phone lines, assaulted a 65-year-old deaf-mute gardener, then stormed the pay office. 'Hit the floor, don't move, don't look at me and don't follow,' said a hooded bandit thought to be Cox. They netted $21,348.10 and escaped in a Holden sedan stolen from the carpark of the Prince Charles Hospital. A hospital carpark—think about that. Cox repeated all his old tricks—phone lines severed, Holden stolen from the hospital, payroll delivered by Armaguard—at Woodlands

Industries, pulling $38,855 in cash and cheques worth $72,389.

Maybe he left the country afterwards. His mate and co-offender in the Pye Industries robbery, Peter Croft, was allowed out of Parramatta Gaol to take part in a couple of fight nights at Cardiff Workers Club, Newcastle. Croft had been knocked out by light heavyweight Peter White on 16 May 1980, then lost on points to cruiserweight Bob Sharkey on August 22. Police combed the crowd on both nights, hoping for Cox to show.

Chris Fraser, then a divisional detective, told me, 'I got heaps of overtime over alleged sightings of Cox. Really helped when you are up to your neck in mortgage and have a wife at home looking after the kids.' Often, a tip-off would be anonymous and Fraser suspected 'some cops wanted some overtime and did it'.

By 1980, even Cox's Queensland family didn't know where he was—and they had lost touch with his surfing champion brother, as well. Cox's mother died in Brisbane in December 1979 and the Queensland Public Trustee placed a sad press advertisement in October 1980, searching for her sons, Russell Anthony Schnitzerling and Melville Peter Schnitzerling, or anyone who knew their whereabouts.

—

Cox was back in Australia by 1981, when he renewed his friendship with Ray Denning and also with Ian Revell Carroll. Cox and Deane lived first in Queensland, then rented a house in unglamorous Nunawading in the east of Melbourne. In July 1982, they moved to Helena Street in Mount Martha, on the Mornington Peninsula, two blocks away from Hawker Beach. They were polite neighbours, who ran in the sand in the early morning—although Cox never went to the beach without a pistol holstered under his T-shirt. They kept a black labrador named 'Devil', after the mountain wolf companion of the comic-strip hero, the Phantom (aka 'the ghost who walks'). Cox sometimes called himself 'Mr Walker' in homage to the Phantom, who was never seen without his mask.

The Mount Martha house was bought from the landlords by Ian Revell Carroll, one of Cox's closest friends. English-born Carroll was often referred to as a former professional boxer, but it seems he only fought twice as a pro, on bottom-of-the-card bouts against novice fighters Hans Gent and Ron Evans, and lost on both occasions. But he was a hard man, respected and feared around Melbourne's docks and beyond. His convictions stretched back to the age of thirteen. In his twenties, he was charged with indecent assault and indecent treatment of a woman. He had been a member of the Victorian Painters and Dockers management committee in 1974, 1976 and 1977, but he didn't get much work despite his union connections. For three years when he listed his occupation as a Painter and Docker, he declared no taxable income at all, yet his interests had included properties at Wonga Park, Springvale, Ringwood, Narre Warren and Williamstown. By his final tax return in 1982, he had somehow become a computer programmer.

Cox was living in Carroll's house in Mount Martha on 26 November 1982, when Brian Kane was shot dead by masked gunmen at the Quarry Hotel, Brunswick.

Police believed one of the gunmen was Cox—but who would know? They were both wearing masks.

12

The Sins of Brett Collins

'I did do the bank robbery,' Brett Collins told me. 'It's a very grudging admission, though, because I was verballed. They never had a case, they never made the case. Am I then justifying the verbal which allowed them to convict me of an offence when they didn't have the evidence? Well, I hope I'm not. But I just want to be real. I think it's much better that I accept responsibility. I did serve, after all, about ten years.'

Until the late 1960s, there had been no Brett Collins—or, rather, Brett Collins had been a different person entirely. The bankrobber Brett Collins began life as David Charles Hass, born in New Zealand, the son of a Jewish doctor from Poland and a Presbyterian schoolteacher. David Hass resented authority. His mother was a fairly strict parent. On the surface, he was an obedient son. Not far beneath, he was a lawless tearaway.

David was an irritant at school, constantly disturbing people. He began shoplifting with his friends. He didn't need the money. When he stole things, he generally gave them away.

He moved up to car theft and joyriding, just for the thrill. He didn't rebirth or resell the cars.

David had too much energy and no useful, satisfying focus. He was expelled from Auckland Grammar School, but entered Otago University, Dunedin, at sixteen, the youngest medical student ever admitted to the faculty. However, he transferred to dentistry and, in his second year of study, got drunk at a party and stole and wrecked a crop-dusting plane.

He was sentenced to nine months in Invercargill Borstal, which he found 'relatively benign'. 'I learned quite early that there was definitely a hard edge to the law,' he said. 'But it didn't really make any difference to me because I continued to push against authority, against borders. I was a little bit overexcited.' Upon his release, he made attempts to study science, then psychiatry, but he couldn't settle down. In 1968, he borrowed the identity of a flatmate, Brett Anthony Collins, to begin a new life in Sydney.

'I needed some basic identification to arrive in Australia,' he said, 'so I asked him did he mind if I had a copy of his driver's licence or something. That was the initial document that meant I had some way of starting afresh in Australia.'

By 1971, the new Brett Collins was an engineering student in Sydney, married with a son. He owned a boarding house in Eveleigh Street, Redfern, bought for him by his parents. As usual, he had no need of money. As ever, he was bored.

On Thursday, 8 April, he pulled on a mask, picked up a sawn-off double-barrelled shotgun, and rode a motorbike to the Commonwealth Savings Bank in Stanmore. At about

11.40 a.m., he burst into the bank and demanded money from an eighteen-year-old teller. When a 69-year-old man tried to disarm him, Collins hit him over the head with the gun then ran out of the bank with about $3000 in a bag and the teller at his heels. The teller caught up with Collins in the street, they grappled and Collins knocked the teller to the ground with his bag of cash.

Collins had no reason to rob a bank. He saw it as a challenge—and a fashionable one at that. In the early 1970s, it seemed to him, everybody was robbing banks. And he thought he could get away with it. He felt invulnerable.

Unfortunately, his bike wouldn't start, so Collins had to steal a four-wheel drive to get home.

Collins thought he had escaped until a few days' later, when he was stopped by police on the Princes Highway at Gymea, in a stolen Holden sedan with the teller's pistol and a pile of numberplates under a coat. Collins took hold of the pistol. The cop later gave evidence that he grabbed Collins' gun hand and forced the gun down and away from him. 'The gun discharged and I felt its recoil while I was holding his hand,' the police officer testified improbably.

The cop fell out of the car and, he later claimed, as he lay on his back pleading, 'Don't shoot, I've two boys at home', Collins laughed and pulled the trigger. The officer said the pistol misfired and, as Collins ran, he gave chase, firing at Collins as he zigzagged away.

'He turned and pointed his pistol at me,' said the cop. 'I heard it discharge and heard the buzz of the bullet as it went past.'

Collins ran into the scrub but was apprehended with the pistol at Sutherland District Hospital. He was arrested, bashed and charged. When he refused to speak to the cops who had brutalised him, they told the court he had confessed to his crimes by nodding his head. 'That's how outrageous they were,' said Collins. 'They were so used to using a police verbal to seal a case where there wasn't sufficient evidence.

'I was treated really badly by Sutherland police,' said Collins. 'We had a pretty heavy confrontation when they did arrest me and I ended up beaten up. They then said that I'd attempted to murder a police. But luckily there were some bystanders who said that hadn't happened.'

Collins' parents came out from New Zealand for the trial and hired Clive Evatt QC to defend him. The attempted-murder charge was thrown out, but Collins was sentenced to fifteen years for the bank robbery and two more for assaulting the elderly witness. Collins felt angry, as if he were the one who had been treated unfairly. 'It left me with a very deep misgiving about the hypocrisy of the police,' he said, 'who could tell lies—break the law—on oath, against me, and act as though they were being honest and straight.'

In jail, the frenetic and inquisitive Collins became an organiser, an agitator, a troublemaker. He taught himself the law and also how to be a prisoner. 'I had to come to terms with living in a community where brutality was the order of the day,' he said. 'I had to mix it in with the others and make sure I learned some survival skills. I learned how to fight and how to avoid fights: that was a long lesson. At different times they had a boxing ring at Parramatta Gaol, and some of the prisoners would teach other prisoners. I used to spar. I learned some skills there.

'The first time I was bashed would have been in Long Bay,' said Collins, 'where I had this prison officer come into the yard and try to beat me up. But I was 23 years old and fit. We threw punches at each other, I then came in and clinched with him, I put him in a headlock, I held him down and then dragged him out of the yard. I made sure he knew he'd lost. After I'd got it over him and he'd thrown his punches, he said, "I fought in Vietnam."

'They had the prison officer on the wall aim his rifle at me and I said, "He came in to me, boss. I didn't attack him. He came into my yard and he took me on as a fair fight. He took his jacket off before he came in."

'It was unusual for him to come in by himself,' said Collins. 'If he was going to come and beat me up, he would normally have come with three or four prison officers. What he was doing was trying to tell me that he was smarter and stronger than I was, and he was going to punish me, and do it because he thought he could do it.

'But the next morning they charged me with assaulting a prison officer. Luckily, I had some prisoner support. Even some of the other prison officers felt it was a fair fight. So I ended up not going to Grafton, but I was held in a black cell for eight days, where all the windows were welded up so the only light you would get would be under the crack of the door at the bottom. Otherwise, it was totally pitch black. So that was a bit of an early awakening about how much control they had of my living space, and it forced me to deal in a very disciplined way with my conditions and how I responded to them.'

Collins staked his place among the hard and damaged men all around him by becoming their champion and their counsellor, as well as their friend. In the life-draining and cheerless New South Wales prison system, Brett Collins finally found a focus for his vigour and vivacity. He was among a group of four negotiators who spoke on behalf of NSW prisoners when the Corrective Services Commissioner came to Maitland Gaol after the Maitland and Bathurst riots. They won the right to elect prison committees and Collins became the committee chair.

He held the record as the prisoner to spend the longest time on the roof of any prison in NSW—a Long Bay roof for three days in December 1977. 'I was happy to fend for myself and stay up there,' he said. 'People were feeding me. It was certainly better to be on the roof than it was to be sitting inside a cell. On the fourth day, I had fire hoses trained on me at about five in the morning and they threw up the ladders. They came from all sides. They had the waterhose and then I got sprayed from the front with the pepper spray and then somebody came from behind and grabbed me. Then I was taken down. They lowered me to probably six feet from the ground—and then they dropped me. I had my hands cuffed behind my back and I came down really heavily on my head. And they put a towel around my throat and choked all the air out of me so I couldn't breathe. I became unconscious.' When he came back around, 'They got stuck into me,' he said. 'They kicked me and kicked me, and then in that state I was taken into the OBS.'

About an hour later, he heard a roar from the yards. The prisoners had climbed over fences and refused to go back to their cells until a delegation was allowed in to see him. He felt the whole jail had acted in solidarity with him. 'You don't forget that,' said Collins.

Mt. Penang Training School for Boys. Among its alumni were bankrobbers Ray Denning and Bernie Matthews. The boys used to joke that the boomerang over the gate meant they would always come back. *Source: New South Wales government.*

Westbrook Farm Home for Boys: a little piece of hell in south-east Queensland that helped forge the man who became Russell Cox. *Source: Queensland Government / Queensland Newspapers.*

Pentridge Prison, once home to Russell Cox and Steve Sellers—and Chopper Read, who made up stories about them. *Source: News Ltd / Newspix.*

Former armed robber and raconteur extraordinaire Bernie Matthews in 1988, the year he helped Ray Denning find Russell Cox—an act he would live to regret. *Source: Steve Christo, Fairfax Media.*

The urbane armed robber John Killick, Australia's first decimal-currency bandit. *Courtesy of John Killick.*

The view upwards from the trac yards in Grafton, where rebellious prisoners were stripped and bashed senseless. *Courtesy of Bernie Matthews.*

The Circle at Parramatta Gaol, where Ray Denning copped his first flogging. *Source: Fairfax Media.*

The Control Room at Katingal, the escape-proof jail from which Russell Cox escaped. And then broke back in. *Source: Fairfax Media.*

A cell in the OBS (Observation Unit) at Long Bay. Former OBS residents include Russell Cox, Ray Denning and Bernie Matthews. *Courtesy of Bernie Matthews.*

Machine guns on the table at the Victorian Club, site of the Great Bookie Robbery of 1976. Russell Cox was in jail during the robbery but is believed to have had a stake in the heist. *Source: Fairfax Media.*

Roger 'Mad Dog' Rogerson of the NSW Armed Hold-Up Squad: dashingly brave, unrestrainedly corrupt. *Source: News Ltd / Newspix.*

Robyn Lawson: Ray Denning's first and last girlfriend. *Source: Greg Newington / Newspix.*

Kim Pascoe, a former girlfriend of Ray Denning who went to the bush to coax him out when he wasn't there. *Source: Fairfax Media.*

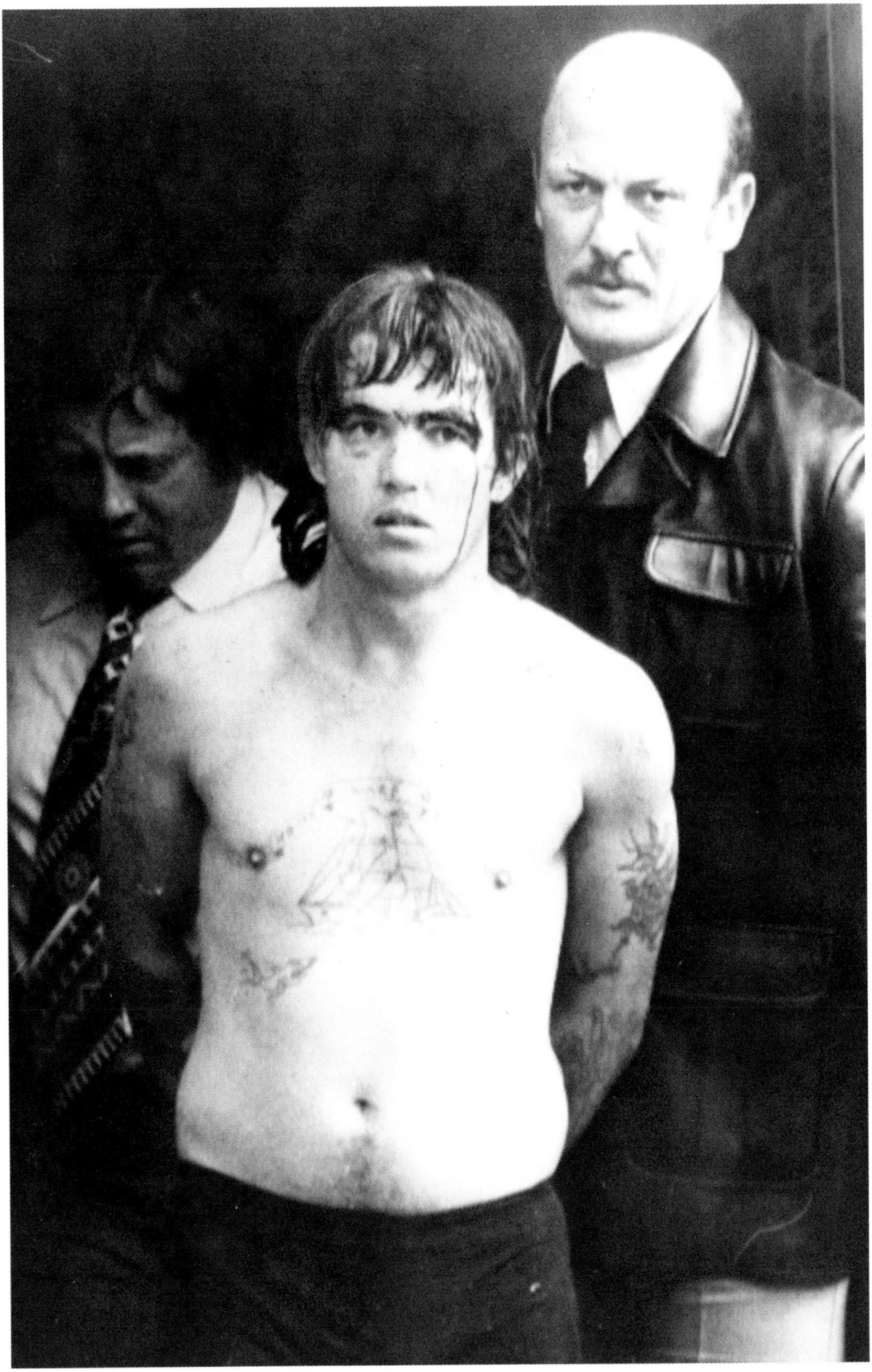

Ray Denning, captured in 1977, with NSW Police officers John 'Bopper' Mooney (left) and former Australian Rugby League representative Brian 'Chicka' Moore. *Source: Fairfax Media.*

Ray Denning's one-time best mate Brett Collins, protesting on a roof at Long Bay jail. *Source: Fairfax Media.*

Ray Denning on the run taunted police by leaving his prints on the door of the Sydney CIB headquarters in 1980. Constable Ian Waterson of the Fingerprint Bureau frowned at them while wearing a jumper. *Source: Fairfax Media.*

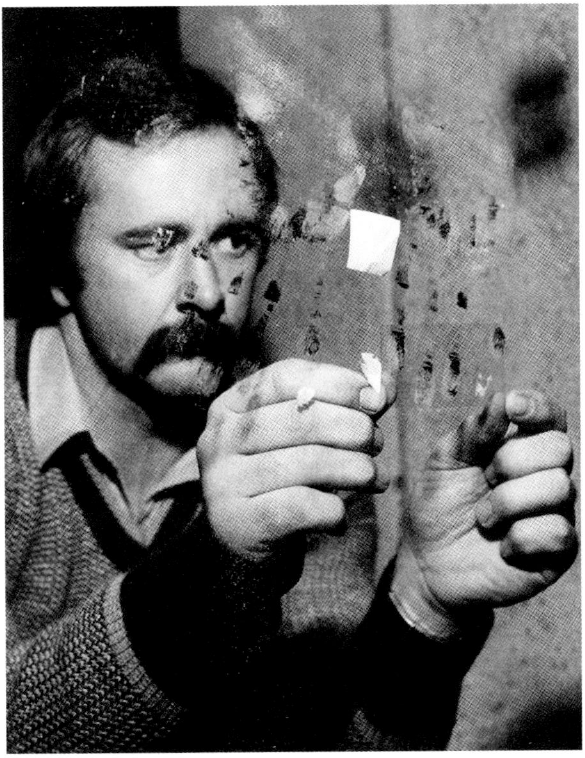

Linda Jobson, the mother of Ray Denning's son. *Source: Fairfax Media.*

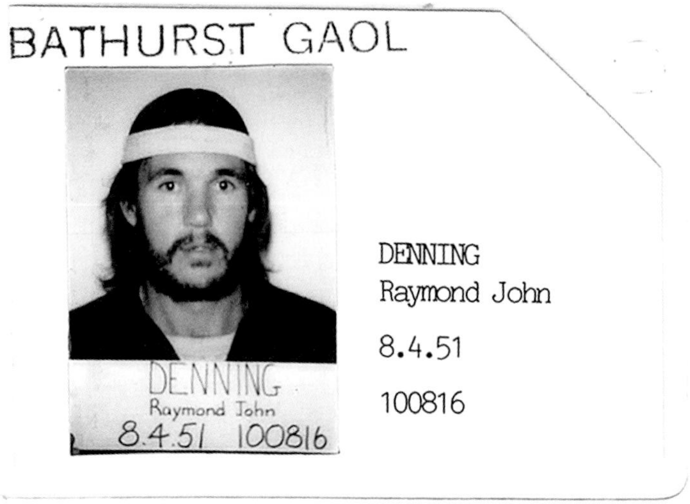

Ray Denning: ID in his real name, for once. *Courtesy of Bernie Matthews.*

Ray Denning and friend at Parklea Prison in the 1980s. *Courtesy of Bernie Matthews.*

The haul of weapons and disguises found in Ray Denning's unit in Mona Vale, Sydney, in 1981. Detective Sergeant Geoff McDowell poses with Denning's pistol (after the gun had been fingerprinted, hopefully). *Source: Fairfax Media.*

Ray Denning enjoying the sunshine in Bathurst, 1986. *Courtesy of Bernie Matthews.*

Ray Denning (top row, second from the left) and friends at the Bathurst Gala Day 1986. *Courtesy of Bernie Matthews.*

Russell Cox captured at Doncaster Shoppingtown, Melbourne, in July 1988. *Source: Fairfax Media.*

Behind every good man is a better woman: Helen Eva Deane, the wife of Russell Cox. *Source: News Ltd / Newspix.*

National Australia Bank, Hornsby, August 1987, site of the first ramraid in NSW, which police initially attributed to Russell Cox. *Source: Fairfax Media.*

Jack the Hat Denning at the funeral of his son, Ray, in June 1993. *Source: Greg Newington / Newspix.*

He first came across Denning in Parramatta, but they stayed in touch while Denning was in Grafton. 'We'd pass messages through,' said Collins. 'It'd normally be a piece of paper rolled up in plastic and put in your mouth or your bottom and carried. There'd be a constant flow. He was involved in cases all the time, and I'd started to get some legal expertise and I was able to give him advice and information and assistance and suggestions of people he might link up to and work with.'

Collins anticipated being sent to Grafton himself and asked Denning what might happen to him. 'I wanted to understand what they were going to do,' he said. 'If they were to attack me first up, what could I expect?

'I really enjoyed the fellow,' said Collins. 'He had such high spirits. He was always happy to smile, always full of energy and was indomitable. I never saw him cowed in those days. He was a little man, he was an inspiring man, a delightful person, the sort of guy of whom you're proud when he's your friend.'

More than 40 years after they first met, Collins still spoke about Denning with love.

—

Denning, Cox and Collins all offered anguished submissions to the Nagle Royal Commission into NSW Prisons, which reported in March 1978. Nagle found that many of the worst accusations made against warders after the Bathurst riots had been substantially factual. The prison officers' union made a blanket admission on behalf of its members at Grafton that the reception biff and punishment beatings—'upon breach of any rules, written or unwritten'—were understood by warders as 'official departmental policy'.

After Nagle, it was clear that everything said by the ratbags and agitators and troublemakers and stirrers and naïve, know-nothing middle-class reformers—fucking *women*, for Christ's sake—turned out to be true, just as their accusations against the police would be vindicated a few years later. The Commission also recommended that Katingal be abandoned because its cost was 'too high in human terms'.

On 4 May 1978, Denning, Pollitt and Sutton were taken from Katingal to the District Criminal Court, Darlinghurst, to face charges of attempting to escape from the prison van, and an alternative count of maliciously injuring a mesh grille. Denning—who no longer seemed to be Lobsang Rampa—pleaded not guilty and represented himself. When Denning asked Chief Prison Officer Victor Coughlan if he had ever bashed prisoners at Grafton, Coughlan admitted that he had. Denning asked Coughlan if he had ever used batons and fists. 'Yes,' said Coughlan.

The Maitland Crew were found not guilty on the van-escape charge but guilty of damaging the grille. Pollitt—who no longer seemed to be a disciple of Lobsang Rampa—hurled evidence transcripts in the air and shouted abuse at the judge. Three women in the gallery yelled, 'Close Katingal!'

The impetus behind the anti-Katingal campaign continued to come from libertarian feminists who'd been blooded in the Vietnam days. Wendy Bacon and Women Behind Bars helped organise with the PAG a traffic-stopping blockade on Sydney Harbour Bridge—an idea Bacon had first suggested during the planning for a Vietnam Moratorium demonstration in 1970.

A number of relationships had grown up between activist women and male criminals, few of which were as successful as the love affair between Vivien Altman and Steve Sellers. 'Some of those guys—certainly not all of them—were very attractive,' Altman told me. 'Now, why are they attractive? How much is to do with them being locked up? I don't know. Maybe they had more time to do a lot of gym. Maybe they had more time to read a lot. Or maybe the men outside were just really boring.'

Many of the crims had grown up getting fucked and flogged. Older, bigger, stronger men had been knocking them into shape almost since the day they were born. The young militants of the New Left were more likely to be the children of parents who put an education ahead of a belting. They couldn't know what to expect from their abused, institutionalised, infantilised new friends.

Burgmann said, 'I always thought that the men had often spent, say, ten years in jail, and not only were those ten years going to brutalise them, but it meant that they didn't grow any older. They didn't become adult males. They remained the sort of teenager that they were when they went into jail. So often they did really, really teenage-boy things, like scratching all the girl's records, or sitting outside the house . . .'

Even when the men hit their partners, 'Often the women involved didn't want it all to be a public mess,' said Burgmann. 'And so often we did what we could at a private level. And there was only one or two occasions that I can think of. And, let's face it, we all knew that our friends were being beaten up by their white middle-class boyfriends too, and so you have to deal with these things as the women themselves want it dealt with, rather than go on a bit of a crusade of your own.'

—

On the afternoon of Sunday, 21 May 1978, a small group of demonstrators walked through a hole in Long Bay's outer fence and marched towards Katingal, where they paraded around the wire then sat down. Twelve people were arrested and charged with trespass on prison property. Radical poster artist Chips Mackinolty was detained with a contingent from Women Behind Bars. 'I always used to get bailed out early, because everyone knew I'd give my right name,' he told me, 'and then my job was to collect as many fake names as I could and remember them for whoever was doing the bailing on the outside. The funny thing was, in the Redfern Court on the following Monday, we had to sign an undertaking that none of us would enter prison. And, of course, if we didn't sign that, we would have been sent straight to jail.'

In a rare unmitigated victory for a radical movement, Katingal was closed in June 1978, after only three years' operation as a jail. Corrective Services Commissioner Ron Woodham later said, 'It was a nightmare for staff to work in there. It was a nightmare for the inmates to be in there ... They broke into it. They broke out of it. They broke the unbreakable glass. They sawed the unsawable bars. It was an absolute nightmare.'

Denning, James, Motric, Sutton and Jockey Smith were among the last men transferred out of the jail. Many maximum-security prisoners from all over the NSW system, including Denning and Collins, found themselves back at Grafton, where the regime had softened but not gone soft.

'The bashings that I heard weren't like they were in the old intractable days,' said Collins. 'I never experienced the biffs that had me urinating and bleeding all over the place. I got punched in the face many times, I got kicked.'

Denning and Collins were locked up in Grafton on 27 August 1978, the day Ray Denning became a killer. Willy Faber had finally succumbed to his injuries and died of a heart attack. His widow, Ursula, said he had suffered from epilepsy since he had been battered. 'The doctors gave him five minutes to live and he stayed with us for four years,' she said. 'There was no warning of when the epilepsy attacks would occur. But in the end, he seemed to have had enough. He just wanted to end it.'

Bob Downes, as chairman of the Long Bay sub-branch of the Prison Officers Association, said, 'Although he was injured performing his duty, the department did not pay him his $130,000 compensation until three years later. Willy often had to survive with the help of hand-outs from his former workmates. It was a terrible thing—he had his brains bashed out by a 7-pound club.' But Denning wrote in his diary: 'I've just heard on the radio the screw has died. I don't feel sorry for the screw because you have to be a dog to be a screw.'

On September 8, Denning was badly flogged by at least eight Grafton warders. They called him a dog and a cunt, hit him, kicked him and thrashed him while he was on the ground. When Denning was taken back to his cell, Brett Collins called out to him. Denning said he was going on hunger strike to protest at his treatment. Collins promised to join him. Because it was the right thing to do, and because Collins loved him.

13

The Martyrdom of Peter Livesey

They pulled off the biggest bank job in Australian history without Steve Sellers. The Katingal break-in attempt had brought Sellers new admiration in the criminal world—but it had also turned the spotlight on everything he did and everyone he knew. So when the Magnetic Drill Gang robbed the Bank of New South Wales in Murwillumbah, they went in without him.

The Magnetic Drill Gang was a loose association of some of the more professional Melbourne crims, led by former Painter and Docker Graham 'the Munster' Kinniburgh, who was thought to resemble Herman Munster, a cut-price sitcom Frankenstein's monster, a clearance-sale grim-faced Lurch.

But Kinniburgh was a respected safebreaker—along with Sellers, he was one of the last of his kind. He was well liked by the kind of people who liked people like him. He didn't big-note himself. He wasn't flash. He paid off the right people. He didn't go around shouting that he'd been verballed and bricked. He didn't fall out of third-storey windows or break into escape-proof jails. He didn't. Draw. Fucking. Attention.

Sellers should have been a member of the Magnetic Drill Gang. He had the skills, the dash, the connections, even the desire—but he couldn't work alongside Kinniburgh because Sellers refused to forget historic feuds or behave like a normal, circumspect, tight-lipped professional crim.

The Magnetic Drill Gang knew there was more than one way into a bank. There was no need to blast out the window and step through tears of glass, bully weeping tellers and dash out into a stolen car. You could break in through the back door of an empty bank at night and patiently work the safe in silence.

The gang had an MO that Interpol hadn't seen anywhere in the world, and it had made them more than one million dollars from thirteen robberies. The equipment they used was a hodgepodge of the medical and the mechanical—the kind of kit a mad scientist might assemble to make a munster. In the early hours of 23 November 1978, when Kinniburgh and his crew came through the rear of the Murwillumbah Bank of NSW and into the vault, they took along a fluoroscope. Fluoroscopic technology is used in airport-security scanners and medical imaging to look inside an object or a body: the gang had adapted it to study the tumblers of a bank safe.

Once the safecracker had familiarised himself with the tumblers, the gang worked a rare magnetic, diamond-tipped drill, which they clamped to the vault door and bore through the lock to penetrate within five millimetres of the point from which the tumblers could be manipulated. Next, they unpacked a cystoscope, an instrument with a lens small enough to use to penetrate the human body via the urethra. They peered down the cystoscope at the mechanism of the safe, then operated a special attachment to turn the tumblers and break the locks.

When the job was done, they left the way they had come in, with $1.7 million in cash that had been delivered to the bank for a Queensland payroll run.

Kinniburgh had pulled off the biggest heist the country had ever known, and now Sellers—who hadn't been in the vault—was demanding a cut. Kinniburgh knew how this kind of thing had to end, so he finished it before it got started. On 2 February 1979, as Sellers answered the phone in the lobby of the Domain Motel in South Yarra Kinniburgh blasted him with a shotgun, three times in the back at point-blank range.

Sellers had $6000 in his pocket.

Sellers was taken to Melbourne's Alfred Hospital. 'Bert Wainer and I went to see him at 3 a.m.,' Robert Richter told me. 'We were concerned because of repercussions of the Beach Inquiry. We saw him and he was all intubated in every way and he was barely conscious, but all he could mutter was, "I'm not answering any questions. I'm not talking to any fucking coppers. I want to see a lawyer." And some people from the NSW Armed Hold-Up Squad and some Serious Crimes Squad came down to Melbourne to interview him about Katingal, and they made up a story that at the very time that Bert and I were seeing him—and he was saying,

"I'm not answering any fucking questions"—he is supposed to have answered them and confessed. Which was obvious bullshit. He wouldn't have given the coppers the time of day, let alone made a confession, but they had the traditional NSW verbal/brick.'

Vivien Altman, who had returned from overseas, also visited Sellers. The police were anxious to find out how much she knew about the shooting. 'That was the most frightening,' she told me. 'The senior police officers were most focused on him, what was happening around him and why he'd been shot, and I thought at the time they were following me around. I'd been in the UK and Europe for three years and I was absolutely terrified. I'd stay with friends in Melbourne and all of a sudden there was this car sitting outside with these really heavy looking coppers, then they'd walk around the back fence and just try to intimidate me. It was totally absurd because I'd barely seen him for three years and I'd had nothing to do with it.'

Robert Richter was happy to represent Sellers in Victoria. When his case looked like becoming a NSW matter, Sellers' then girlfriend, Sky Blue, contacted a young Sydney barrister, Peter Martin Livesey, unwittingly beginning a process that was soon to destroy two promising legal careers.

There was no Sky Blue, of course: she'd been born Doreen Jacques, but had apparently changed her name by deed poll in 1976, with the idea she might publish a book about cosmology.

—

Peter Livesey was the son of an English father and a Lebanese mother, and educated as a boarder by the Marist Brothers at St Joseph's College, Hunters Hill. His features had what used to be called a 'Levantine cast', so he was picked on by the athletic, idiotic sons of the confident, Caucasian rich. 'Ignorance has no bottom,' he told me. 'They thought I was a black Jew. I got a note under my pillow—"We don't like black Jews".'

The first time Livesey was arrested, he was bricked. On 25 January 1972, he was standing near Meredith Burgmann at a demonstration against the Springboks in Orange, NSW, when he was picked up by police and charged with possession of an article capable of causing bodily harm—a Pains Wessex handheld distress flare. 'I never had a flare,' Livesey told me. He was represented by Maurice Byers QC, an old boy of St Joseph's. 'When he walked into court, everyone just went, *Yes, Maurice*,' said Livesey. Byers—who later became the Commonwealth Solicitor-General—quickly established the flare was not capable of causing bodily harm, so the court did not hear that Livesey had never seen it before. 'I beat that case because of the old school tie,' said Livesey.

Livesey's arrest headed his Special Branch file, but there was no mention of his acquittal. The political police later noted him in and around demonstrations, meetings, courtrooms and a police station and, once, nude on a beach. He was spotted at the Court of Petty Sessions after a protest outside Katingal. He was seen near Silverwater when a demonstration was planned by Women Behind Bars—although the protest never took place—and he was recorded as appearing for one of about 100 people arrested on Oxford Street during a demonstration organised by the Gay Solidarity Group in the week of Sydney's first Mardi Gras in 1978.

Livesey worked pro bono at Redfern Legal Centre—largely, he said, as the 'long-haired barrister' for demonstrators and dope smokers. He visited Katingal with a colleague, Helen Golding, and met some of the prisoners—including Denning—who were Golding's clients. 'They'd all been kicked from arsehole to breakfast,' he told me. 'Every one of them was a kind of Royal Commission in himself.' Golding represented the four Maitland Crew who had been charged with trying to escape the prison van. After she died in a car accident, one of them wrote to the legal centre and asked, 'Can that Aboriginal-looking guy who came out with Helen take over my case?' And so Billy 'the Kid' Sutton became Livesey's first criminal client.

Livesey met with Denning several times, as a potential witness in Sutton's case 'or some other thing I'd bodgie up just to visit him', he said. 'I'd more or less visit anyone who asked for me. At the time, I thought he was one of the massively damaged boys' home products that had been made into a radical by sheer dent of their mistreatment of him. I thought he was one of us.'

Along with others, Livesey later smuggled out some of the handwritten pages of what would become *The Ray Denning Diary*. 'I did a lot of shit that I got away with,' said Livesey. 'I smuggled a glass needle into the jails so they did not have to use the same one—so they could boil it up. It was a lifesaving thing. I smuggled in, obviously, letters from girlfriends.'

Billy Sutton and three other prisoners were charged with setting fire to paper and linen in a Katingal workshop on 21 January 1978 with the aim of causing malicious injury to the jail. Sutton escaped conviction when Livesey proved it was impossible to set fire to Katingal because no part of the jail was flammable. 'This all got written up in the *Telegraph*,' said Livesey. 'Everyone in jail reads all this shit assiduously, and next thing Jimmy Smith is writing to Redfern Legal Centre and says he's got a bit of a murder case . . .'

Jockey Smith's case turned out to be the shooting of bookmaker Lloyd Tidmarsh, which led to high-profile proceedings that brought Livesey to the attention of Steve Sellers.

Redfern Legal Centre put Sky Blue in touch with Livesey, who flew down to see Sellers. 'I first met him in Melbourne in the hospital in a morphine haze,' said Livesey. In the same ward, he was to encounter Wainer, Altman, Richter and Blue, the exotic congregation around Sellers' bed. Livesey found Sellers 'incredibly charming, frustrating and stubborn and a little bit self-obsessive' with 'an element of selfishness' but 'he could charm the birds out of the trees', said Livesey. 'He had the gift of the gab, the absolute gift.

'There's nobody else in Australia who would ever have tried to break into a jail and free everyone except Steve Sellers,' said Livesey. 'He's the only guy who you could point to who had the balls.'

Sellers asked Livesey to take a statement: 'I'm not prepared to say anything to the police unless I have a lawyer present.'

'It's what's known in the law as a "self-serving statement",' said Livesey. 'It says that's your intention, but you can easily change your mind, basically. So it doesn't really prove that you haven't on some occasion given a statement, but every prisoner thinks this is some form of protection. It's one of the great jail myths.'

Sellers asked Livesey to recover the $6000 he had been carrying when he was shot. ('I think he probably always had a large amount of cash—or as much as he could—against contingencies,' said Livesey.) Sellers told him to deliver the money to Wainer for safekeeping.

The NSW Police wanted Sellers extradited. Richter went to court and raised the fact that Katingal—the jail Sellers was supposed to have admitted breaking into—had never, in fact, been gazetted as a jail. 'I can't remember whether it was me or Steve who found it, but there's a government gazette that proclaims the area inside the Long Bay stone fence as a jail,' said Livesey. 'But Katingal was built outside that fence, in a kind of no-man's land between the stone fence and the much-further extant wire fence.'

That argument was ignored. However, said Livesey, 'Robert had kudos even in those days, so he said to the magistrate, *This man isn't well enough to fly and even if you allow the extradition you should put a stay on it for two weeks*, and the magistrate, because it was Robert, accepted it. Well, the coppers weren't having any of that.' On March 8, 'After about a week, they just pumped him full of morph, took him out to the airport and flew him up. And I get this frantic phone call that Sellers is missing in action.'

Sellers was taken first to Maroubra Police Station, where the cops thought Livesey looked like Corporal Klinger, the desperate-for-a-discharge crossdresser on the TV show *M*A*S*H*. Sellers noticed Livesey's photograph attached to a dartboard on the station wall, with a handwritten speech bubble that said, 'You're all mad. I'm not Klinger. I'm a barrister.' Because just as the cops hated Sellers and Sellers hated the cops, the cops hated Livesey.

Sellers arrived at the Central Court of Petty Sessions in his hospital pyjamas. Livesey explained to the court that he was wearing pyjamas because he needed surgery for his gunshot wounds but was refusing treatment in protest at his extradition. The magistrate granted Sellers $10,000 bail on the charge of having conspired with Cox to effect the escape of Jockey Smith, Marko Motric and others, but the police immediately executed a bench warrant against Sellers and took him to the District Court on a six-year-old break-and-enter charge. The judge refused bail and Sellers went back to the cells in his pyjamas.

At his committal hearing, Sellers lodged a plea of not guilty, and complained that he should still be in hospital. He also repeatedly attempted to discover if the police were planning to claim he had made an unsigned, untaped confession. He accused them of conspiring to perjure him.

'You've been doing it to me since I was sixteen,' he said.

Sellers played with a cigarette in the dock.

'I would ask you to ask the defendant not to light his cigarette in court,' said the prosecutor.

'I haven't got matches,' said Sellers. 'I'm not lighting a cigarette. Don't verbal me. Don't verbal me. That's what I'm talking about. How can I light cigarettes when I haven't got matches? I'm being verballed by the prosecutor now.'

Then Livesey made his stand.

'Without wishing to be colourful,' he said, 'this defendant was kidnapped from Melbourne by the police.'

Livesey argued Sellers was not going to jump bail, as he was a horse trainer and breaker who owned ten horses in Melbourne and had last been convicted of an offence in 1968—although, Livesey had to admit, he had failed to answer the old break-and-enter charge. However, when that warrant had been issued, Livesey noted, Sellers had been in the Alfred Hospital waiting for an orthopaedic operation 'as a result of his being thrown out of the window in 1974'. This time, Livesey argued, Sellers should be granted bail because he needed physiotherapy every six hours for his broken scapula, and had already suffered pneumonia in one lung and a puncture in the other, as well as a haematoma which made it hard for him to breathe. 'He is also carrying in his body at the moment hundreds of lead pellets which could cause lead poisoning and for these reasons he is in dire need of proper medical attention,' said Livesey. 'He is also going to receive a skin graft to his shoulder when the flesh has sufficiently granulated.'

Livesey painted Sellers' arrest and extradition as a national scandal.

The magistrate refused bail anyway.

The break-and-enter case against Sellers should have been an easy win for the police. Sellers had been caught at the scene of the crime and stopped to help a co-offender who had been shot. 'They got that trial on very quickly because they figured it was simple, open and shut, and he'd get a sentence,' said Livesey. 'Once he had a sentence, they could relax about Katingal, because they knew that was going to be a horror show.'

Sellers represented himself on the break-and-enter charge, with help from Wendy Bacon, who attended court as a McKenzie friend (an unpaid legal adviser). Livesey turned up to watch the trial on his days off work. He said it was one of the funniest cases he had ever seen: 'Steve had everybody, including the judge, in his sway. It was wonderful theatre.

He did the whole thing in his pyjamas and dressing gown. And on the last day—he's getting the transcripts every day; this simple case has gone on for two weeks—when he's summing up, he turns to the jury and he rolls his sleeves up incredibly theatrically and he goes, "Now, I could take you through every page of this transcript"—and that's stacked up fifteen-inches high on the dock—"and I could point out every contradiction but"—he said, rolling up the sleeves—"I don't think I have to do that. I think you're smart"—and they're nodding their heads—"I think you can already see I'm not guilty." And they're like, *Yeah, yeah, just fucken let us go*.

'And, of course, they duly find him not guilty.'

After he'd beaten the break-and-enter charge, Sellers was eligible for bail. Livesey flew down to Melbourne and collected the $6000 from Bert Wainer, but Sellers still needed another $4000. 'We basically gathered it from people,' said Livesey. 'Some of it was his, I think. Bert might've put some money in. And then somehow we passed the hat around a bit and scraped ten grand together.'

Wendy Bacon was asked to give surety for Sellers. 'As far as everyone was concerned, Vivien Altman loaned the money to Wendy,' said Livesey. 'Our story has always been that Vivien brought the ten grand in a bag over to my place in Queen Street on the afternoon that we were going out to bail Steve, and that it was a loan from Vivien to Wendy.'

The bail was lodged and Sellers was released from Long Bay in May 1979 and collected in a car by Livesey and Bacon. They were followed from the jail. 'When Steve gets in the car he's like, "Go up this one-way street, go through this red light!" said Livesey. '*Okay, okay.*—I thought I was humouring him. *Okay, Steve*. We thought he was being paranoid.'

But Livesey's Special Branch file described how a 1975 Renault 12GL Sedan (registered in the name of a woman who was 'no doubt Peter Livesey's mother') was 'lost' by its tail outside Long Bay 'after the driver, LIVESEY, employed anti-surveillance tactics'.

—

Livesey and his Queen Street housemate John Crittle—a couturier whose Chelsea boutique, Dandie Fashions, once made clothes for The Beatles—bought a farm together at Thumb Creek, about 45 kilometres inland from Macksville, NSW, 'and about as deserted as you could ever get', said Livesey.

'We got 50 head of cattle with the farm,' said Livesey, 'Funnily enough, just after we bought the farm, the cattle prices went up. And we were actually able to pay the mortgage by selling off the vealers. And so for a couple of years, John was drinking the excess and I was technically a Pitt Street farmer—I went up there and I rode around the edge of the cattle. Neither of us did any farming. Steve came up there once to the farm and basically he slept. He had this thing with horses and my mate next door was a horseman and I thought they'd get on and they didn't.'

Ultimately, despite his need for daily physiotherapy, his impending skin graft, his punctured lung, his haematoma and the hundreds of lead pellets lodged in his body, Sellers did not turn up for committal proceedings on the Katingal matter on 16 July 1979. He jumped bail instead.

While Sellers was on the run, the police circulated his description and the full extent of his criminal career. He was 1.8 metres, of medium build, a labourer/waiter and his aliases included 'Spano', 'Bradman', 'Jorgie', 'Peter Spana' and 'Ron Harris'. Since 1957, he had been convicted in South Australia, Victoria and NSW on charges including car theft, break and enter, goods in custody, conspiracy, possession of explosives, assault police, assault occasioning actual bodily harm, and several variations on those themes. He was thought to model a full beard and an 'Afro-Cuban hairstyle', and was considered extremely dangerous.

But in September 1979, Sellers gave himself up without a fight when he and Blue were arrested at Bondi and he was charged with theft of a car and possession of a gun. The car had been stolen from the street behind Livesey's house in July. Blue, who was wanted in Victoria in connection with an art robbery committed by Sellers, was extradited and granted $3000 bail. (It was this robbery—the theft from Melbourne art dealer Joseph Brown of Australian paintings worth $617,000, with the idea of returning them if the government promised an inquiry into police corruption—that led to the later characterisation of Sellers as an 'extortionist'.)

Another of Livesey's clients, Brian O'Callaghan, had escaped from Silverwater jail and was recaptured in his wife's panel van in March 1980. Livesey visited O'Callaghan at the police station, then appeared for Sellers at his committal hearing for the Katingal break-in. 'In removing everything in his wife's panel van, the police came across some unused tampons,' said Livesey, 'and, as a joke, they put one on my chair which I pulled out in court the next morning. They've gone, *Ah, fucking tampons. O'Callaghan must be a cunt. Oh, Livesey's a cunt too. Why don't we put one on his chair? Oh, that'd be fun.*'

—

That same year, Billy Sutton and his girlfriend spent about a week at the Thumb Creek farm. 'Needless to say, it all went wrong,' said Livesey. 'And I get a frantic phone call saying Billy's shooting at her with a .303 as she is trying to walk out of this property.' Sutton 'had a screw loose', said Livesey. 'God knows what happened to him as a kid, but none of it was good. He visited another farm, owned by my brother, and we stupidly left him and my brother's girlfriend alone in the house while we went to the beach. And something happened which made me suss about him, and it was borne out being he got charged with other things—doing wrongness with younger girls. And it was always, *She sort of was leading me on . . .*' Prison psychologist Tim Watson-Munro told me, 'I liked Bill a lot, but a lot of work had been done by influential people to secure his release from prison, a lot of people believed in him.' When, in October 1980, Sutton was arrested for a robbery and shooting at Warringah Mall, Brookvale, a lot of people were disappointed.

—

When the Katingal matter finally came to trial in March 1981, it was another open-and-shut case as far as the police were concerned. Two detectives advised the court that Sellers had admitted breaking into the jail with Cox and a 53-year-old pensioner named Raymond Herbert Goodwin, who had apparently supplied the cutting equipment. Of course, Sellers maintained he had confessed to nothing, and Livesey was at his side to help him in court. Once again, Sellers chose to represent himself at the trial proper. Once again, he infuriated the judge, who appeared at times the exasperated parent ('I have ruled it irrelevant at least 15 times!') and at times the pained expert ('It is extremely difficult to explain to a layman what a leading question is': people might, he thought, think it was a good question) but always imperious, upper-class and impatient ('Gilbert and Sullivan would regard this as even ridiculous. I have never seen anything like it in all my life'). But Sellers bludgeoned on, regardless of the notional opinions of dead composers. If the judge could accept the unsigned statement tabled by police as evidence, Sellers could not see why he wouldn't admit Sellers' earlier statement that he would not give a statement.

Sellers hoped to show that the police were habitual verballers. More than once, he raised the issue of the 'Klinger' photograph on the dartboard at Maroubra Police Station. He called Livesey as a witness.

'That photograph is totally irrelevant,' said the judge.

'Since I have had words put in my mouth by these two detectives, your Honour,' said Sellers. 'I do believe I am entitled to try and put this.'

'How can Mr Livesey give evidence about words put into your mouth?' asked the judge. 'He wasn't there.'

Ah-ha!

'Mr Livesey,' said Sellers, 'were some words put virtually in your mouth on that photograph in the form of a caption? . . . Have you ever spoken those words in your life?'

'No, certainly not,' said Livesey, who had never been called upon to confirm being Corporal Klinger from *M*A*S*H*.

'Assuming those words were put there by a policeman at Maroubra Police Station,' said Sellers, 'could it be said that that can be a classic example of just how police verbal does work?'

'I reject that,' said the judge.

Robert Richter gave evidence about Sellers' condition at the time he was supposed to have confessed, and, at some point, it must have become clear to everyone in the courtroom that Sellers would not have admitted to being a carbon-based lifeform, without endless hours of didactic, semantic and philosophical argument—let alone spontaneously owned up to having broken into Katingal with Russell Cox. The case became a trial of the verbal rather than Sellers, a popularity contest between the men in suits and the bloke in his pyjamas.

'After the jury had been out for a while,' said Livesey, 'the judge called them back in and said, *Look, you must decide this case on the facts before you, not on the personalities. You've heard the evidence, don't be swayed by what you think of a person*. Stuff like this. He's basically shafting Steve. The jury goes back out. Well, when they came back in, the judge was beside himself. He's like, *This is it. They've listened to me*. As Steve said, "They had a cup of tea, did a U-turn, came back straight in and found me not guilty."'

Sellers was acquitted in April 1982. The only man who could have broken into jail with Russell Cox, was judged not to have done so—which, as it turned out, was truer than the facts might suggest.

—

Law graduate Wendy Bacon's application to join the bar was rejected by the Barristers Admission Board, as the board did not find her to be a fit and proper person to be made a barrister—largely because of the unwitting part she played in the handling of Sellers' bail money.

Livesey also fought a losing battle to remain at the bar. He was held to be too close to his clients and to act inappropriately. It was Sellers who had raised Livesey's connection with the bail money at the Katingal trial, and the Bar Council was unimpressed that Livesey had gone running after money for his client. Justice Reynolds said, 'This young man has no concept of the noblesse of the robe, the collegiate pride of a learned profession . . . He has no chambers in the accepted sense, he owns no wig and gown, possesses a minimal library and has distanced himself from his colleagues in the profession.' ('I used to just borrow Frank Lawrence's wig,' said Livesey, 'because, conveniently, he was in jail.')

In fact, Justice Reynolds was wrong. The concept of 'noblesse of the robe' had nothing to do with professional pride. It refers to a time when, in the French court, knights of the realm would stand up on behalf of some poor, impecunious indigent and argue their case. Livesey had more noblesse of the robe than almost anyone else at the bar.

But, said Reynolds, 'He has allowed himself to become too close to his criminal clients and lost the detachment which is essential to proper practice. He has willingly allowed himself to be placed in a position where he became a witness in criminal trials and has sought to intrude himself into situations where persons charged with crime are escorted in custody by police officers. This is not barrister's work.'

Livesey was disbarred in August 1982 and moved permanently to the country. He did not see Sellers again. 'I thought we were friends, at one stage,' said Livesey. 'Steve is far too mercurial a character to ever think that you actually have a handle on a friendship with him. He was a very, very fun guy to be with. But he'd sit on your bed in the middle of the night and wake you up, with no notice. He'd run up phone bills on your phone. He arguably did a lot of things to a lot of people without thinking through the consequences, and people allowed him to get away with a lot of stuff—ostensibly because we were all fighting for a cause, but, with hindsight, in reality the cause was much more about Steve than some vague political notion of reform.

'But Steve Sellers did things for no gain for himself. Breaking into Katingal—if he did it—clearly, there was nothing in it for him. There was no money, there was no kudos. No one would ever know.'

14

Wrong Ray, Go Back

The Sun reporter Michael Robotham was already a journalist at twelve years old when he interviewed Gough Whitlam for the student radio station at Orara High in Coffs Harbour, New South Wales. Five years later, Michael aced the HSC and scored the marks to study Arts/Law at Sydney University. 'And my dad, with tears in his eyes, said, "I can't afford for you to go,"' Robotham told me.

In 1978, straight from school, Michael applied for a cadetship with Fairfax newspapers. He passed a battery of tests and outscored about 6000 other hopefuls but was told he probably wouldn't land a job. The Robothams had no telephone, so Michael had to learn by telegram the result of his final interview. No word came on the promised day, nor the next, nor the day after that. Despairing, Michael borrowed the family car and drove to cricket practice. Then the telegram man came to his parents' front door.

Forty years later, Robotham wept when he told me, 'My mother ran all the way from home—which was a long way—holding this telegram. And then I had to phone up Fairfax and accept the offer. I had spoken on the phone probably two or three times in my life. My father, a big man, was squeezed into this phone box with me. When you're not used to the phone, it sounds like you're talking to someone in a wheat silo—they were talking back at me and I was trying to hear.'

He started the job on 9 February 1979, a baby-faced eighteen-year-old country boy, born in Casino and raised in Gundagai and Coffs, surrounded by older, more worldly graduate cadets. He grew a moustache as soon as he could, to make himself look more mature. But his youth worked in his favour. As a junior reporter, he was routinely assigned to the 'death knock'—the most reviled task in journalism, when a writer turned up at the home of a grieving family, asked how they felt about the loss of their loved one, then tried to talk them into handing over a photograph. Robotham, nauseous with nerves, would vomit in the rosebushes before he reached the front door, but he was a tremendously successful death-knocker because even the recently bereaved could feel sympathy for the frightened boy trapped in their trauma. He did fourteen death knocks in one day after the Appin coal mine disaster in July 1979, when fourteen miners died in an explosion 600 metres underground.

—

In the country towns where Robotham was raised, the local copper was a well-respected man who knew everyone, shepherded kids through their driving tests and punished young tearaways with a slap around the head and the threat to speak to their father. When Robotham first came to Sydney, he had never been inside a building more than three storeys high. He had never pressed a button in a lift or travelled up an escalator. And he didn't know there were police who fabricated evidence or beat up suspects in the cells. But newspaper editors were well aware that NSW was rotten with dirty cops. 'I was taught really early on, when you got word on someone being corrupt—that decision on whether to expose that person's wrongdoing was weighed up against the number of good stories that person gave you,' said Robotham.

He was quickly to encounter a new and unexpected source for his crime stories—and, in fact, become a part of the story himself.

When Ray Denning escaped from Grafton, it was the first successful jailbreak of his adult life and the first time in history an inmate had broken out of Grafton. Like Cox, Denning was a patient observer. He watched the garbage trolley as it was wheeled through the prison, stacked with cardboard boxes packed full of jail trash. At about 8 a.m. on 2 April 1980, Denning climbed into a box, which prisoners covered with other containers and loaded onto the trolley which they pushed out of the gates, under armed guard, to the incinerator where the rubbish was to be burned. The guard left, Denning climbed out of his box and jogged away.

Forty cops beat through the dense bush north of Grafton, aided by mounted police, police in four-wheel drives, police on dirt bikes and the obligatory helicopter. They said they believed Denning was hemmed in by their roadblocks and 'possibly living off wild lemons'. The police mounted a cordon around Grafton and searched empty buildings. 'There have been no sightings elsewhere,' said a spokesman, 'so we have no reason to believe he is not still here.'

Police found fresh footprints on a bush track near the barely populated locality of Whiporie, 50 kilometres south of Casino. Officers followed them for five kilometres before their trail disappeared into hard ground. *The Sydney Morning Herald* reported, 'Scientific squad police from Grafton confirmed that the tracks were made by Denning' who was 'wearing track shoes with a distinctive pattern on the sole'. More footprints were detected the next day, ten kilometres to the east, and a calf was discovered slaughtered in a paddock in New Italy. The animal had been killed with a knife and a large piece of flesh had been sliced from its rump, so Denning now had rump steak to eat with his wild lemons. The latest police theory held that Denning might be hiding in a cave during daylight hours and emerging at dusk like a dingo to hunt for food.

A tape Denning had made in jail the year before, in which he talked about his own case with sadness and anger but also delivered an aggravated, perplexed and frustrated attack on the Australian criminal justice system, was delivered to the ABC's youth radio station 2JJJ. There was something disarming and endearing about the way Denning expressed himself. He sounded sincere, trustworthy, horribly wronged, hurt without measure, vulnerable, artless and, desperately, heartbreakingly . . . cute.

Denning wrote a colourful account of his escape that was passed on to *Playboy* magazine by Women Behind Bars.

According to Denning, he couldn't hitch a lift so he ran 'five or six miles' before he was stopped by a police officer who thought he recognised him, and who asked his name. 'Ray,' said Denning. 'Ray Denning?' asked the cop. 'No,' said Denning, 'Ray Massey.' (Massey was Denning's mother's maiden name.) Outwitted, the police officer supposedly allowed Denning to carry on.

As he would.

The story continued with Denning hitching a short ride on a postal worker's Mini Moke, before running off into the bush chased by police who shot his transistor radio out of his hand.

Although no such incident was ever reported.

Denning tore off all his clothes except for his shorts, and lay pepper—which he had handily thought to bring along from jail—to cover his scent and confuse tracker dogs. He then dug a hole and buried himself, but was able to hear searchers walking all around him saying, 'He's in there somewhere, the bastard.'

Which was narratively convenient.

Denning claimed to have remained buried alive (which Lobsang Rampa would have identified as catalepsy) for three days. On the third night—only one day earlier than Lazarus of Bethany—Denning crawled out of his pit and 'by a miracle' came upon a waterhole, then he climbed mountains, swam rivers, waded through swamps and lived 'like an animal', eating grass and lizards and bitten by 'at least three snakes', until he finally hitchhiked to Sydney. All the while, he was lent strength by a mysterious voice urging him on (which Lobsang Rampa would have identified as Denning picking up impressions from his 'Silver Cord').

There was no more truth in Denning's *Playboy* story than in the works of Lobsang Rampa or Chopper Read, but it was not substantially more fictitious than most of the newspaper reports of Denning's flight. On April 10, eight days since his escape, police became captivated by the strange idea that Denning had fled to Blackheath—a chilly, misty Blue Mountains town, named for its rough, dark shrubbery. This belief was prompted by the theft of a Holden panel van from the western Sydney suburb of St Marys. The day after it was taken, the vehicle was spotted near Blackheath Pool by a council worker who heard noises coming from inside. As he moved closer, somebody threw a bra from a window then a group of men climbed out and pelted him with stones. Surprised and indignant, he called the cops, and Constable Alan Tohm was dispatched from Mount Victoria to investigate. The van—whose number-plates were covered over—drove off as Tohm approached. After more than four kilometres of high-speed chase, it bombed down a dirt track and careened into thick scrub, where it crashed.

Tohm parked 200 metres away and waited for reinforcements. It took police half an hour to get to the van, where they found four men and a woman. When the woman, nineteen-year-old Julie Ann Martin, was shown photographs at Katoomba Police Station, she identified one of the men who'd been in the van as Denning. She said he had run off into the bush wearing only a T-shirt and jeans, leaving even his thongs behind.

Another passenger in the stolen van, nineteen-year-old Gavin John Nicholson, was supposed to have served time with Denning—although it's hard to see how, since Denning had been locked up in tracs sections ever since Nicholson was old enough for adult jail. In those days, however, everybody confessed to everything and, according to police, Nicholson 'admitted picking up Denning in the stolen car with a number of other people and driving him to Blackheath where they stayed overnight'. Police successfully opposed bail for Nicholson and his mate who, according to the police and media reports, was eighteen-year-old convicted car thief Ray Pedrana, who had been released from prison the day before the vehicle was stolen. Police were concerned that, given the chance, Pedrana and Nicholson might team up with Denning and 'make good their escape'.

A dragnet was thrown over the area, roadblocks were raised on the Great Western Highway. Scores of police, a helicopter and a tracker dog named Kane joined the hunt.

Michael Robotham had driven up from Sydney for *The Sun*, and his archrival, Mike Munro, arrived to report on the search for the Murdoch tabloid, the *Daily Mirror*. Both men turned up at Katoomba Police Station, hoping for an interview with Julie Ann Martin.

'We were told in no uncertain terms—*guaranteed* by the station sergeant—that she wasn't going to be released,' said Robotham. 'So I made a call, when I went back to the car, that we would go down to where Denning was last seen and stay with the police.'

Munro's car was parked facing up a hill, so he had to do a U-turn to leave. 'As he drove back past the police station,' said Robotham, 'he saw a woman leaving and it was her—the police had let her go. So Munro snaffled her, put her in a hotel room that night, and got an exclusive interview in the *Daily Mirror* the next day. I almost lost my job over that.'

The cops pronounced Denning 'cornered' although deadly—as he was supposed to have armed himself with a .30-30 Winchester rifle and six silver-tipped bullets stolen from an unlocked cabinet in a railway-fettlers' camp two days before, when Denning had not yet reached the mountains. It was unclear by what mysterious means Denning might have acquired the weapon, but an Inspector Pomroy assured the media there was 'reason to believe that he has the stolen rifle'.

'With that gun, Denning is as dangerous as a rattlesnake,' said a police officer.

Another officer—or perhaps the same one—said, 'If he doesn't watch himself in the dark, he could easily fall down a ravine. That's if the spiders and snakes don't get him.'

That night, the police constantly patrolled the streets of the Blue Mountains town, although they expressed confidence that they had Denning bottled up in the Blackheath tip. 'We will get him this time and it will be this morning,' promised Inspector Noel Golledge at sunrise. 'No one moves in this sort of terrain at night.'

A police spokesman said, 'We've got him surrounded on three sides,' presenting Denning with a fairly clear escape route.

Mike Munro's interview with Julie Ann Martin appeared in the *Daily Mirror* on April 11 under the headline 'My 2 Days With Lifer'. Martin told Munro she had been moving house from Mount Druitt to Blackheath, with her fiancé, two other men and a boy, when they stopped to pick up a bloke called 'Bob'. They all spent the night at Blackheath swimming pool park but, in the morning, Bob—who she had since discovered to be Ray Denning—was eager to get out of town. When a police car began chasing the van, 'everything went insane', she said. 'This Denning bloke was driving and he went off his head. He kept repeating over and over again: "The cops want me, the cops want me but they're not getting anywhere near us."' He drove 'madly' into the bush until he hit a tree, whereupon everybody jumped out of the van and scattered. All except Bob/Denning were caught by the police. 'Denning was edgy and never stopped looking around,' she said. 'I did think it was pretty funny when he insisted on driving all the time.'

Blackheath became quite crowded. The Channel 10 helicopter flew in with Denning's onetime-girlfriend Kim Pascoe and filmed her at the edge of bushland pleading to Denning to surrender if cornered. Brown-eyed and broad shouldered, with a blank expression and some rather vague memories, Pascoe was variously reported to have lived with Denning and been engaged to him. However, nothing she said to journalists was particularly helpful to him, and most of it seemed likely to put his life at risk

'If Ray's boxed in and armed, I know he'll shoot it out,' she declared. 'He would even take hostages.

'Ray has told me he would rather be dead than spend the rest of his life in prison,' she said—although a Kim was not mentioned in his diaries as a visitor—unlike a Wendy, Virginia, Beatrice, Ellen, Judy, Denise, Julie, Kay, Debbie, Irina Dunn, Christine, Pam and Donna, a seventeen-year-old penpal whose poems, Denning thought, were 'really beautiful'.

Pascoe drew upon her extensive knowledge of Denning in tips to pronounce, 'He can survive anywhere, even in bush like this.' While she conceded there was 'no future' for her and Ray, she consoled herself with the thought that 'at least he knows that I would do anything to help him stay alive'—even though she appeared to be doing the opposite.

Meanwhile, people kept on coming to Blackheath. One newspaper reported that 'thousands of thrill-seekers' had 'flocked to the mountains in the hope of seeing a Hollywood-style shootout'—although that seems fantastically unlikely. Journalists took to filing colour pieces to meet the demand for news. Reporter Bill Mellor observed that Kane the tracker dog was 'so excited by the abundance of trees in the search area that he spent more time cocking his leg than following scents'. To fill space, and to demonstrate that nobody had any idea where Denning was, Mellor interviewed several people who had no idea where Denning was. As his investigation widened—rather than deepened—Mellor discovered that 'the manhunt may have helped the Blue Mountains tourist trade, then again it may not'.

But one person who was not in the Blue Mountains was Ray Denning. On April 11, the PAG held a press conference in Sydney, where law lecturer and barrister John Basten, who had apparently been briefed to act for Denning, laid out conditions for his surrender. Through Basten, Denning demanded assurances from the Attorney-General, the minister for corrective services and the police minister that no charges be laid against him for his escape from Grafton; that he be given safe conduct to a police station; that his lawyer be present during his police interview; that he would not be placed in solitary confinement or tracs; and that he would not be bashed or harassed in jail. Basten would not explain what kind of contact he might have had with his client. 'I don't wish to say whether I have spoken to Denning or not,' he said. But whatever way the two men had communicated, it seemed unlikely the barrister had penetrated the bush around Blackheath tip.

In a *Daily Telegraph* front-page story headlined '"Houdini" escapes rugged bush ... Denning Eludes Police Dragnet', reporters repeated police theories that Denning had employed 'bush cunning' to get from Grafton to Blackheath and that 'barefoot and wearing only jeans and a singlet against near-freezing temperatures' he had slipped past searchers in the mountains. 'Cunning as a fox', he had managed to 'sneak through bushland past a seemingly impregnable police barrier' to earn another day of precarious freedom. A senior police officer wondered if Denning had 'edged his way through deep gullies and ravines, past roadblocks and perhaps jumped on a passing coal train'.

He had not.

There were certain problems with the story that Denning had travelled from St Marys, where he wasn't, to the Blue Mountains, where he didn't want to go, with a group of people who didn't know him and who brought scrutiny to themselves by covering their numberplates, throwing underwear out of the window and hurling stones at a council worker. And that he had then crashed a van he wasn't driving and stolen a rifle that had already disappeared—at which point a TV station flew in a woman who wasn't his girlfriend to urge him to give himself up.

In fact, Ray Pedrana, the convicted car thief in the stolen van, had just been released from Emu Plains Detention Centre in Sydney's south-west. 'I was only fifteen,' he told me, 'and I was with my cousin and his brother, Brownie, and some sheila. I really didn't know the sheila or like her.

She was Brownie's girlfriend. And we'd gone up to Blackheath and, before we knew it, there was police thinking that we were going to do something. So they chased us, and we got chased through the bush by about 100 police officers. We got taken back to the police station when they finally caught us, and they're asking me who Ray Denning is. And I didn't have a clue who he was, being a juvenile. They actually thought I was about eighteen. They started beating me and that. When my mother and a priest who used to look after all the boys in the boys' homes saw me on TV, they came straight up to Blackheath—and that's when the police found out they'd been beating the fuck out of a fifteen-year-old for the last hour or something. I kept trying to tell them I didn't know Ray Denning, there was no Ray Denning in the car. But I didn't know that that sheila was saying that there was Ray Denning in the car and he was with us and all this shit. She might have thought that me being Ray and just being out of prison, it might've been me. That's all I can think of.

'It done no good for us,' said Pedrana. 'I ended up back in prison, I think, for stealing a motor vehicle. Until they realised that Ray was still in Grafton, they charged us with everything like harbouring a criminal and blah blah blah. The males went to prison and the sheila got let off, I think.'

—

Late at night on April 20, Wendy Bacon delivered a cassette tape to the offices of 2JJ. It was another recording made by Denning, setting out new conditions that would have to be met before he handed himself in. 'They say that justice has got to be done and seen to be done,' said Denning, 'and I've got to be charged with me escape because that's the law.

Well, fair enough. I'm willing to be charged with the escape. All I want in return is all the prison officers that've been proved to be bashers—and committed any crimes against prisoners—I want them charged also.'

Denning talked like a battered boxer with butterfly stitches across his brows, sometimes struggling to squeeze thoughts into words. He pronounced 'escape' as 'eck-scape', like a child. He told the tape it was not fair, that he had been robbed of his right to shield himself from harm. He could be stripped and beaten at the whim of his guards. He could be crippled or murdered. Nobody would come to help him, and people who didn't know him would say that he'd got what he deserved. He would be punished forever, not for what he had done but for what he had become—worthless. And the screws, who were paid a wage to bend him over and baton him, routinely committed worse crimes on the prison population than most crims had ever done on the outside.

'It's just so unbelievable how the government has let these people get away with it and then promoted them into higher jobs,' said Denning. 'And now they're running the screws' union! You've got barbaric, sadistic men running a union—all they call for is for hanging, for flogging and for cages. It's like the Nazis' war camps all over again. Next they'll be wanting gas chambers built—not for the crimes that are being committed outside but just to make their jobs easier, so that they can sit back and do nothing.'

He said, 'When all the prisoners who are classed as intractable, kept in these bloody cages that are smaller than the average man's bathroom, for 24 hours a day, week in, week out, year in, year out: when all these sections are closed, I will give myself up.

'They say, "You're now classed as uncontrollable, you're an intractable prisoner, you're dangerous to society." But the thing is, you're already away from society. So the only danger you are to anyone is to the prison system. The only reason you ever go to these trac sections is you're rebelling against the system itself, against the atrocities and the barbaric things that go on in it . . .'

He called for a full public inquiry into his alleged confession to the Faber bashing. Denning sounded desperate, victimised, abused and indignant. But, most clearly, he sounded innocent—in every sense. He made you want to hug him, to hold him, to take him to bed and either tuck him in or fuck him, whichever would best ease his pain.

He probably didn't sound that way if you were Ursula Faber, though.

The words 'Run Free, Ray' appeared overnight in two-metre high black letters on the sea wall at Bondi. On June 15, Denning appeared on Channel 9's *60 Minutes*, clean-shaven and dressed smartly for primetime TV. The show's film of Denning was taken from a homemade video tape that had reached the producers through Wendy Bacon at Women Behind Bars. Denning repeated all his political demands and his claim to have 'scientific evidence' that he was verballed over Faber, and he threw himself at the mercy of the Australian people. 'I'm leaving it in your hands to decide for me what you think I should do,' he said.

However, he also said, 'I feel that now I have at least a little bit of support from the public in general as regards to me not giving myself up and, as a result, I'm definitely not gonna give myself up until there's at least an inquiry into all my allegations.'

No prison escapee had ever made their case on Australian TV. In the wake of the broadcast, Channel 9 executives were questioned by police, but *60 Minutes*' Ian Leslie said, 'Detectives said Denning had done them a favour as the most recent picture they had of him was seven years old.'

On July 12, Denning made his strangest demand. The first episode of the *Prisoners' Program*, opened with a tape of Denning haltingly congratulating 2JJ on going FM and acquiring the new call sign 2JJJ. 'All I want to appeal to now,' said Denning, 'is all your listeners to write to the Minister of Post and Telecommunications demanding instead of the ten kilowatts which 2JJJ got—we all want them to be put on an equal footing with the ABC FM program that has 50 kilowatts.'

—

Meanwhile, Michael Robotham was immersed in a twilight world of fatal accidents, gruesome murders, hopeless suicides, and various other public tragedies that did not happen much in Coffs Harbour. Throughout his training, he was rotated through the various newspaper disciplines, with three months at a time working on lottery results, or captioning, or the racing form guide. Like every cadet, he hungered for a position where he would actually get to write something and, in 1980, he had been given the night shift—an important position on a tabloid newspaper whose lifeblood was sport and crime. Sport happened during the day. Offences often occurred at night, when Robotham was the only reporter working at *The Sun*. He shared the shift with a photographer, a copyboy and a driver who waited to be called to a job. All night, Robotham sat in the police-rounds room on the fourth floor of the Fairfax building on Jones Street in Ultimo, scanning police, fire and ambulance frequencies.

The radios argued among themselves, hissing, crackling and screeching though the static. A young reporter's ears grew attuned to their babble. There might be a dozen cops and operators talking across each other and Robotham could pick out one keyword then turn down all the other speakers to listen in.

Nobody ever phoned the nightshift reporter. He made his calls and he waited. If things were dead quiet, he'd slip out to Kings Cross for a coffee. Because Sydney was a city that slept—apart from the Cross, where the hoons and whores would gossip and glare in the early hours, with the journos and cabbies and easy marks and mugs.

'Working nights, your big enemy was the *Mirror*,' said Robotham. 'To the point when you knew at times they were parked outside your offices and they knew that you were sometimes parked outside theirs. We'd play tricks on each other. You'd try to get them sent out of town and you'd try anonymous phone calls and all sorts of shit. Munro made my life a misery.'

When the first edition of the paper dropped from the printers, Robotham would grab a bundle, drive down to the Water Police and hand deliver them—you never knew, they might have fished a body out of the harbour. Then Robotham would take the fresh tabloids around the various police stations, where he'd play matey with the desk sergeant, keeping good with the cops. *We're not such bad blokes are we, us journos? You and me, we're in this together, eh?*

Robotham might catch a scrap of chatter between two cops, and perhaps he'd come back later with his notebook drawn. But the roundsmen generally knew when there was going to be an operation, because the police radios fell silent—tumbleweed rolling across the airwaves—while the cops prepared for their dawn raid, their swoop on some mug in bed with his moll, sleeping with a pistol under the pillow.

Then one morning, at about one o'clock or maybe two, the phone rang—the one that never rang—and Robotham thought it was Munro, the only other journo awake, asking if he fancied a coffee. It took the caller a long time to convince Robotham that he was Ray Denning and not a prankster from the *Daily Mirror* wasting his time, trying to divert him from a big story.

They shot the breeze, two young blokes talking about the footy at two o'clock in the morning—the footy and police verballing and unsigned statements. Robotham madly scribbled notes in shorthand, afraid that he'd ask the wrong question, that he wouldn't ask the right question, that he'd somehow get into trouble with his boss because Australia's most wanted man had called him at the office. When Denning put the phone down, Robotham worried he had missed the story. And what is a story anyway? Was there a story in the fact that Denning had phoned? It was a yarn for the pub, but was it news for the paper?

The Sun didn't notify the police or run a piece and, a few days later, Denning rang back. Once he was confident the cops weren't tapping the phones or tracing the calls, he got in touch again. And again.

Denning spoke about his life. He said he'd been a good kid when he was first locked up. He'd just been wayward, stray. He had lost his family, lost his home, then he had been brutalised, hosed down, stripped naked and beaten.

'I wasn't a killer when I went into prison,' he said. 'It was prison that turned me into a killer.' But he never admitted attacking Faber. That was always one of the things they 'said' he'd done. And it didn't matter what Denning told them, they always put words into his mouth. Even when he was a kid, he said, the police verballed him, the coppers lied. They made up things that they said he had done, and then they punished him.

'I was ready to believe Ray,' said Robotham, 'because I'd seen police lie often enough. Even though I was friends with a lot them by then, chummy with them and having beers with them. Within the newsroom, we all knew the police. Police roundsmen in particular, if you were working early morning shifts you'd finish at lunchtime and you'd often go to barbecues with coppers—and you'd try to befriend the homicide detectives because these are the guys who are going to give you the drum on the next murder.

'But even being up and down the Cross, you'd see police dropping into brothels and police getting favours and some of that you'd figure is just harmless, but some of it's not.' On July 26, Denning phoned Robotham to say he had left a note for the police on the front window of the Criminal Investigation Branch (CIB) headquarters. He called other news outlets too, but Robotham arrived to photograph the letter before the police even knew it was there. They only came out from behind the desk when they saw the flash guns fire off *The Sun* photographer's camera.

The note was headed 'Ray Denning—No Fixed Address'. It read, 'I heard that there was another strike by prisoners against police verbals today and its [sic] about time the Government explains to the prisoners and public that unsigned confessions and verbal alleged statements by the accused no longer will be accepted in a court of law.' Fingerprints deliberately left behind matched those on file for Raymond John Denning.

In their embarrassment, police tried to confiscate the photographer's film.

In September, it was revealed that police looking for Denning had earned about $85,000 in overtime between Denning's escape on April 2 and the end of the financial year on June 30. The NSW deputy Leader of the Opposition, Bruce McDonald, suggested it would have been cheaper to offer Denning $50,000 to give himself up. On September 27, Denning reviewed the new Australian movie *Stir* for 2JJJ. He liked it: it was based on the Bathurst Riots, written by former prisoner Bob Jewson and included in the cast former armed robber and escapee Les Newcombe and the PAG's Kevin Storey—as well as Gary Waddell in one of the leading roles. Denning watched the film at a preview and someone left a cassette recording of his critique on the radio station's doorstep.

But he wasn't the only person to give an opinion on *Stir* for the ABC. The radio show *City Extra* featured a long discussion of the movie with NSW prison officers' union leader Bob Downes. Unflinching and perceptive, with a grim, wounded humour, Downes didn't like the movie at all, although he conceded, 'Some of the bashings and happenings shown in that film did take place.' Asked if he had known prisoners were being flogged at the time, Downes looked for cover in epistemology. 'Well, I didn't *know* that it was going on,' he said, 'because you only *know* what you physically see. I didn't see any.'

Downes explained how the bashing of maximum-security prisoners had become commonplace in the 1970s. 'We had come out of a very violent period, leading up to World War Two and following off World War Two, where societies all over the world became accustomed to brutality—became, to a degree, brutalised themselves,' he said. 'And the fact that prisoners—who were put into jails sometimes for pretty horrific crimes—were being flogged . . .' He raised his voice '. . . really didn't disturb anybody at all. If anybody tells me that the people of New South Wales as a whole didn't know what was going on in jails, and that the government and the ministers and the controllers of the system didn't know, I just won't believe it.' Although not ten minutes before, he'd claimed he himself didn't know.

'Everybody knew,' said Downes finally. 'Everybody accepted it.'

—

So let's take a moment to look at things through the eyes of the prison officers. As Downes said, 'There's nothing sinister or magical about a prison officer. He's a working man in a slightly different environment which, by its nature, is almost closed off from public view.' Most prison officers weren't bashers. As long as there were wings like Grafton tracs, they didn't need to be. The troublemakers could be shipped off to the bloodhouses and stripped and knocked around by 'robust' blokes who liked that kind of thing—and earned a special 'climate allowance' for taking part. When Grafton closed the tracs, there was Katingal for the stirrers, where the torture was mental and largely unintentional. Without special units, ordinary prison officers had no final sanctions for rioters and cell blockaders, psychopaths and anyone else who threatened good order.

It was bad enough for honest jailers. Crims were the flavour of the fucking month, the stars of judicial inquiries, pulling hot women at arty dances. Nobody ever invited a prison officer to their radical dinner parties. No one shed a tear for a warder's busted skull or got arrested defending the rights of screws. No braless feminist painted graffiti around town supporting the men who kept rapists behind bars. As Downes complained, nobody could imagine *Stir* had been written by a prison officer.

Many squareheads had always been suspicious of screws, and now some of them were openly contemptuous. Public distrust drove prison officers closer together. If they didn't defend each other, who else would stand up for them in a society where morality had turned upside down, making the bad guys the good guys and jailers the real crims?

—

In November, Denning sent a new tape to 2JJJ, calling on all prisoners to go on strike and for men to resist entering the tracs sections. 'If you refuse to go in,' he said, 'all the screws can do is look in on that empty yard. If they want to drag you out to the yard, let 'em drag you out every day and charge them with assault every day.'

He threatened retaliation against prison officers who bashed inmates. 'If those prisoners are attacked in any way by the screws then I'm going to attack them,' he said. 'And I don't care how far I have to go.'

In the earliest hour of the morning of November 12, a message came over the police radio that shots had been fired at a guard tower at Parramatta Gaol. From the *Sun*'s radio room, Robotham called for a photographer and, as he was hurrying out to pick up a car, the office phone rang and a voice on the line said, 'I want to claim responsibility for the shootings at Parramatta Gaol. This is the Reform Justice Devils.'

Robotham scribbled a note in his pad: 'RJD' for 'Reform Justice Devils'—and also, of course, for Raymond John Denning.

'That's you, right?' said Robotham.

'No,' said Denning.

'Come on,' said Robotham. 'I recognise your voice.'

'It's not me!' said Denning.

Denning advised Robotham to go to a mailbox outside a house in North Parramatta, where he and the photographer collected a note from the Reform Justice Devils: 'This is only the beginning for those who are immune to prosecution. If there is no equal weight in the scales of justice surely then next time there will be a killing. So it's up to the Government to act now.'

The house turned out to belong to a former deputy superintendent at Parramatta Gaol. The stunt was supposed to commemorate the one hundredth anniversary of Ned Kelly's execution on November 11, but the shots were actually fired at 12.10 a.m. on November 12.

'Police fucking were furious,' Robotham told me. 'Because we went and got the letter and photographed it before letting them know. Even though I was really careful not to put fingerprints, they fingerprinted me.'

A gunman in a yellow car had opened fire at a warder in number-one tower. 'He had just seen that a hand was protruding from the window with a gun when a bullet thudded into the bricks just below the window,' said a detective. The prison officer dived for cover and the rest of the volley missed him.

From his cell in the jail, Timothy Edward Anderson had heard the shots.

Denning did not phone Robotham again, although somebody claiming to represent Reform Justice Devils called Australian Associated Press and warned that a prison officer would be picked out at random and killed if any harm came to Denning.

The police went public with an intriguing theory as to why they had failed to apprehend the fugitive: it was suggested that he might have altered his appearance. A police spokesman said it was likely Denning had grown a moustache or beard or dyed his hair.

Kevin Storey told the media Denning had turned up at a prisoners' art exhibition at East Sydney Technical College, among invited guests including Justice Michael Kirby, Tony Vinson and two Long Bay prison officers. A police spokesman said police had never regarded Denning as an art lover and there was no proof he had attended the show.

In December, Brett Collins—who had been released from Parramatta in June ('They didn't want me there,' he said)—held a press conference on behalf of the Prisoners' Action Group to present the 'scientific evidence' that Denning had been verballed. This took the form of an expert analysis of a carbon copy of Denning's unsigned record of interview after the Faber bashing. The examination was the work of James Buglio, a founding member of the Australian Society of Forensic Document Examiners. According to the transcript, Denning was supposed to have been given the interview to read before he had taken it and replied, 'I just read the bloody thing out.' Buglio examined the alignment of typed words on the paper and found that the document had never left the typewriter, so Denning could not have read it.

'It means the statement was fabricated,' said Buglio, 'a verbal, and casts strong doubt on the whole of the police evidence in the case.'

Denning was supposed to have slipped into NSW State Parliament House while parliament was in session, and sat in the public gallery 'glaring at Corrective Services Minister, Bill Haigh'. On December 20, police found a note signed by Denning tucked into the visitors' book of the police launch *Norman T.W. Allan*, the largest police boat in Australia. The vessel had been named after the former police commissioner Norman Allan even though Allan had been forced to retire early after responding to allegations that he had falsified crime statistics by trying to have his accuser declared insane.

Reporter Bill Mellor had mused that 'if the Denning story is ever filmed, much of the credit must go to the anti-hero himself, who presents some of the qualities of a combined Rocky, Papillon and the Fugitive'. It was a sound point: Denning was a man for his time, a tender tough guy; a beaten-up, beaten-down poor boy; a romantic revolutionary at war with 'the system' and determined not to live on his knees. He was half-Ned Kelly and half-Che Guevara. If his life had ended differently, there'd be knockabouts in Wollongong wearing Ray Denning tattoos.

The police despised him. 'He was making them look foolish,' said Robotham. 'And they hated that more than anything else. The public were enjoying the sport of it all. The more he goaded the police, the longer they took to catch him—and the more it seemed as though he wasn't robbing—the more the public seemed to want him. And the more the police hated him.'

Denning acted like he cared about the mates he'd left behind in jail. When he spoke, he tried to represent all of them. He wasn't simply campaigning on his own case: he wanted every prisoner out of the tracs. Denning did not behave like a normal human being. Abused children grow up swearing revenge, but they don't take it out on their abusers. They find someone weaker—usually a woman or a girl—and they humiliate them in the way they themselves were once debased by parents, priests or prison guards. They don't turn their guns on the guard tower. Real life doesn't work that way.

After eight months on the run, Denning's life stopped working that way too. The stunts came to an end. The campaigns trailed off. Politically, Denning disappeared.

The truth was, he had returned to armed robbery.

15

Left Behind

In real life, Denning probably didn't bury himself alive, or swim rivers in his shorts while carrying a transistor radio pierced by a bullet, but he did spend a few days around the bush in April 1980 before he rang Redfern Legal Centre to ask for help. The lawyers could not get involved, but they didn't feel they could abandon him either, so Denning's appeal was passed on until it reached an anarcho-feminist prisoners' rights activist, who agreed to go and pick him up in her Volkswagen. The weather was rough, but she and a friend battled hailstorms as they headed towards a campsite near Scotts Head. They were stopped at police roadblocks, but the cops barely gave a second glance to two young women in a shitbox car.

When the women found Denning, they expected him to be dressed in his prison gear, but he said he had been breaking into houses to get food, hiding out near a camping area and stealing clothes from washing lines.

Rather than eating lizards.

For his own reasons, Denning refused to squeeze into the Volkswagen—which had no place to hide a fugitive—so the women had to drive home through the roadblocks without him, regularly stopping because the car's windscreen wipers were too weak for the rain.

The next day, Billy Sutton—who was working with the PAG—arrived with his girlfriend in a bigger car and they took Denning down to Sydney, hidden under boxes in the back seat. It was decided that Denning should be safe-housed with political activists, draft-resister style. Even today, nobody would name names, but it seems contact had been made with anarchist Peter McGregor, a long-time leading figure in the anti-apartheid movement. Peter had suggested Denning could stay at his mother, Alice's, rambling old home at Roseville. Alice was a grandee of the left, who had campaigned to free the jailed African National Congress leader Nelson Mandela since the mid-1960s. Peter, however, had not always backed the prisoners' cause. In 1967, he was supposed to have demonstrated in support of the execution of armed robber Ronald Ryan, the last man hanged in Australia. The genius of housing Denning with Alice was that it would be impossible for the police to imagine an escaped armed robber staying with a middle-aged, middle-class matron whom he had never heard of—let alone met.

After a couple of days in Roseville, Denning told activists he had overheard Alice on the phone to a friend saying, 'You'll never guess who I've got staying here . . .' so he had to be moved on. His accommodation coordinator was the woman with the Volkswagen. In the first fortnight, she rehoused him every two days. She favoured unlikely hosts—friends of friends—and she would only deal personally with her direct contact. So, although she would know the place Denning was to be picked up from, she would not know where he would be taken. Many of the people who safe-housed Denning were unaware of the identities of any of the others.

The coordinator was appalled when Denning suddenly had money and she realised it must have come from a robbery. She told him he couldn't do that kind of thing if he wanted to stay out of jail, but the truth was Denning didn't have a plan to stay out of jail. He didn't know where to go, what to do, or how long he might last on the outside. He had just spotted an opportunity and seized it. He wasn't like Cox, who had an extended family and an interstate network. Ray Denning had virtually no one.

But he had Donna, the Bondi teenager who had composed poems for him. 'I used to write to him constantly,' Donna told me. 'He used to write me cards, and write my name into a poem and things. He said that his dad was a mean, nasty drunk; was horrible to his mother; that his mother used to live in fear. He said, "I raised myself." He said, in one of his first letters to me, "I was growing up to be nothing, and I didn't want to have nothing, and that's why I did what I did and I robbed banks. But I didn't murder anyone."'

One day in April, two detectives came to the house where Donna lived with her parents and told her that her last letter had arrived at Grafton the afternoon after Denning had escaped.

Donna told them there was no chance Denning would contact her. 'And I honestly thought that,' she said. One of the detectives gave her his card and said, *There's my number.*

Now listen, $10,000 is a lot of money for a young girl like you. All you've got to do is when he gets in touch with you, meet him at a hotel and ring me, and you go to the ladies and we'll nab him. A few weeks later, Donna answered a knock on her front door to find a pair of green running shorts and a map of New South Wales on the doorstep.

—

Denning had acquired a plan, although other people had developed it for him. Irina Dunn, who had safe-housed draft resister Michael Matteson (and, incidentally, coined the feminist maxim 'a woman needs a man like a fish needs a bike') had become a prisoners'-rights activist and editor of the NSW prisoners' newspaper, *Inprint*. She told me, 'Denning was directed pretty much by some people who said, "Look, you might as well make use of your escape"—because it was an extraordinary escape from Grafton Gaol—and somebody said to Denning, "Look, if you're going to be on the front page of the newspapers, we might as well give you a reason for your escape and draw attention to the appalling conditions at Grafton." So he agreed. So thereafter little notes kept popping up on the underside of phone booths and the media were directed where to find these little notes about what was going on. So it was a very effective campaign, thanks to Ray's escape. It was not Ray's idea. He just wanted to get out of jail.'

Like Matteson the draft resister, Denning couldn't just disappear if he was going to make a political point. He had to keep popping up around the place, shaming the system, daring it to do its worst. So Denning made his tapes, and also two films for broadcast on TV—the first with Sutton, the second with Brett Collins, who was reaching the end of his sentence but had education leave to study law at the University of NSW. According to Collins, while Denning was still up north, the PAG ran a campaign to suggest he was in Sydney, as a distraction. Not only did Denning not write his own scripts—he didn't do his own stunts.

But that's not fair. Denning's words were torn from his heart, and he took all the risks himself. As time passed, he began to stay in one place for weeks at a time. His coordinator became concerned that people were harbouring him for the wrong reasons—almost to be close to a celebrity—and other women took on looking after him, including his first girlfriend, Rosalyn Lawson.

'There were many women who absolutely loved him and were delighted with him,' said Collins. 'It wasn't just the excitement of being with somebody on the run. He was a very attractive personality, full of spirit and fun, and he knew how to laugh and was quite happy to joust with authorities in risky ways, in cheeky ways.' Collins and Dunn began a relationship. 'A lot of sex was involved' in the crim-feminist axis, said Collins. (The couple later married, then divorced.)

Meanwhile, on a rainy Thursday afternoon, the phone rang at Donna's house.

'It's your old mate,' said Denning down the line. 'Meet me outside Newtown train station at five o'clock.'

'I went there,' Donna told me, 'and it was like a movie. I'm standing outside the station and it's all gloomy and people are coming from work, and this guy comes walking past. He had two dogs, a black one and a white one, and he had bandages all over his hands. And out the side of his mouth he goes, "Follow me."

'And we got to these terraced houses and I went *Hey!* and we gave each other a hug, because I'd only ever seen him through glass.' In Denning's room, 'He had a police radio,' said Donna, 'and he could hear all the police channels. And on the floor was stacks of paper. And he goes, "This is my book."' He showed Donna the handwritten notes for what was to become his published *Diary*. He'd recorded having to cut short a visit with her at Long Bay on 12 December 1979, and his happiness at opening a letter from her on 25 February 1980. 'I was just flabbergasted,' she said.

In the weeks that followed, 'He'd just pop up out of the blue,' said Donna. 'One time, he came to my house and I've made him something to eat, and Mum and Dad have come home from work, and I've gone *Eeeeuw*! I've got them at the front door and I've taken them into their room and I went, "Now, look, you know my friend that's been on the news lately? Ray Denning? He's in the lounge room."

'And Mum was, like, *fucking what*?'

'He's not a murderer, Mum,' said Donna. 'He's just visiting. And I'm just letting youse know.'

'So my dad goes, "Yeah, cool."'

'Mum and Dad have had something to eat,' said Donna, 'they've gone into the lounge room, and they've sat with Ray until two in the morning. Chatting.

'I've seen Ray blond,' said Donna, 'I've seen Ray with long hair. He'd turn up sometimes with a moustache. One time, I went out on the weekend and didn't come home on the Saturday night. And on the Sunday, I've gone to throw my bag on my bed, and all my stuffed animals were different on my bed. So, I've walked through, and Ray was sitting at the table having a big cook-up with Mum and Dad!

'He's come over to visit and Dad's entertained him. He was watching TV and it got late, and my dad said, *Look, she's not going to come home at this time of night. Just go and crash in her room.* My bedroom was done up in pixie pink. I had exposed white beams, I had puppets hanging, white and gold furniture—a very feminine, pretty bedroom.

'Ray's told me, *I woke up and I could hear your mum and dad walking around and, the next thing I know, there's a tap on your door and your mum's brought me in a cup of tea in bed.* He goes, *I lay in your room, and it was so pretty. I've never woke up in a room like that in my life.*'

'I just loved it,' said Donna, 'that it was something he experienced.'

And Donna cried when she told me. She cried and cried again.

'Me and him were never romantically—sexually—thingo,' she said, 'but he said to me, "Donna, if I'd ever met you in any other circumstances than this, I would marry you." And I think that's what he wanted, really. Stability. He never had anything stable in his life. The only thing that was stable in his life was fucking jail.'

And Donna cried.

'He was a very sensitive man—you wouldn't think so, robbing banks and things like that,' said Donna.

But not everyone was seduced by Denning.

'I only ever met him once,' said Meredith Burgmann, 'for about ten minutes. And he was quite a thoughtful bloke. He wasn't dumb, and some of the stuff he wrote and said was quite insightful really. But I remember thinking, *Oooh, he's little and quite unassuming*. He certainly wasn't the sort of person you'd remember.'

Brett Collins was on the board of Glebe House, a halfway house for prisoners near Burgmann's home (Burgmann said she was occasionally called to sort out disputes there). Gary Waddell, who had met several PAG activists on the set of *Stir*, first came across Denning on a visit to Glebe House. 'And he came around my place at one stage,' said Waddell.

'I was living in Annandale. He was with Kevin Storey—Chickenman in *Stir*—and they were looking for some weed and I couldn't help them. (I don't know whether it was Ray that wanted it.) A couple of things happened around that time, like my car got stolen. I don't know whether Ray Denning did that or not.

'I thought he was a completely out-of-control human being,' said Waddell. 'He was just chaotic. He didn't have any long line of thought. He'd jump all over the place and he was always incredibly nervous.'

Certain police seemed to make a sport out of verballing and bricking ex-prisoners campaigning against verbals and brickings. In November, PAG activist and paroled burglar Kevin Street was arrested and warned that he would be loaded up with dynamite if he didn't tell the police where to find Denning. They impounded his car and, while Glebe detectives interrogated Street, other police searched the vehicle—in front of a TV crew—and 'found' two sticks of gelignite.

Police testified in court that Street had admitted possession of the explosives—although, of course, he had made no signed statement. They presented a complicated story that had Street taping a note to a wall at Long Bay. According to police, Street told them, 'This time, it's only a note.

Next time, it'll be gelignite and I'll blow up a jail.' The gelignite was never fingerprinted and Street was eventually acquitted, but only after nine months on remand in Long Bay.

—

Bernie Matthews was also on parole, and living in Liverpool, NSW, with Lee Gadd, who had recently been released from Mulawa Women's Detention Centre after serving ten years for the murder of her partner. Gadd was a friend of a nurse who was involved with Women Behind Bars. The nurse rang Gadd and Gadd asked Matthews if he wanted to go into the city for dinner. Matthews didn't, but Gadd persuaded him. They were supposed to meet in a pub in East Sydney. Matthews was with another former Katingal prisoner. 'And I saw this bloke at a pool table,' said Matthews. 'I looked at him, and he had his hands covered with bandages. I said to the bloke with me, "That's Ray Denning."'

Denning had dyed his hair and used bandages to cover his tattoos.

'Ray wanted to talk to me,' said Matthews, 'because I was in a position to network him with other crims.'

Matthews was the first contact for a network of ex-tracs, which he called 'the Sydney Tattersalls Club of the NSW Prisons System'. He said Katingal had created 'a unique system that's never been replicated' of hard prisoners 'who all bonded together but didn't necessarily work together'.

Trust between tough guys had been built up in the tracs.

'There were blokes who went up there and got flogged and they'd fucking scream their head off,' said Matthews. 'I'm not saying they're weak, I'm just saying it's a sign of weakness. That's how we gauged each other—how you could take physical punishment. Because, at the end of the day, if you can handle a flogging, then if I'm pinched with you, I know if the coppers are going to backhand you, you're not going to say, *Oh yeah, he* . . . We had no TV, we had no radio, we had no books, so we had to have something to create some sort of sensibility.

'In Grafton', said Matthews, 'you didn't know what happened outside the walls. So you'd talk. I'd know everything about you since the day you were born. You'd know everything about me. I guess you became . . . a family's not the right word to describe it, but that's the closest thing there is to it.'

We'll call the 'family' the 'Blockhouse Network'. It wasn't a syndicate or a crime gang, it was more like a mutual aid society. 'It was a network that was impregnable,' said Matthews, 'because if you hadn't been to Grafton or Katingal you didn't get into the inner circle. And that inner circle were privy to things that normal prisoners weren't privy to—and that the police and prisons certainly weren't privy to. Say, if you're in that network and you're in Perth and you ring up and say, *Listen, Bernie, I need a gun or I need a fucking driver's licence* . . . Well, I'm not obligated to help you, but because I know who you are, and because I know that you've been through the same shit as I have, I'm gonna help you—but expect the same in return. And that was usually the way it was. It was a system that came into being under extreme violence.'

Not every trac was welcome. 'You wouldn't trust the kid-killers with fucking anything,' said Matthews. 'Or a fucking informer. Of course not. But others, yeah. And Denning, of course, was part of that network. It was a situation that will never be replicated, and unique to Australian prisons. I don't think the coppers or the police really realised what they'd created.'

Denning told Matthews his safe house had been blown, and they all went together to Billy Sutton's unit to talk. Denning couldn't stay at his mate's home for long, so they decided to ask for help from a popular and affable criminal we'll call 'Unknown' because he doesn't want to be known.

Unknown, who had done time for armed robbery and break and enter, had met Denning in Parramatta Gaol. He now lived like a squatter with his partner in the driftwood-and-stone fishermen's huts at Crater Cove, nestled into the rugged cliffs at Dobroyd Head, Middle Harbour. They used to do their laundry at Sutton's place.

Unknown was happy to help out Denning, who he thought was a great bloke. Denning sat around Crater Cove and gazed across the harbour, and went out fishing in a little boat. He was introduced to other people to run around for him, and he passed through in about a week. Unknown gave him a joint and believed it was the first Denning had ever smoked.

On 15 December 1980, police acting on a tip-off descended on Chippendale in inner-city Sydney. After a house-to-house search, they arrested Rosalyn Lawson and another woman, and accused them of harbouring Denning.

The political campaign ended and Denning once again picked up the balaclava, gloves and gun.

Although it's possible he had never put them down.

16

The Sins of Ron Chester

Some of the blokes you meet in the underworld might not be as deeply committed to feminism as your new squarehead friends. Take Ron Chester, for example. Back in April 1976, New Zealand–born Private Ronald Glenn Chester of the Australian Army was on leave from his posting at Puckapunyal, Victoria, and driving up to Sydney, when his car broke down on the Hume Highway, 40 kilometres south of Yass. A married couple who had stopped for a tea break on a reserve helped Chester try to get his car started again.

So Chester pulled a sawn-off shotgun on them, forced them through a fence, tied up the bloke and stole five dollars from his wallet before raping the woman, who didn't struggle because she was frightened Chester might kill her husband.

And she was right: Ron Chester had a murder coiled up in his heart, biding its time, waiting for its moment. But he kept it suppressed on that day. He just stole their car and drove away. That fucking showed them, eh? Taught them who was boss. A valuable lesson about trust. You can't just go out of your way to help a bloke in trouble and expect to get away with it. Not when that man was Ron Chester—a good soldier, keen on his job—who could do anything to anyone.

But the jacks caught Chester, because it's not so clever to leave your own fucking wheels behind at the scene of the crime. It's what those in the trade call 'a clue'. Like the clue that the judge didn't have when Chester came to court. Why would a good soldier—with a 'big future' in the military—want to terrorise people with a weapon?

Justice Taylor pronounced it 'a mystery' and sentenced Chester to twelve years for rape, with four more for armed robbery—of five bucks; not exactly the Great Bookie Robbery—and an extra two years for stealing the car.

In September 1976, the judge directed that Chester would have to serve five-and-a-half years before he could be considered for parole. In June 1980, after nearly four years in the nick, Chester escaped from Cessnock Correctional Centre. He wasn't interested in any 'big future', except at the easy end of a gun.

On 17 December 1980—the day after Robyn Lawson and her friend appeared at Central Court charged with harbouring Denning—Gary John Carter, an electroplater living in Marrickville, received a telephone call from professional criminal Stuart Harold Tange, who asked him if he could put up three men for the night. Tange turned up about half an hour later with Ray Denning, who introduced him to Chester and his mate, David John Hately. Carter didn't know Denning, but he knew who he was, and he was willing to look after him for a couple of hundred bucks.

The next morning, the boys told Carter to go to Glebe and look for an Armaguard truck and any signs of police movements in the area. Later that day, Chester, Hately and a juvenile trailed the security vehicle into a dead-end street and waited while the guards delivered the payroll to a Glebe engineering company, Sydney Mechanical Services. As the guards counted out the money, Chester and the kid burst in and forced everyone up against the wall. Chester fired a shot into the floor, and the raiders escaped with $9300 and a .38 revolver. Hately drove the getaway car, until the crew transferred to a second car, driven by Denning.

Carter came back home to find Denning, Tange, Hately and the juvenile, all of them armed. Denning had plugged in a mobile police scanner and he asked Carter to monitor the broadcasts. A message came over about a robbery in Glebe and the juvenile said, 'They've got my age wrong!'

Chester burned the pay packets from the robbery in Carter's incinerator, and paid Carter $523, largely in twenty cent pieces and small bills.

It was the one thousandth armed robbery reported in NSW in 1980.

Denning was back in the world he knew best, but not every criminal trusted him. According to Vivien Altman, Steve Sellers had his doubts: 'Towards the end of 1980,' she said, 'Steve called me to say, "Watch out for Ray Denning"—I don't know if he used those words—"He's a dog."'

In the new year, Denning and his robbery crew gathered a hoard of guns, including a .357 Magnum, a .308 rifle, a sawn-off pump-action shotgun, a .32 Fabrique Nationale pistol and a .30 calibre M1 rifle, and headed down to South Australia. On 21 January 1981, Denning, Hately and another man attacked a delicatessen run by an elderly couple in Beverley, a western suburb of Adelaide. The three bandits walked into the unassuming little shop and bought a few small items, then drew pistols on 64-year-old Mary Vallance and her husband. They tied up her husband with a chain and padlock, and Mary yelled for the police.

'One of the men grabbed me and put his hands on my face and mouth to keep me quiet,' she said. 'I think that was when I punched him in the stomach.'

Mary came out of the scuffle with a couple of cuts to her face. The bandits told her they were waiting for the Armaguard truck whose crew often called in to buy drinks from the store. They stole some cash and left after about 45 minutes.

The hapless Gary Carter was still mixed up with Chester and Hately in March 1981, when everything went to shit. Carter was just a crooked electroplater looking for an earn. He couldn't stand up to Chester and nor could Hately. They did whatever the older man told them, because they thought he'd kill them if they didn't. Just like the woman who'd tried to help him, who he raped in a field, they could see Chester's hungry murder waiting to be fed.

Maybe Alan Boyd 'Woody' Woodard knew as well. Some people set their own deaths in motion, by accident or design.

Back in Sydney, Chester told Carter that Woodard was trying to blackmail him and Hately over some armed robberies in South Australia. Chester paid Woodard's train fare up from Adelaide so they could have a chat about old times. He met Woodard from the station and brought him to Carter's unit a little past midnight.

After a sleep and a feed, Chester, Hately, Carter and Woodard drove out to bushland near Buxton, to bury some guns. On the steep track down from the parked car to the burial ground, Chester told Carter, 'That was Woody's last ride.'

Chester ordered Woody to dig a hole, and he must've been salivating while he watched Woody sweat. Chester would have liked that—getting Woody to do the hard yakka himself, leaving only the good bit for Chester—because it meant he'd tricked Woody, just like he'd conned that couple on the Hume. He had Woody trusting him, helping him. But when the pit was dug, Chester, of course, raised his sawn-off at Woody and told him to take off his clothes and lie in the hole. And he did. He stripped himself naked and arranged his own body for the bullet. Chester told Woody he was going to shoot him through the teeth so he'd die in one go and nobody would be able to identify him. After Chester shot Woody, Carter vomited and Chester told him he should be ashamed of himself. Chester wanted Carter to cut the hands off Woody's corpse with a bayonet.

This was the kind of bloke Denning was running around with when he wasn't drinking coffee with his political friends. You want anarchy? *I'll show you anarchy, mate. It's at the bottom of this hole.*

The killers filled the grave with the dirt that Woody had dug, and covered it with branches and twigs. Three weeks later, Carter went to the cops at Petersham. He'd had enough. He hadn't agreed to any of this. He gave up Chester over Woody—a murder the cops hadn't even noticed—and threw in Denning for the Sydney Mechanical Services job.

It was a good score for Aarne Tees, come out of nowhere like that, just walked in straight off the street.

—

Denning took love where he could find it. Some time around March 1981, he met transvestite Margarete Ngatai from Para Hills on the northern hemline of Adelaide. Denning spent time with Ngatai in South Australia, where they lived together for three weeks before they returned to NSW for a week in Nelson Bay, a fishing-and-chip-shops beach town near hardscrabble Newcastle. Next, they checked into the Ritz Private Hotel, a grandiosely named boarding house for the luckless and workless on Milson Road, Cremorne Point. Ngatai paid Denning's rent for a few days until the couple split up on April 21. The police extradited Ngatai from South Australia to face charges of harbouring an escapee, and there was a certain desperate glee in newspaper reports of the unemployed 31-year-old fronting up at the Central Court of Petty Sessions 'wearing a maroon dress, red high-heel shoes and a bright red satin jacket'.

Ngatai said they had split up once he realised who Denning really was—which must have become fairly obvious on April 21 when Denning returned to the Ritz with close to $8000 from a morning's work. Denning had stepped into the Bank of NSW in Summer Hill at about 9.25 a.m., just after bank teller Antoinette Matrone had taken the wallets out of the night safe. She was about to move the wallets from the floor when Denning tapped on the glass front door, with a Colt .45 pistol in his hand.

'Open the door or I will kill you,' said Denning.

Matrone picked up the wallets and ran. Denning fired three shots into the glass and walked in through the hole he had made. Matrone felt glass spray the back of her legs. She dropped the wallets onto the desk of the bank's accountant as she ran to her teller's box.

'Anyone who moves will die,' promised Denning.

He took three wallets containing a total of $20,260, then left the bank and jumped into a Valiant sedan. A taxi driver, who was in touch with his radio base, tailed him to another car, which Denning had purchased under a false name. In the second car, Denning activated a radio scanner and heard the police broadcast the progress of a vehicle through the streets of the inner west. 'He suddenly realised it was his progress that was being monitored,' said Aarne Tees later.

Denning abandoned the car, leaving behind one night-safe wallet packed with $12,500, but his fingerprints were later found on the vehicle, and his image had been captured on the bank's security camera.

Denning travelled north to Queensland, where he met up with Russell Cox, whom he seemed to have no trouble finding even though the police had no idea where he was. In August 1981, police intelligence had him in Brisbane with an acquaintance of Cox named Linda Jobson, and he was seen jogging with Cox on Bribie Island. Denning and Cox bought and repainted cars on the Gold Coast, at Bribie and in Geebung. On September 22, Denning and Cox, unmasked, walked into the brutalist Railway Centre that clawed at the elegant Victorian Central Station in Brisbane, and waited in the foyer with the morning crowd until a Transurety armoured truck delivered the payroll at 9.43 a.m. The guards climbed out of the truck and stacked a trolley with four metal boxes containing $327,000. Denning and Cox drew their guns and warned, 'This is a stick-up.' Denning was wearing an earpiece attached to a pocket radio, probably tuned to police broadcasts.

One man grabbed the money and the guards' guns and radio while the other held a pistol pointed at a guard and ordered everyone to lie on the floor. Cox and Denning left the back way, warning ticket collectors to 'keep their fucking mouths shut' as they passed. They made it to a nearby getaway vehicle—a stolen white ute fitted with Commonwealth government plates—and escaped the city centre before ten police cars could catch them.

It was the biggest payroll robbery in Queensland's history.

After the raid, Denning, who never, ever had any kind of plan, blew $110,000 at the races.

Denning and Linda Jobson returned to Sydney where, on September 8, Detective Sergeant Roger Rogerson was honoured with the Peter Mitchell Award for the most outstanding performance by a policeman in any phase of police work, for his success in apprehending two teams of armed robbers. It was the same year Rogerson had shot dead the probably unarmed drug dealer Warren Lanfranchi in Chippendale—a killing that prompted his girlfriend, Sallie-Anne Huckstepp, to go to the NSW Police Internal Affairs Branch and the media with all kinds of allegations about Rogerson and his mates.

The newly decorated Rogerson was deeply concerned about bank robberies and he couldn't help but think that bank staff weren't doing their bit and the unions were mostly to blame. Time and again, he suggested, bank tellers were told by their unions not to follow robbers outside the bank. 'We do not want bank staff to become heroes or put themselves at risk,' said Rogerson. 'No amount of money is worth a life.' That said, 'There have been occasions when staff have been an impediment to the immediate investigation by not getting *even basic details* such as the description of the getaway vehicle.'

It wasn't the cops' fault when they couldn't catch a bandit, it was the chicken bloody tellers. The information the bank staff didn't get because they were too busy hiding under their desks or sobbing into their blouses 'can be vital because there are now three police helicopters', said Rogerson, 'one of which has been ordered to be constantly on the ready for armed hold-ups'.

Rogerson already had an army of cops, now he'd been given an air force—but how could the choppers be deployed if nobody could identify their targets? Also, businesses needed to look at raising their game. 'We are still seeing the same little girl carrying the same calico bank bag along the same route on the same day of the week to the same bank ... No wonder so many robberies happen.' It wasn't that the cops weren't keeping the streets safe—it was this girl's fault. 'Use a man to carry the money,' Rogerson advised a Sydney seminar of the NSW Chamber of Manufacturers. 'Or at least a male escort.'

He also told the bosses to 'stagger the hours of delivery and use different cars and different routes'. He said at least 80 per cent of armed robberies were committed by junkies, and heroin was 'the greatest scourge on society we have ever seen'. Whether or not Rogerson had yet begun his own career as a Sydney heroin dealer, organiser of armed robberies and convicted murderer is a moot point. The press and public loved him. He was Sydney's 'Dirty Harry' (although Dirty Roger didn't have quite the same ring). Go ahead, make his day.

Five years later, Sallie-Anne Huckstepp was found floating face down in a pond in Sydney's Centennial Park. She had been strangled and drowned. She'd had to ask herself a question: *Do I feel lucky*?

But back in 1981, NSW Police had been told by an informer that Denning's girlfriend Linda Jobson was going to visit her sister in Pelican Street, Swansea, near Newcastle. Police installed an illegal interception device on Jobson's sister's phone and monitored her conversations from a van parked near the house. The eavesdroppers heard the sister send her love to 'Jack', the Jobsons' name for Denning.

On November 8, Denning met Linda in his Valiant at Manly Wharf. A team of at least a dozen officers lay in wait, some patrolling the beach dressed as beachgoers, hiding pistols in eskies and shotguns wrapped in towels. Denning picked up Jobson from the ferry and was on his way back to their unit in Surfview Road, Mona Vale, when a detective wearing beach shorts stuck a shotgun through the window and said, 'Ray, get out of the car.' Denning had a .45 pistol under the seat but he wasn't given the chance to reach for it. Jobson was in tears.

At the unit, police found three rifles, a .357 Magnum, a gas mask, a blond wig, ammunition and a radio tuned to police frequencies, as well as five legal Queensland driving licences in five different names.

New South Wales' most wanted fugitive had finally been caught. And it was soon revealed that he had been planning a new and spectacular stunt that was guaranteed to catapult him back into the public eye.

At least, that's what Aarne Tees told the judge.

17

Cops and Robbers

The Ray Denning captured by the Armed Hold-Up Squad and interviewed by Aarne Tees in 1981 seemed not to be the most recent Ray Denning (the anonymous, unrepentant, state-hopping armed robber) but the Ray Denning before that (the flamboyant, vengeful political campaigner). Although they hadn't mentioned it at first, police had apparently discovered in Denning's unit a number of Christmas cards along with the home addresses and phone numbers of certain New South Wales judges. Instantly, Denning had admitted to Tees that he had collected the cards because he planned to 'stir something up' on November 11 since, 'That is the day they hung Ned Kelly.'

Denning had not committed any kind of political act for a year, so it was fortuitous that the Hold-Ups had caught him just as he was planning a reprisal of his most notorious stunt, when he had opened fire on the Parramatta Gaol watchtower on the centenary of Ned Kelly's death.

If he would commemorate 100 years, why not 101?

Or, indeed, why?

Who the hell does that?

It was as if Denning's scriptwriter had become lazy and repetitive—or the task had reverted to Aarne Tees. There was no reason for Denning to draw attention to himself on 11 November 1981: the list of judges (which was certain to ingratiate Denning with any judge) probably came from a similar place to the gelignite found in Kevin Street's car, or the noose in Allen McDougall's cell, or even—perhaps—the hat discovered at the scene of Jack Denning's housie robbery all those years before.

—

Aarne Tees himself seemed surprised by the likeable, polite and talkative Denning he had encountered (and probably invented). Denning wasn't fleeing brutality—or even hardship—at Grafton. Instead, he supposedly offered a breezy explanation for his escape to one of the arresting officers: 'You can't spend year after year of your life in there. You need a holiday sometimes.' Tees's Denning was impressed the cops had found him and gave cheerful praise for their sterling work on his case: 'Congratulations,' he said. 'I have obviously dropped my guard somewhere. I would love to know where.' When the police asked if he had planned to use the pistol found in his car, he candidly admitted to contemplating murder: 'It crossed my mind,' he said, 'but there were too many of you.'

It would be difficult to believe Denning had said any of this—unless you were a magistrate at the Central Court of Petty Sessions, in which case you heard this kind of evidence, from this exact character, scripted by Tees and his writing team, every week of the year.

Tees claimed he had told Denning they had film of him at the Bank of NSW at Summer Hill, where he'd left behind fingerprints and witnesses who could identify him. Denning agreed Tees had got him. Tees said he then asked Denning if he denied involvement in the Summer Hill robbery or the Sydney Mechanical Services hold-up, to which Denning replied, 'No.' Which meant, yes, he did it. Although, this time, he stopped short of actually congratulating Tees.

Sadly, there was no signed record of interview, and Tees had not thought to record Denning's confession with newfangled video equipment because he hadn't known it was available to the Armed Hold-Up Squad. Under cross-examination, Tees said the record of interview had not been made directly after he had spoken to Denning but on the same day.

The campaign in support of Denning was reignited with his arrest. The PAG handed out flyers calling for a re-examination of the Faber case to journalists at Central Court—where Denning's barrister denied his client had made any admissions—and a small group of protesters ('mostly women', according to the *Daily Telegraph*) later gathered outside Central Police Station chanting, 'Free Ray!'

Even though Denning had been found with Linda Jobson, who was charged with harbouring an escapee, his former girlfriend Kim Pascoe made a surprise reappearance in *The Sun* with her familiar promise that she would always love him. 'I love him in a special way, but I know there's no future for us,' said Pascoe. 'I will stick by him no matter what.' *The Sun* revealed she had been divorced four years previously after a three-month marriage. Pascoe said police had regularly checked on her house in Bidwill, NSW, but Denning had not. She couldn't have him there, she explained, because she didn't want her kids' heads blown off with a shotgun.

The PAG and Women Behind Bars staged events to pay for the publication of *The Ray Denning Diary*, written by Denning at Grafton and Long Bay between September 1978 and March 1980 and described by Liz Fell in the *National Times* as 'a devastating account of the violence meted out to Denning by NSW prison officers (with the consent of the Department of Corrective Services)'.

The diary was dense and detailed and authored with an ear to audience reaction. While it succeeded in expressing Denning's overboiling frustrations with the injustices of prison life, it didn't cover a particularly colourful period in his jail career. He and Brett Collins took on the system and lost. He was excited and then disappointed by the Corrective Services Commissioner Tony Vinson, whose attempts to change the prison system in line with the recommendations of the Nagle Royal Commission were stymied at every turn until Vinson resigned in 1981. Denning raised a case against floggers and bashers and it failed. He met members of the Ananda Marga sect, imprisoned after an arrest by Rogerson and verballed and bricked over an imaginary assassination attempt on an Australian Nazi. Denning made particular friends with the strongest character among them, Tim Anderson. Denning flirted with Margi beliefs—just as he flirted with every idea and every person who came his way—but decided their discipline was a little too strict for him. He received several letters from Jack the Hat, who told him he was proud of his son for making a stand.

The *Diary* was given a book launch at Balmain Town Hall. One of the women who had harboured Denning took Donna along, and Donna found her name in the pages of the book. 'I was in touch with Ray for a while after he went back in,' said Donna, 'but then I just grew up and we grew apart and I had my children. One's called Ray and one's called John.'

—

In December, a coy and curious story appeared in *The Bulletin*: a boatshed owner had been approached by 'a personable young couple' who had paid $10,750 cash for a small runabout that had been previously owned by a diplomat. A few weeks later, the seller had received a call from the CIB identifying the buyer as 'Raymond Charles [sic] Denning'. The boat came up again in the press before Denning went to trial, when Tees described the haul Denning had brought in from his armed robberies—'More than I could save in a year,' Tees mused. Denning had ownership papers for the boat, a Land Cruiser and a car; TAB slips for several thousand dollars worth of bets; and a state-of-the-art colour TV set with 'a video attachment for playing Space Invaders games'.

Denning made a new cassette recording in Long Bay, predicting another outbreak of prison riots if conditions didn't improve. The tape reached the media through Brett Collins and the PAG. While Denning awaited his own trial, he gave evidence in a case brought by the PAG and Women Behind Bars, which had ten prison officers and a prison doctor summoned to answer charges related to the Grafton bashings of the early 1970s. The hearing took place before Stipendiary Magistrate Kevin Waller, and the case was driven by Collins. Waller made it clear that he didn't approve. 'Character is a factor to be taken into account when assessing the credibility of every witness,' said Waller. 'Not to put too fine a point on it, the character of most of the prisoner witnesses was appalling.'

Waller said he was astonished that Collins had called to the stand men such as Ray Denning and Marko Motric, who had been convicted of 'the most heinous crimes'. Although he conceded Denning was 'softly spoken and his evidence in chief was given in a moderate fashion', in cross-examination he demonstrated a 'bizarre attitude to life, firstly, claiming that to point a loaded .38 pistol at bank tellers or a bank customer was not an act of violence, and then that every person in court could well have committed an armed hold-up in his (or her, presumably) life. He has apparently no conception of the law-abiding citizen who does not and could not resort to violent crime . . . He was an unreliable witness.'

In other words, Denning might as well have just stayed in his cell and kept his mouth shut because nobody outside jail would take the word of a crim like him to mean anything at all.

And maybe Denning had found in his life that every law-abiding citizen could resort to violence, because most of the squareheads he had known since he was a boy were police and prison guards, and they'd been knocking him around—naked when they could—since at least 1966. Only Denning wasn't allowed to use violence; he was the only man whose body was not sacred. So, once again, no prison officer was going to be held to account for the Grafton bashings and if the prisoners were so fucking worried about being bashed, maybe they should have thought twice about committing the kinds of crimes that had seen them end up in Grafton in the first fucking place.

Linda Jobson pleaded guilty to harbouring Denning. She claimed she had met him at a 'dance' in Newcastle in mid-1981, they had been together for three months and she was expecting his baby. She was given a $1000 fine and a two-year good-behaviour bond.

Denning's son, Benjamin, was born in July 1982, and Jobson joined other prisoners' partners campaigning for private visits. 'Ray and I want to be alone with our baby, just like other parents,' she said. 'Ray hasn't got much to look forward to, he's serving a life sentence, but just being able to share affection for a few hours a month must help him cope better with prison life.' Another of Denning's regular visitors was Dot Bach, a 50-year-old woman who ran a service station in Yass, NSW. It was unclear how Dot had come to meet Denning in his current incarnation but she felt they had been lovers in a previous life, so perhaps the shadow of Lobsang Rampa had risen over Denning again. Dot was a married mother of four children. She wrote to Denning on heavily scented paper, promising she would never abandon him, and sent him a picture of a cat sitting in the middle of her bed. At first, Denning laughed at the letters, but she began to send him money, too, and regularly remind him that all his so-called radical friends had abandoned him (although they hadn't) as all they'd wanted was a martyr for their cause. And in the background all the time waited Dot's volatile husband, John.

Aarne Tees later told a court that Denning and the PAG began to drift apart after activists pressured Denning to plead not guilty to the charges brought against him by

Tees. 'Notwithstanding that we had his fingerprints and a photograph in a bank concerning an armed robbery matter,' said Tees, '... admissions were unsigned and the Prisoners' Action Group wanted to turn the trial into a three-ring circus, which he did not want because he held the view that he is going to be convicted and he pleaded guilty'.

It seemed that Denning made an arrangement with Tees—which was somehow brokered by Dot Bach—not to contest the Hold-Up Squad's verbal. Denning wrote to Brett Collins: 'I would fight all these things regardless of the odds but I have made commitments to other people plus I have interstate blues that I have been promised will be dropped and my Lady Dot has put a lot of work into a deal for me that is just too good to throw out the window, then if all goes as planned I will be out in about 3 or 4 years at the most. Otherwise if I do not go through with the deal the boots really go in and I am in big trouble mainly interstate, so see I am really over a barrel and they know it. Keep this to yourself and destroy this letter mate, OK?'

Denning ultimately did plead guilty and Tees offered surprising testimony in court before Justice Alfred Joseph Goran. Tees said Denning was 'far more intelligent than what he was in 1972', that he had formed a friendship with the Bachs who showed a 'keen interest in his welfare and his future' and—astonishingly—that it could not be said that, during his time on the run, he was 'an associate of the criminal element'. Tees said that Denning was 'not causing any problems whatsoever' in jail. He also offered a variation on Denning's testimony—deemed 'bizarre' by Waller—that his armed hold-ups weren't violent. At Summer Hill, said Tees, 'The bank has bullet-resistant glass and the girl who picked up the money from the night safe actually ran in between the glass and they were really quite safe.' Incredibly, police made no mention of Denning's spectacular attack on the gun tower at Parramatta.

John Bach also gave evidence, as a company director whose business operated the Yass service station, its restaurant and store—which apparently comprised the largest service station in Australia—and the 'Glengullen' Murray Grey Stud. John said he was prepared to support Denning to the hilt while Denning was in custody. He said he had visited Denning three or four times in jail, and his wife went to see Denning once a week. He promised to take Denning into 'a managerial situation' whenever he was released.

The judge was unmoved by Tees or Bach, or anything else. Apart from the fact that Denning's mum had burned herself to death in Denning's presence, said Justice Goran, there was nothing remarkable about his background or his criminal history except perhaps that he moved from state to state committing his offences. Goran was an educated man, who knew irony when it crouched in his courtroom with a self-satisfied grin across its cheeks, and so he felt obliged to identify it for the less able. Goran told Denning that evidence that he had undergone some change of heart 'ironically enough comes from the detective sergeant in this case; a police officer, and one who knows that in some of the claims you have made you have consistently attacked police officers for falsely having led to your convictions'. Goran did not consider that the change of attitude might have come from the detective rather than the defendant, and been motivated by the possibility that Dot Bach had sold Denning's boat and given the proceeds to police.

It would be some years before that idea was raised in court.

On 29 March 1983, Goran gave Denning a further ten years' jail for the escape and two armed robberies. On April 8, however, he reversed his judgment, on the grounds that he didn't have the authority to make an additional sentence cumulative to a life sentence which, in some ways, could have been seen as accommodating the theories of both Lobsang Rampa and Dot Bach that Denning could have more than one life. So instead of sentencing Denning to remain in jail for ten years after he had notionally died, Goran announced the sentence would run concurrently and therefore have little practical effect on Denning's imprisonment. It seemed a life-sentenced prisoner might break out of jail, taunt the police, shoot at a prison guard, rob a few banks and remain on the run until he was finally recaptured and suffer no serious legal sanction.

Whether or not the judge's lenience had anything to do with the Bachs, John and Dot became known to other prisoners. Dot's contacts included three lifers and Billy Sutton, who was doing his time for the Warringah Mall robbery when he escaped jail on 5 April 1984. Sutton was arrested in a car driven by John Bach, which had been tailed by police. John drove Sutton from Yass to Canberra and gave him about $100, but John was not charged in relation to the escape and the recapture involved Aarne Tees, so it seems likely John had tipped off Tees. It's not known how Tees met the Bachs—and they may, of course, have been introduced in another life—but Tees later told a court that Dot had visited him at his home, cooked at his barbecue and perhaps met his wife.

Coincidentally, another of the old Maitland Crew absconded a couple of months later. Roy 'the Red Rat' Pollitt had become an accomplished painter in Katingal (Denning had also produced some surprisingly deft canvases) and Pollitt would have been the ideal person to launch Brett Collins' latest venture, Break Out—an arts-and-crafts centre run by ex-prisoners—were he not incarcerated on a prison farm in the NSW Riverina. On June 27, Pollitt allegedly stabbed a fellow prisoner and escaped. He was recaptured on June 29, but escaped Wagga Wagga Police Station on July 1 by impersonating a drunk who had been held overnight. Break Out celebrated its opening on July 14, the shopfront wrapped in a green and gold ribbon. To the surprise of most—but probably not all—of the guests, Roy Pollitt broke out of the Break Out shopfront, broke through the ribbon, announced 'I declare the joint open', and ran off into a waiting car.

Pollitt remained on the run for a few months until he was caught and charged with an October armed robbery in Altona, Victoria, where he took $11,000 from the local branch of Westpac.

But before we can move any further forward, we have to go back to 3 January 1983, when Ian Revell Carroll visited his Mount Martha house and ended up in an argument with Cox. Both men were armed. Carroll had a pocket sewn into his pants to carry a small pistol; Cox later claimed he had been given a gun to protect himself from 'criminal elements'. It is thought Cox had differences with other members of the milieu on account of the Great Bookie

Robbery. Police investigator Ken Ashworth told me Cox 'was involved in the planning of the Great Bookie Robbery. Cox was incarcerated at that time so he didn't participate in the hold-up but was entitled to some of the proceeds, and that's what the argument with Ian Carroll at Mount Martha was all over.'

There was a fight. A woman was heard by neighbours to shout *Don't shoot him!* or *Don't point that at him!* A man and a woman wrestled over a pistol. Carroll shot Cox, and somebody shot Carroll dead.

Deane and Cox fled to NSW, where they persuaded a doctor in Gosford that Cox had been injured in a firearms accident in Papua New Guinea and therefore there was no need to report his wound to the authorities in Australia. Police searching the Mount Martha house found three false-bottomed chests in the loft, containing an arsenal including machine guns, submachine guns and a pistol stolen in Northern Ireland, as well as medical kits, bullet-proof vests, handcuffs, balaclavas, Armaguard uniforms, gas marks, false magnetic vehicle signs and flashing lights, and disguises including false moustaches, hair dyes and make-up.

'It was an armed robber's paradise down there,' said Ashworth. 'Every tool you ever wanted.' A panel van that had been parked on the property was later found in Oakleigh. 'I remember the registration was BEL 890,' said Ashworth, 'because I've typed it so often it still sticks in my mind. And that vehicle had been purchased by a fellow by the name of Santo Mercuri.'

Santo 'Sam' Mercuri was a Calabrian who had grown up around North Fitzroy and Preston, and lived with his son in Gladstone Park while his ex-wife looked after their daughter in North Fitzroy. Mercuri deeply loved both his kids and did whatever he could to spend time with them. And he tended to have time on his hands since, although he gave his trade as 'butcher', he was in fact a professional criminal. Like the Russell Cox of legend, Mercuri had his first contact with the cops when he was charged as a juvenile with stealing a bicycle. He had fronted courts on charges of theft, handling stolen goods, burglary, assaults and deception, but he was not without friends. Cox and Deane, for instance, had been guests at the wedding of his sister on 18 September 1982. A picture from the wedding day showed an empty seat where Cox had been sitting before the photographer took his shot. Cox wasn't going to be caught on film. He didn't make mistakes like that.

Aarne Tees came to see Denning in jail with a photograph of guns and clothes, and asked him about the shooting of Ian Revell Carroll. Denning told Tees he knew nothing about it. Six months after the shooting, police returned to the Mount Martha property and found an empty barrel buried in the ground. It hadn't been empty when it was buried and it hadn't been found in the first search of the house. At some point in between, someone had gone back to collect it.

Police believed the barrel had contained some of the proceeds of the Great Bookie Robbery. So maybe Cox won the argument in the end. But it seems to have been around this time that Cox became widely known as 'Mad Dog', perhaps in reference to the nineteenth-century bushranger Dan 'Mad Dog' Morgan, a drunken murderer who was shot dead during a hold-up. Cox hated the nickname—if a mad dog escaped, you'd have no choice but to put it down—and he was always known in the milieu as 'Cox the Fox'. Back in Katingal, the only mad dog had been Archie 'Mad Dog' McCafferty, a psychopath and serial killer. John Silvester, the fine crime writer who claimed to have coined the epithet for Cox, later said he regretted it. Anybody willing to call Cox mad or a dog to his face would have to be mad or a dog themselves.

—

Ian Revell Carroll came from a large family of boxers and waterside workers with branches in both Sydney and Melbourne. He was a once-removed relative—'like an uncle'—of Mark Royston Carroll, the son of Sydney boxer and wharfie Roy Carroll and brother of boxer John Carroll. 'I'd met him as a child,' Mark told me, 'Uncle Ian.'

Mark was a handy fighter who trained from the age of about six at Punchbowl Diggers Boxing Club in south-west Sydney and fought as an amateur until he was about twenty. He grew up mates with the ill-fated criminal Warren Lanfranchi and the boxer Bob Holt, and various other men who would make impressions on the fight game or the underworld or both.

At seventeen, Mark pulled an armed robbery on a drug dealer. 'You never would've called it armed robbery in them days,' he said. 'I mean, they got their money illegally, so no harm done.' He was 22 years old in 1984 when he served his first real jail term for another shakedown on a better-connected and wealthier pusher. Carroll went straight to Long Bay, where he met Ray Denning.

Denning had picked up a charge in Maitland on 14 January 1983 for possession of money and a dictaphone, which suggests he was about to make another tape recording, but the plan—if there was one—came to nothing. On February 22, Denning was back in the Bay, where he was to return every few months for the following four years. Carroll became mates with him in 3 Wing at the CIP. 'We got along really well,' said Carroll. 'To me—being a bit younger than him—he was a bit of a hero. Balls on him like a brass monkey.' He was 'a very quiet bloke and a real gentleman', said Carroll. 'Not everybody would have a TV and a radio—they were hard to come by, really—but because I knew a couple of his friends and I'd met him, he got me a TV and food and a couple of good tracksuits and T-shirts.'

'He was an organiser too,' said Carroll. On 8 September 1985, Denning led a sit-in in support of a list of demands for better conditions in a jail where 474 prisoners were jammed inside a facility built for 350. The protest was monitored by the Malabar Emergency Unit (MEU), a riot-response and high-risk prisoner-escort squad housed in the old Katingal building.

When the sit-in began, 'the MEU got wind of it', said Carroll. 'And in the CIP, facing the entrance to the prison, there was a big corrugated steel fence about a foot or so off the ground. You couldn't see through it, but you'd see underneath it, and all I could see was all these pairs of boots. Within minutes of lockdown, the superintendent came in with a bullhorn and said, "Are you going to go back to your cells?" Ray was the spokesman and said, "No." And, basically, he's turned around and said, *Alright. Go on. Give it to them.*'

Dave 'Emu' Farrell was in charge of the MEU, which advanced at the prisoners firing tear gas canisters and blast-dispersion grenades. An officer in the tower started shooting his automatic rifle over the heads of the protesters (and the MEU). There were about 300 prison officers on hand, and the rank and file went in after the riot squad.

'I was standing next to Ray,' said Carroll, 'and they were firing tear gas canisters at us and one was on the ground—there was stuff coming out of it—and a screw ran over with a baton and went to hit me over the head with it, and Ray's grabbed his helmet and stuffed the tear gas canister up there.'

Bill Dodson was an officer with the MEU team at the demonstration. About eight years younger than Denning, Dodson was tall and imposing and fiercely fit—he loved his job. Once the fighting was over and the prisoners subdued, 'We'd rounded them up,' Dodson told me, 'segregated them into yards and, after that, the process was to escort them back to their cells and lock them down in the wings. But, as Denning's getting escorted by one of the officers, he's taken a baton off him.' Denning wrestled control of the club but didn't have a chance to use it. 'There was a couple of other Emergency Unit officers, sort of jogging on the spot near him,' said Dodson, 'because everyone was keeping an eye on him because they knew who he was. So then he's had to be upended again and restrained. But that was the guile of the bloke.'

Dodson was contemptuous of Denning. 'Younger crooks looked up to him,' he told me. 'A lot of these old "good crooks", they're not the smartest guys academically, but they survive by their wits. The common traits that they have is that they're manipulative, they're cunning and they're ruthless.'

That evening, the ringleaders were transferred out of the Bay. Denning was sent to Parklea. 'Those sort of crooks got shanghaied a lot,' said Dodson. 'Any serious incident that happened in any maximum-security jail, there'd be people shanghaied all over the place.' Dodson moved Denning several times. 'We had a list of about 40-odd of the most dangerous prisoners in the system,' he said. 'So anything that had to happen with those, as in court escorts or medical appointments outside, or transfers to other jails—we did those.' The list of prisoners included Denning, and also the Anita Cobby murderers, the Bandidos and Comanchero bikies, serial killer Archie McCafferty, and a fiery young armed robber named Ray Carrion. According to his best mate, armed robber Mark Merriman, Ecuadorian-born Carrion was once driven from Goulburn Gaol—where he was in segregation—to Penrith Court, flanked by prison officers. Merriman told me that Carrion made a plastic spike from a toilet brush and was hiding a handcuff key in his mouth. During the journey, said Merriman, 'Ray opens up one cuff, pulled the pick out and stabbed the screw under the neck with it, and said, *Pull over or I'll kill him*! With that, he was overpowered.'

Remember Ray Carrion: he was always trying to escape.

Dodson never met Cox, but his five years in the MEU often brought Cox to mind. 'There were 25 of us, full-time, working out of Katingal,' said Dodson, 'and we were servicing the whole state's maximum-security system. It was very good for a unit like ours, because we could use it as a training venue as well. Because essentially it was a jail. Each Emergency Unit officer had his own cell in Katingal, so when we were on stand-bys for riots and stuff we used to stay down there. We sort of semi-lived in there as well.'

A reminder of Cox's escape was ever-present in the old Lower Green yard. 'You could actually walk out into that exercise yard and see where he'd cut out,' said Dodson. 'You judge good crooks by how much time they spend in jail, really. Because the good ones either don't get there or they can manage to survive outside and spend a long time out of jail—which Russell Cox could do.'

Denning was transferred to the new privately managed jail at Parklea for the first time on 3 May 1985, and was regularly brought back and forth from the prison in the following two years. In September 1986, he tried once again to bring alleged bashers to account. At Central Court, handcuffed and under guard, he accused former rugby league forward and prison officer Chris Withall of beating him while other prison officers held him down, naked. Denning had refused to lift his testicles and bend over without a nurse or senior officer present, when the prison officers had pinned him to the floor and left him with a cut eyebrow and lip. All the officers were cleared in October, when a judge said it was not proven that Withall had caused Denning's injuries—it could have been any of the guards. A previous magistrate had found there was no evidence of common purpose and dismissed the case against the other men named by Denning. So they hadn't all done it together but one of them had done it alone but since they were all doing it together it wasn't possible to tell who had done it.

That was the last case Denning brought against prison officers. Anyone could see there was no fucking point.

Parklea in north-western Sydney was probably the most comfortable jail in NSW. Prisoners were one-out in the cells with only twelve to a wing. They cooked for themselves and had their own televisions. John Killick—arrested for three bank robberies in May 1985—was at Parklea with Denning. 'He was very quiet,' said Killick. 'He never came out of his cell half the bloody time and when he did come out he didn't look that well. He used to wear a hat.'

Armed robber Ray Brownlowe had met Denning at Parramatta but only became friends with him at Parklea. 'He was very well liked,' Brownlowe told me. 'But he only hung around with a few people he got close with. He was not very trusting of everyone, but he was friendly with everyone. He was easygoing but he had that respect. I think people were a bit worried about him because of his reputation—and he knew some pretty brutal people.'

Among the small crew that hung around with Denning at Parklea was armed robber, kidnapper and rapist Arthur Loveday, who was not a particularly popular man in jail. Loveday didn't seem like Denning's type. 'I couldn't see what the relationship was between Arthur and Ray,' said Brownlowe.

—

Meanwhile, the Bachs' servo had come under heavy pressure from Shell, which had reclassified the business as a commissioned agent and reduced the size of its restaurant. The Bachs were forced to sell some properties to keep the servo going, but it went into liquidation anyway. One day at Parklea, Dot told Denning she had to get away on holiday. She was thinking of visiting the Gold Coast.

'Hong Kong is cheap,' said Denning, who had never been out of Australia. 'Why don't you go there?'

18

Cox on the Run, Denning on the Turn

Russell Cox found the cops before the cops found Cox—or, at least, before they realised it was him.

After the shooting of Ian Revell Carroll in 1983, Cox and Helen Deane travelled up through New South Wales to Queensland. In November, police were tipped off that Cox was planning to hold up the payroll at the Mayne Rail Yard in north-east Brisbane. They didn't know the date of the raid, so cars were sent to sit off the yards whenever the payroll was due, waiting for Cox to show.

On Wednesday, 30 November, the officer-in-charge of the Brisbane Armed Hold-Up Squad, Detective Sergeant George Sharry, was on patrol with Senior Constable Kim Roylance, in an unmarked police car. 'We just happened to be two of the arrest team—for want of a better word—that were allocated to that day,' Roylance told me. 'There were a number of undercover police and Special Weapons Teams all the way around the place. We were listening to the radio calls and there was a discussion about a car: it had been seen driving around but had left the area.'

The suspicious vehicle was a cream-coloured Valiant, and Sharry and Roylance were the first to see it. 'We pulled the car over,' said Roylance, 'as a normal process, just to find out who the driver was. He parked his car. We parked ours behind. Then he got out of his car. We started to walk over towards him. And then he just pulled a revolver from under his shirt.'

Cox had grown a beard and a moustache. He strode towards the detectives, carrying a .38.

'We didn't have weapons drawn,' said Roylance. 'We didn't even have any weapons on us—they were still locked in the car. Because we weren't supposed to be in that situation—we were to come along after he had been apprehended.

'So he's just pulled the gun on my partner and I, and my partner lay down on the ground. I was on the other side of the car, away from him. I ducked down behind the car, but then he threatened my mate. He said, *Come around here or I'll shoot him*. So I just walked around and I lay down on the ground with him.'

Cox stood over their bodies with his gun.

'Move an inch and I'll turn you into dog meat,' said Cox. 'I'll blow you so far away you'll think eternity is only in the next street.'

'Your adrenalin is pumping,' said Roylance. 'You do have a heightened sense of fear as to what might happen, but you've got to take into account where you are: you're on a busy road, he'd stopped outside a car-rental place, and there were people around.' And Cox wasn't a mad dog. Not really.

'One murmur, one move, and I'll shoot both you bastards dead,' warned Cox.

'Because we'd jumped out of the car, we hadn't taken the keys with us,' said Roylance. 'Once he had us on the ground, he's gone and grabbed the keys, and locked the doors so we couldn't get back in to use the radio. He also took the briefcase on the back seat where we had our guns. And then he's driven off. And we couldn't chase him. We had to race into the car-rental place and make a call into the operations area to get more cars. He drove off and parked his vehicle in a brickyard and just put a cover over it.'

The car was found a few kilometres away in Alderley. Roylance's and Sharry's briefcase and guns were still inside. Cox later told a judge that he had ditched their weapons once he'd established they really had been police. Also in the car were a home security manual, books about running and yoga, and *The Prophet* by poet-philosopher Kahlil Gibran, which was widely read in the 1970s and early-1980s—although probably not by many Australian armed robbers.

Cox enjoyed and understood weapons. He used a Victorian firearms licence in the name of Gaetano Vella to buy two high-powered rifles—including an $1800 West German assault rifle—from a gun shop in Tarragindi, in Brisbane's south. Cox paid in cash, which he said he had won on the Golden Casket lottery. (This is probably the incident that gave rise to Chopper Read's idea that Cox had collected $15,000 lottery money on the run.) The Tarragindi gunsmith told police Cox had acted like a 'bit of a dill' who'd had to be shown how the gun worked. It's unlikely Cox would have learned anything he didn't already know.

Over the years, Cox had refined his robbery techniques. He preferred to hit Armaguard trucks after Ray Chuck had introduced him to an Armaguard worker whose son was struggling with a drug addiction and who was willing to pass on intelligence about possible jobs in return for ten per cent of the take. Cox carried out his own target surveillance for two to three weeks, sitting in a panel van—sometimes behind tinted windows—wearing a disguise and watching. He put on wigs, false beards and false teeth for his raids, and often wore an earpiece connected to a police scanner. He and his crew generally dressed in jackets or floppy shirts worn outside their trousers to hide the bulge of their firearms. At first, Cox liked to steal Valiants as getaway cars, using their ignition barrels to get the engines going, but later he made a skeleton key that worked on most Fords too.

His tradecraft was noted by his pursuers. The task force hunting him was led by the Victorian Homicide Squad's Detective Sergeant David Sprague, who made a strange statement to the press, announcing the high regard he had for Cox. He said, 'A policeman probably shouldn't say this, but you have got to give him credit for his professionalism. He is a very skilful criminal. I am sure he is trying to outdo Ned Kelly . . . The way Cox escaped Katingal was remarkable.'

Since the death of Ian Carroll, Sprague had searched for Cox across every Australian state and made inquiries in the US and the Philippines, although he thought Cox had recently been living in Noosa and was still in the Brisbane area. 'He has no fear of living openly like an ordinary citizen,' said Sprague. 'He can melt so easily into the suburbs. He avoids the inner city and pubs where other criminals are likely to spot him and give him up.'

But Cox was only invisible to people he didn't want to see him. Vivien Altman met him in the early 1980s. 'He was brought around to a house I was living in, in Annandale,' she told me. 'He came with his girlfriend, Helen. I know he was a big hero and he broke out of jail, but I just found him really unremarkable . . . He didn't form a strong impression.'

Which was the only feeling Cox would've wanted to leave—an imprint on a cushion, a shadow over a coffee table, an empty seat at a wedding.

—

Cox later claimed he went back to England in December 1983. And perhaps he did, but the Australian Bureau of Criminal Intelligence (ABCI) was still hunting for him in Australia. 'I was put on the team that was looking for Cox,' former detective Michael Kennedy told me. 'It was just an ongoing job we had. We believed he was living in Darwin.'

Police also thought Cox had teamed up with Colin Creed, a former South Australian policeman who had become a rapist and armed robber. (This idea resurfaces occasionally but is furiously disputed by some of Cox's associates.) Aarne Tees—'a good bloke,' said Kennedy—suggested Kennedy should speak to Cox's former de facto, Audrey, who was still living in Ultimo.

'Audrey was an old knockabout crim,' said Kennedy. 'We never had any trouble with the old knockabout crims. Publicly, it was all *Fuck off and don't come near me, you cunt* but privately, we came from the same class, we spoke the same language. It was very easy to talk to them—providing you weren't going in looking for confessions.

'I went back to see her quite a few times,' said Kennedy. 'I'd go around and I'd have a cup of tea, or I'd meet her at the Pudding Shop and we'd have a bit of cake and coffee together. You'd give her a bit of a heads-up on something if someone was getting a bit too close to her, and she'd give you the heads-up on some information.'

Kennedy said Audrey's child with Cox found a good job with the Bank of New South Wales. 'Audrey was very, very proud.'

Audrey told Kennedy about Cox's younger years, when he came out of jail to face demands for weekly 'rent' from the police. She never said where Cox might be, but the ABCI pursued the idea that he was in Darwin with Barry Dunks and another criminal, David Hopes. They passed on this intelligence to the AFP, where the matter was taken over by the AFP–NSW Police Joint Task Force—'which I didn't want to happen,' said Kennedy, 'because they couldn't be trusted'—and the task force went in and arrested Dunks but found no trace of Cox or Hopes.

NSW Police had growing problems of their own. On 6 June 1984, undercover drug squad detective Michael Drury was shot twice though the kitchen window of his home in Chatswood. Drury, who almost died from his wounds, alleged Roger Rogerson had tried to bribe him to drop charges against heroin dealer Alan Williams. When Drury had refused Rogerson's money, Rogerson had contracted Chris 'Mr Rent-A-Kill' Flannery to shoot him. Rogerson was eventually acquitted of Drury's attempted murder but dismissed from the police force and later convicted of perverting the course of justice in a related matter.

But, of course, Rogerson had been perverting the course of justice for a long time.

On 26 April 1985, the hardy and unafraid Australian boxer Jeff Fenech knocked out IBF world bantamweight champion Satoshi Shingaki in the ninth round of a ferocious fight in Sydney. Russell Cox, always a keen boxing fan, phoned Fenech's trainer Johnny Lewis to congratulate him on the new Australian world title. Cox and Lewis arranged to meet on May 18, when together they watched Collingwood beat Hawthorn at Victoria Park.

Chris Flannery disappeared in May 1985, never to be seen again. Laurie Prendergast vanished without trace in August. The next year, Cox and Helen Deane—calling themselves John and Carol Andrews—rented a retreat in Thane, Queensland. The closest town to Thane is Warwick, the ancestral home of the Schnitzerling family. In 1986, in his ninth year on the run from police in every state and territory, Melville Peter Schnitzerling, Australia's most wanted criminal and sometime public enemy number one, chose to move to a property on . . . Schnitzerling Road, Thane.

—

While Cox's life returned to its roots, Denning's flew off to a place he had never visited. The thriving, thickly populated area known as Lee Garden, just west of Causeway Bay on the island of Hong Kong, was named after Lee Hysan, the one-time 'Opium King' of Hong Kong and Macau. Lee Hysan was gunned down in a Hong Kong street in 1928, but his legacy was the foundation of the wealthy and powerful Lee family dynasty, which opened the luxurious 22-storey Lee Gardens Hotel in 1971. When it was first built, the hotel stood as the tallest building in the area, before it was dwarfed by sunflower skyscrapers on three sides. In its heyday, it attracted such era-defining guests as Diana Ross, the former queen of Motown pop; Ronald Reagan, the former president of the United States; and John Bach, the former owner of a failed servo in Yass.

William John Bach, born on 24 March 1939, was known in Yass and Wilton as 'John'. That was the name on the passport he used when he travelled to Hong Kong on Qantas Flight 28 on 30 June 1986 and booked into room 2115 at Lee Gardens Hotel. And that was the name he gave police when he was arrested at Kai Tak International Airport attempting to return to Australia a few days later.

John was interviewed by Detective Inspector Robin Victor Milner of the Joint Drug Task Force in Sydney at the Narcotics Bureau at the Royal Hong Kong Police Force Headquarters at 11.30 a.m. on 9 July 1986. John told the cops the Bachs were going broke, and Ray Denning had offered to lend them some money. The catch was, they had to go to Hong Kong to collect it. According to John, Denning had talked about $200,000 that was waiting for him in Asia. The Bachs, he said, could have a loan of half of it.

'We were losing everything and Shell were going to bankrupt us,' John told the cops. 'It became clear that the things might be connected with drugs but my position was so desperate that I went along with it as it appeared it was my only way out.'

As John spoke, Milner typed, laboriously correcting as he went along. John told the cops he was going to bring back heroin to Australia strapped to his body and legs, using 'some little plastic containers, some small ones and large ones'.

He said, 'I had never seen heroin before. I had practised with icing sugar at home to see how bulky it was.'

The initial plan was to smuggle three pounds of the drug, but John decided his cut of the deal would not be enough to save his house, so Denning offered him another pound of heroin for a further $100,000 fee. John travelled to Hong Kong with Dot and a former prison officer who was to be known as 'Mr White'.

Mr White was supposed to go to the Citizen Travel Agency in Hong Kong, find a woman and say, 'Hullo, I'm Mr White.' She was supposed to reply, 'I'm Mrs Black.'

However, when Mr White met Mrs Black, 'She indicated to me that she didn't know what I was talking about,' Mr White later told police. 'I told her I was sent there by a mutual friend, but the only name I knew was Mr White.

'She seemed confused,' said Mr White, 'so I left the agency and returned to the hotel.'

Relations then soured between Mr White and John, who possibly should have been called 'Mr Brown'. Conventional wisdom may have held that John should have kept a low profile while organising an international drug deal in a foreign country, but John was not a conventionally wise man. John felt he was being kept in the dark, said Mr White, 'which led to violence on several occasions, one being a brawl in the lobby of the hotel between myself and him'. Further mayhem resulted in 'the destruction of his room when he cut himself up putting his fist through the window'. John 'had to go to the hospital to get fixed up'.

In Hong Kong, John picked up $68,760 from the Wing Lung Bank. It wasn't enough to pay for the heroin and, after what Ian Temby QC later described as 'much muddle and fuss', John did not take delivery of the drugs anyway.

John Bach was hopelessly confused that everything had gone awry. After all, he was just a simple bloke who used to own a servo in Yass, way over his head in a business deal that no one could imagine might go wrong when a prisoner who had never been out of Australia, and was serving a life sentence in Sydney, had offered to lend him a spare $100,000 that he had lying around in Hong Kong.

Although the debacle had only begun a few weeks earlier and ended a couple of days before, John had already had ample time for reflection and remorse. 'I regret having been involved in this,' he told police, 'and I am glad that the heroin never arrived as I couldn't live with myself knowing I was getting myself out of my own predicament . . . causing grief and death to other people.'

While he was away in Hong Kong, police found 34 marijuana plants growing on his farm in Wilton.

The Bachs returned to Australia on 12 July 1986, and Dot went out to Parklea to visit Denning. According to a statement Dot later made to the Joint Task Force on Drug Trafficking, Denning asked her, 'What the bloody hell happened?'

'*You* tell *me* what happened,' said Dot.

She said she and John had been arrested, held for two days, questioned and searched for drugs. Denning wanted to know if the police had asked about him. She said they had.

'If I had any drugs on me, I would've been there for life,' said Dot.

'Well, now you know what it's like,' said Denning, the lifer. 'You've only done 48 hours.'

Later Dot told the cops, 'He gave me the impression that he couldn't have cared less. In fact, he seemed angry that it hadn't come off.'

The Commonwealth Director of Public Prosecutions (DPP) later discussed whether to indemnify the Bachs and use them to give evidence against Denning and another man, but Inspector Kilpatrick of the Joint Task Force said that the lives of the Bachs would probably be endangered if they were either charged or indemnified. The DPP doubted the Bachs could be used as effective witnesses in a prosecution that would serve little purpose anyway, in part because Denning was already doing a life sentence, and also since 'no heroin was imported because the plan was frustrated by its own apparent ineptitude'.

The mess in Lee Garden left Denning in a desperate position at Parklea. The money in Hong Kong had come via an imprisoned heroin kingpin, a former boyfriend of the late Sallie-Anne Huckstepp, who had used Denning to recruit John as a mule. The kingpin—in deference to tradition, we'll call him Mr Big—knew John had been arrested at the airport. He knew John would only have been released if he had given names to the police. Therefore, Denning's mule had not only endangered a lucrative heroin-smuggling operation, he had also implicated Mr Big. Since John was a squarehead, the blame lay with Denning, who was supposed to be a good crook. It made the picture even worse for Denning that Dot was still permitted to visit him in the jail even though the prison authorities must have been aware of the smuggling scheme.

A major reason some men tended to enjoy their time at Parklea was the fact that the prison was awash with drug dealers and drugs. Inmates included some big international names among wing dealers such as Arthur Loveday, who sold heroin to other prisoners. It was an easy place to get on the gear and a terrible jail to earn a reputation as a man who messed up supply lines.

If Denning knew what was good for him, he would get out of Parklea and away from Mr Big's possible reprisals. He had almost no choice but to strike a bargain with Corrective Services. On 23 July 1986, less than two weeks after John Bach had been arrested in Hong Kong and told police that Denning had set him up as a heroin courier, Denning's security classification was downgraded from A2 to B. On August 24, Denning was transferred out of Parklea to Bathurst Gaol.

Towards the end of the year, Bathurst threw a gala day, when normal prison discipline was relaxed and prisoners' families and friends were invited onto the sports oval. Bernie Matthews was out of jail and running Glebe House, but he and his new partner, Cheryl, came in for the event. They were chatting with another prisoner under a marquee when Denning came over.

'Fucking how come you're here, Ray?' asked Matthews.

'Aw, they've farmed me through medium security,' said Denning. 'I think I'm on my way out in the next four or five years.'

'That's fucking good, mate,' said Matthews.

Matthews' friend—in deference to Cheryl—said, 'Listen, Bern, do you mind if me and Ray have a shot up?'

'It's got nothing to do with me,' said Matthews. 'Ray who?'

'*Ray*.'

'Denning?'

'Yeah.'

'That's the first time I knew he was on the gear,' Matthews told me. 'He had a shot, and that should've been a warning sign for me—but it wasn't.'

19

The Sins of Santo Mercuri

The slow death of Jenny G began on 11 July 1988 when Russell Cox teamed up for a robbery at Barkly Square in Brunswick, Victoria, with Melbourne underworld identity Mark Moran and Cox's friend Santo Mercuri, whose car had been parked outside the Mount Martha house on the day Ian Revell Carroll was killed. Cox had completed his usual preliminary work. The crew had chosen their loose clothes and disguises, their wigs and the weapons. Cox had lent Moran a .44 Magnum and a yellow bulletproof vest that came down to his thighs.

Moran was an unlikely collaborator for Cox. His half-brother, gangster Jason Moran, had married Les Kane's daughter, Trish—so working with Cox put Mark in a crew led by a man suspected of killing Mark's sister-in-law's father (whose brother Brian, in turn, was believed to have been involved in the murder of Helen Deane's brother-in-law, Ray Chuck). But if these matters are not deliberately broached, they rarely arise in casual conversation. Mark was the bright, generous, charming, measured Moran—private-school educated and necessarily mysterious. His ambition was to own nightclubs but his destiny was to rob security vans.

At 7.45 a.m., Swiss-born security officer Dominik Hefti turned up for his shift at the Armaguard depot in Bakers Road, North Coburg. Hefti, who had migrated to Australia from Switzerland in 1981, joined two other guards in an armoured truck to head out on their usual round of escorting and collecting cash tins from businesses around Campbell-field, Broadmeadows, Fawkner, Brunswick and Coburg.

Hefti was designated as the unit's Number Three—the helper, whose specific duties were to carry the cash tins between the customer and the truck. The driver was Number Two and had instructions not to leave the truck under any circumstances. The guard in the front passenger seat had position Number One: armed with a .38 Smith & Wesson, Number One was tasked with providing extra security for Hefti.

The morning was uneventful. The afternoon was a disaster. At about 3.10 p.m., the driver reversed into the loading bay behind Coles New World in Barkly Square and passed an empty cash tin to Hefti and Number One, who climbed out of the truck. They rang a bell, called out 'Arma-guard!' and a steel door opened, and Hefti marched to the pay office with Number One behind him.

The manager let the guards into the office, where he took $33,000 dollars from the safe. The guards sealed the money in the tin and carried it through the security door and back towards the loading bay, along a narrow warehouse track with packaged foods stacked on pallets on either side.

Out of the blue, Number One heard a yell and turned around to see Santo Mercuri running towards him along the warehouse passageway, pointing a gun. Mercuri was only a couple of metres away when Number One slipped and fell against a freezer door.

Mercuri was supposed to attack the guards from his end of the passageway, while Cox and Moran came up in the other direction to jam them in a trap. But Cox and Moran were imitating idlers, staring into shop windows, when Mercuri made his move too early. He thought his mates could see him, but they couldn't.

When Mercuri made a grab for the money, Hefti pulled out his gun.

'Dominik was holding the cash tin with his left hand at about stomach height between himself and the male person,' said Number One in a statement. 'Dominik's revolver was pointing toward the male person. However, during the course of the struggle Dominik and the male person were pulling the cash tin away from each other.'

Mercuri expected Cox and Moran to arrive at any second, but he was left on his own.

'All of a sudden,' said Number One, 'I heard either two or three gunshots and saw the colour of Dominik's pale-yellow shirt change to red.'

Mercuri had panicked and shot Hefti. Cox and Moran didn't even know the raid had started until they heard the bark of Mercuri's handgun.

Number One took out his revolver but he didn't have the space to shoot safely. Hefti fell to the floor and lost his grip on the cash tin. Mercuri grabbed the tin and ran back into the supermarket.

Number One fired three shots after him.

There was chaos in the passageway by the time Cox and Moran entered, so they headed instead to the carpark. Number One turned to Hefti. 'I saw that there was blood all over the place,' he said, 'including a trail of blood leading from the warehouse into the actual supermarket via a small passageway with plastic flap doors.

'Dominik was bleeding heavily from his chest and his mouth.' A doctor was trying to help him. 'I was very scared for my life and very scared for Dominik,' said Number One.

Mercuri pelted through the supermarket, still clutching his handgun and trailing blood, then fled into the carpark and realised he didn't know where the getaway car was parked. So he rushed up to a white Nissan Pulsar hatchback driven by Jenny G, who had just stopped at the shopping centre on her way back from work to pick up something for tea. She later told police, 'He had a gun which he was knocking against the window. He had something in his other hand which looked like it was either a white or grey sack or material bag which he had wrapped around by hand to hold on to.'

Jenny G was startled and bewildered.

'The man became quite frantic,' she said, 'wanting me to open the door. I pushed my door button down and locked my door then he became really frantic and started waving the gun at the door button. I thought, *Oh my God*, and pulled the button back up and jumped out of my car. It must have still been running, because it kept rolling and bunny hopping.

'This bloke jumped in and started the car, turned it around and went back out the same driveway I had come in,' she said. 'I watched him for a while as he was turning around and I thought, *My God, what am I doing? He might shoot me or something*. So I ran and hid behind some cars for protection and then I saw he was gone and ran to the State Bank for some help.'

She struggled to remember the thief's appearance. 'He was fairly unkempt and grubby looking,' she said. 'I was just so scared. I thought I was going to die.'

Mercuri did a U-turn and sped off in Jenny G's car. Cox and Moran couldn't see Mercuri in the carpark so they headed back to the house in Bowen Road, East Doncaster that Cox and Deane had rented together.

Dominik Hefti did not recover consciousness. If he lived, doctors said he would be brain-damaged and paralysed. But he died from his wounds two days later, leaving a widow and a three-year-old son with only the memory of his touch. Hefti's widow said if his attacker was caught she would 'cut him to pieces'.

Jenny G's Nissan Pulsar was recovered around the back of Evans Street, Brunswick. Mercuri had left behind a light-coloured wig and the stains made by his blood, but he had taken Jenny G's car keys and her RACV membership tag. Mercuri arrived at Bowen Road before Cox and Moran. His little finger was badly lacerated—'half-hanging off'—and Deane bandaged it up. Later, Cox helped her treat Mercuri, picking embedded teeth of metal out of the skin where a bullet from Number One had travelled through the cash tin and into Mercuri's hand.

The take from the robbery—the price of Dominik Hefti's life—was $33,000. The crew had expected at least $100,000. Mercuri divided the money into thirds. Cox didn't want to take his cut because he thought Mercuri would need the lot to help him disappear, but Mercuri said they were all in it together and insisted Cox accept a share.

On July 12, Armaguard announced a reward of $100,000 for information about the shooting of Dominik Hefti.

20

The Hardness of Michael Yabsley

Michael Robert Yabsley was born in Lismore, the son of Robert 'Bob' Yabsley, a prominent grazier whose pioneering ancestor William Yabsley had been the first permanent settler in nearby Coraki. At the age when Ray Denning's mother burned herself to death in front of her son, Michael Yabsley was a private schoolboy taught by the Marists. At the age when Denning was sentenced to two years for vagrancy—the crime of having no money—Yabsley was a prefect at St John's College, Woodlawn. In between school and the Australian National University (ANU), Yabsley took a year out to visit South Africa on a Rotary exchange.

This was the same apartheid South Africa that Peter Livesey and Meredith Burgmann had been arrested for campaigning against during their student days—although Yabsley insisted it wasn't. In 1977, he wrote in the ANU's student newspaper that the machinery of apartheid had been dismantled, that the current South African government's policy was 'separate development (Note, not apartheid)' and, anyway, 'the blood stained aspirations of African despots . . . make even the most iniquitous aspects of apartheid a preferable alternative'.

In March 1984, after a lengthy, creative and vigorous election campaign, Yabsley won the New South Wales seat of Bligh for the Liberal Party. At only 27 years old, Yabsley was the youngest member of the NSW Legislative Assembly. In 1986, he said, 'I have never supported South Africa's apartheid regime'—a statement consistent with his belief that apartheid had been dismantled in the mid-1970s.

From the beginning, Yabsley was firmly of the opinion that prisoners should serve their full sentences. He was particularly incensed by the case of Frank Meola, who was awarded early release from Long Bay in August 1986 by fiat of the acting minister for corrective services. Meola, an unemployed man from Yabsley's hometown of Lismore, had been caught altering one word of a piece of graffiti near the Sydney offices of the charity Community Aid Abroad. The original vandalism read 'Community Aid Abroad, a front for terrorism in South Africa'—a catchcry of Jim Saleam's white-supremacist National Action party. Meola—described in the press as an 'anti-apartheid activist'—had replaced the word 'terrorism' with 'freedom'. He was arrested and sentenced to one month's imprisonment, and his appeal was rejected by Judge Roger Court, a former official in adman John Singleton's right-wing Workers Party. Meola missed the birth of his first child while incarcerated but, to the chagrin of Yabsley, now shadow minister for corrective services, he was released after serving only a week of his sentence.

'Justice must not only be done, it must be seen to be done,' thundered Yabsley.

Later in the year, Yabsley took to the media the jailhouse furphy that HIV-positive prison rapists were deliberately infecting child molesters with AIDS. 'The government will deny it,' Yabsley predicted, correctly. In September 1986, Yabsley reported to the police that he had been robbed of his wallet at knifepoint. Yabsley was often described in the press as a 'hard man', but he wasn't hard like working-class hard men. He wouldn't take his fists to a knife fight, so he gave up his wallet and let his attacker leave. So if he wasn't a hard man like, say, Mark Carroll—who was reputed to have thrown a man off a balcony for pulling a knife on him—then what kind of a hard man was he?

Yabsley lost Bligh in the state election of March 1988, but the Coalition won government. Yabsley took a job as a lobbyist for the colourful stockbroker Rene Rivkin (later a convicted criminal). On a trip to London, where he stayed at a luxury Piccadilly flat owned by Rivkin, he met and befriended the author Jeffrey Archer (later a convicted criminal). Upon Yabsley's return to Sydney, the sitting Liberal member for Vaucluse died suddenly—aged just 44—and Yabsley inherited both his seat and his portfolio as Premier Nick Greiner's minister for corrective services.

Under the previous Wran government, courts in NSW imposed a head sentence, which was the maximum time a convicted person would spend in custody, along with a non-parole period, which was supposed to be the minimum time served. But compliant prisoners could earn remission from their non-parole period—the celebrated 'time off for good behaviour'. A man serving an eight-year sentence with four years' non-parole ('eight on the top with four on the bottom', in the argot) could be out in three years if he kept his head down. This arrangement had been cynically abused by the desperate and corrupt Wran minister Rex Jackson (later a convicted criminal), who sold remissions to drug dealers to pay off his own gambling debts.

Under Yabsley, the Coalition was set to abolish remissions and ensure no one was released before the end of their non-parole period. This would do away with time off for good behaviour, thereby removing an important incentive for prisoners to behave well. Under Yabsley, men with long sentences would have to spend more time in jail and, the minister claimed, more would be done to stop inmates from escaping. So one of the inmates with the longest sentence decided to escape.

—

Redfern-raised Ray Carrion was a fit, young armed robber and a handy touch footballer. Like his younger brother Roy, Ray's life was punctuated by a sad trail of dynamic, self-defeating criminal offences followed by extended terms in jail. But his mates loved him. 'He was the quietest, most humble bloke,' said armed robber Mark Merriman. 'He was a good-looking guy, and he was very broad, always muscular, always fit. He had your back. He never made a statement.'

Carrion was a friend of Ray Denning in Goulburn Gaol, where the two men were classified as 'C1' medium-security prisoners. Denning had been transferred to Goulburn on 19 April 1988. He had been C1 for only a few months when Carrion supposedly complained he was ready to escape. Carrion had organised a car to meet him at the back of

X Wing the next day—on 15 July 1988. He had been planning his escape for about two weeks, and—according to the story Denning later told—Denning chose to go with him because of a comment made by Yabsley that lifers would have to do a minimum of 20 years.

'The other reason which also caused me to escape,' said Denning, 'was a comment by a senior prison officer to all prisoners at a muster that if there was a further escape (there had been one from W Wing the week before) all C1 prisoners would be returned to maximum security. As Carrion was going to escape, I would be returned to maximum security.'

The fact that Carrion planned to escape forced Denning to join him on 'the spur of the moment'. However, two weeks before the spur of the moment, Denning had asked a woman named Anne Denton to visit Brett Collins and see if she could get some money and a couple of driving licences from him.

Margaret Anne Denton was a young single mother of three who lived in Ashfield, New South Wales. Anne had her first baby at seventeen, and her husband seems to have left her around the birth of their third child. She started writing to Ray in prison, after she had read his *Diary*. Some of her letters ran to fifteen pages.

In January 1988, she had begun to visit him in jail. Anne told her family Ray was a sweet, kind man who'd never committed a violent crime. She said seeing Ray put some romance and excitement in her life. Because there wasn't much of that, you know, in Ashfield, and it's not what you expect, when you give a bloke a family, to have to watch him walk away with another woman. To have to hear him say he'd be happier with someone else.

—

Just after midday on Friday, 15 July 1988, Denning—'a bit fucking paranoid of what the new system was going to be'—and Carrion used a makeshift ladder to climb the three-metre-high barbed-wire-topped back fence near a toilet behind X Wing, dropped to the ground on the other side and made their way down a hill to a waiting Ford Escort. It was an unspectacular escape. Almost any fit, determined prisoner could have pulled it off. The skilled part had been for a lifelong professional criminal like Denning—a screw-basher and serial escaper—to convince the authorities to lower his security classification to C1 to get himself to Goulburn in the first place.

Dog Squad and Tactical Response Group cops combed the area around Goulburn without much hope, looking for a maroon Holden sedan—rather than a brown Ford Escort—last seen heading south on the Hume Highway. They set up six roadblocks to catch a misidentified vehicle that had already shot through, driven by a man with heavily tattooed hands.

Denning and Carrion had been picked up by Roy Carrion and a woman, who drove them two hours' east to Wollongong, where Roy booked the escapees into a motel at the ocean end of Crown Street. It was Denning's idea. He believed he was hiding, but Wollongong's most famous outlaw had returned to the place he grew up and taken a room on the main drag.

The boys had swapped their prison greens for clothes passed onto them by Carrion's family and they waited in the motel room until early that evening, when Denton came by with photocopies of false driving licences in the name of Ashcroft and Hartley. She'd been told the documents could only be used as identification—if Denning and Carrion were pulled up by the cops, they would find their licence numbers were not in any computer system.

They drove through the darkness to Sydney where they looked up an old-time crook who lived on Hastings Parade, Bondi, between parklands and the beach. The crook gave them a sawn-off .22, a chrome-coloured .22 pistol and ammunition, and about $60 in crisp, new bills which, he told them, had come from a bank robbery that same day. Ray Carrion took the rifle. Roy lent them a car to drive to Potts Point, where Denning dropped in unexpectedly on an old contact from the PAG days. Startled and disturbed to see Denning, she phoned Bernie Matthews.

Matthews was running Glebe House, helping former prisoners make their way back into society, but he was also still at the hub of the Blockhouse Network. He holstered his .357 Magnum, and a mate drove him to pick up Denning, Denton and Carrion.

Denning wanted to go straight to Queensland to find Russell Cox, but Matthews couldn't take him because his wife had the family car. So the Blockhouse Network had to kick in to move Australia's highest-profile prison escapee over state lines to meet Australia's most wanted man, who had broken out of NSW's escape-proof jail and remained hidden for eleven years. They'd be taking the piss, if they could do in a day what the cops hadn't managed in more than a decade. Every man and woman with a badge was going to be left looking like a dithering, blithering gronk.

They couldn't even find Denning and Carrion. 'Every single police officer in the State is on the lookout for them,' said a spokesperson for NSW Police. 'There is no physical search, though, as no one has any idea of where the hell they are.'

Matthews took Denning, Carrion and Denton to Dee Why in Sydney's Northern Beaches, where they met, for the first and only time, Alan John Weir, known as 'The Pom'.

And we'll get back to Weir, but first let's look at what Yabsley did next.

In 1990, the minister for corrective services oversaw the confiscation of several categories of personal property from maximum-security inmates, including crucifixes, jewellery and pet birds. Yabsley's 'reforms' had no positive effects. The prisons burned again and, of course, inmates continued to escape. Later, after the gang rape of a young minimum-security prisoner, Yabsley pronounced prison rape as 'inevitable'. This has often been remembered and repeated, but few commentators recall the all-important context that politicians like to pretend their words are taken out of.

So before we return to July 1988, we'll take a peek through the bars at February 1991, when a non-violent offender, with a two-year sentence for break and enter, was raped by three convicted murderers and a convicted rapist in the minimum-security section of Long Bay.

After the attack, the young man jumped the fence and ran to his mother, who met him at Bondi Junction and took him back to prison, where they told his jailers he had been held down and sodomised. The victim was promptly charged with escaping from lawful custody. 'I just thought that it could not possibly happen,' said his mum. 'It's not fair.'

'In the eyes of the law,' said Yabsley, 'that still constitutes an escape, regardless of the circumstances.'

The rapists were charged and the raped man was put on protection in a cell with a child molester. As an escapee, under Yabsley's policies, he was never entitled to return to minimum security. The minister for corrective services pronounced that rape, while regrettable, was inevitable. The jail could not reasonably be expected to prevent a prisoner being raped, but a prisoner could reasonably expect to serve an additional sentence if he tried to get away from his rapists, even for a day.

Because the rules, son, are the fucking rules.

And that's what they meant when they called Yabsley a hard man. He wasn't hard like a street tough who could fight off a knifeman. He wasn't even hard like a firm-but-fair jailer who could stamp out the scourge of prison rape.

He was hard in his heart.

21

The Sins of the Poms

You want a real gangster called Jack the Hat? An East End charmer in a stiff felt trilby? A rough head from the glamour days, the truly gilded age, when gunnies partied with popstars, slept with models, and ended up in bundles at the bottom of the sea? I give you Jack the Hat McVitie. Now, Jack the Hat was born into the working class, but he made his name—in so far as you can 'make' a name like 'the Hat'—in the criminal class. He had worked for Ronnie and Reggie Kray, the twisted, psychotic princes of the 1960s London underworld, but the Krays distanced themselves from McVitie because he was a pill head who drank too much and couldn't always be trusted to kill their enemies. One night, McVitie turned up, drunk and trouble-thirsty, at the 211 Club in Balham, which was run by the Twins' associate Freddie Foreman, a teak-tough gangster and handy boxer. Foreman and McVitie exchanged words and Jack the Hat left. A little later, McVitie went too far on one night too many. He took a sawn-off shotgun to the Krays' favourite club, the Regency, and word got out that he'd threatened to use it on the Twins.

McVitie was invited to a party at Blonde Carol Skinner's basement flat on 28 October 1967, but Ronnie Kray cleared out all the women before McVitie arrived. As soon as McVitie came through the door, Reggie pointed a pistol at his head and pulled the trigger. The gun jammed. McVitie, it's said, ran to a garden window and tried to climb out but was hauled back in by the Krays and their associates. McVitie lost his hat and Reggie stabbed him to death. While associates scrubbed McVitie's blood out of the carpet, somebody went into the garden to retrieve his hat—vital evidence if it came to an identification.

The body was left with Freddie Foreman for disposal. Foreman, who had also been among the crew who had killed for the Krays the wildly erratic prison escapee Frankie 'the Mad Axeman' Mitchell, wrapped McVitie's body in chicken wire attached to weights and sank him at sea.

A boy named Alan John Weir was a nephew of Freddie Foreman, on Foreman's mother's side—his grandparents were at the wealthier end of a family that straddled some of Britain's post-war social divisions. Weir was a pupil at the prestigious Royal Alexandra and Albert School in Reigate, Surrey, until he was expelled for stealing. He went from public school to an approved school for delinquent and neglected boys—Knotley Hall at Chiddingstone Causeway, Kent. He was released at the age of fifteen and became a handy amateur boxer.

'I grew up with villainy,' Weir told me. 'All my family were villains. I was introduced to villains when I grew up.

Freddie opened a pub, the Prince of Wales, and that was my local pub. I was best friends with his oldest son, Gregory, and it was just life.

'I was a witness in the trial of the Mad Axeman for Freddie,' said Weir. 'I worked opposite the Prince of Wales, at the Electrical Company. It was just before Christmas, and he was bringing in all the booze for our Christmas party, and that was the time he was supposed to have shot Mitchell.' The stocky, fast-talking Weir came to Australia in 1974 and quickly became a part of the criminal milieu. Through a set of circumstances too complicated to relate here—or, perhaps, anywhere—he came to be working around Glebe House with Bernie Matthews and also in a repair garage in Dee Why.

'I was in the garage, doing night work,' Weir told me. 'Bernie walks in, he's gone, "Listen, Pom, can you do me a favour?" So we go over to the flat, and then up the stairs comes Ray Denning, Ray Carrion and Anne Denton. And I had my girl over there. Well, one of my girls. And Bernie brought them up there and he says, "Can you take them to Queensland?" So I said, "Oh yeah, alright," thinking, *Another fine mess you've got me into!*'

And so the son of Jack the Hat met the nephew of the man who made Jack the Hat disappear, and the criminal dynasties of two continents cracked stubbies in Sydney's Northern Beaches. Weir had never seen Denning but knew him by reputation. 'He was one of the most well-respected crims in jail,' said Weir. 'And on that night, he was the most wanted in Australia.

'I got my girl to go to bed with Ray Carrion, the poor sod,' said Weir, 'because she was like, not my proper girlfriend, you know what I mean—and I felt sorry for him and I gave him my Nike shoes.'

The next morning, they all drove north in Weir's yellow Toyota Celica (later remembered by Denning as 'one of those bloody Japanese car hatchback, sort of thing') far away from anywhere the cops would think to look—since Queensland was one of the few states where Denning had never been arrested.

Denning didn't seem worried to see his name on headlines caged in newspaper boards. When Weir pulled into a service station to fill up the Celica, Denning wanted to get out and walk around.

'And then he wanted to drive the car,' said Weir. 'I said, "No, no way in the world."'

Weir drove Denning, Carrion and Denton past the seaside town of Coffs Harbour to Woolgoolga, where an ivory-white Sikh temple rose above the highway like a shabby, suburban Taj Mahal. At Woolgoolga, Denning got out in a caravan park where he met a mate from Grafton tracs, an armed robber and drug dealer who lived in an on-site caravan.

Weir left the crew at the caravan park and drove back to Sydney. Denning later said the former trac gave them a couple of beers and $500 and borrowed his business partner's Ford Fairlane to drive them 360 kilometres to Brisbane. At about 11 p.m. the fugitives checked into the Hamilton Motel, close to the racecourse and near the home of one of Cox's brothers, Karl, who we last met when he went into national service in 1957.

—

Denning hadn't seen or heard from Cox since his last escape, but he knew Karl was the person who'd know how to find him. It is not an offence to be able to contact your own brother, and Karl said he might get back to Denning with Cox's contact number the next day. Danny from the network came up from the Gold Coast with a Mini Minor booked from Avis Car Rental. But it took Karl longer than a day to get Cox's number—or perhaps Cox's permission to pass it on. The crew moved to a motel half an hour up the road in Redcliffe.

To kill time, Denning, Carrion and maybe a couple of others paid a visit to the Commonwealth Bank in Zillmere. They arrived in the Mini Minor at 1.05 p.m. on July 19 and left a few minutes later with $44,474. Denning went in ballied up and carrying the sawn-off shotgun, but was caught on a security camera taking off his balaclava.

Denning had expected Cox would come and meet him but, when he was finally given Cox's number on July 21, it turned out Cox wasn't even in Queensland—he was in Victoria. Denning rang Cox at about 9 a.m.

'He said that he was in a bit of bother,' Denning said later, 'and it would be better if I came to Melbourne; that he would have guns and money for me to pick up.' Cox also promised 'a good earn' and arranged to meet Denning at Doncaster Shoppingtown.

Denning, Denton and Carrion returned the rental car, spent $9000 on a Commodore station wagon for sale by the side of the road, and headed back south, avoiding the coast, skirting Bathurst and going through Orange.

They drove through the night. In Melbourne, at about 11 a.m., Denning called Cox again.

'He arrived within about five minutes of my ringing him and told me he couldn't take me to his place,' Denning said. 'It would be okay if I was by myself but because I had the sheila with me and another bloke that he didn't know, he said, "I can't take you there and I've got somebody at my joint that I'm looking after who's been shot."'

Cox didn't want a full house at Bowen Road while Mercuri was recuperating, so he offered instead to book Denning into a motel just outside Doncaster. He took Denning to look at the motel while Carrion and Denton did some shopping.

—

Twenty-nine-year-old Glen Iris–born Detective Senior Constable Ken Ashworth had joined Victoria Police in 1977 at the age of eighteen. 'I always had a strong sense of doing the right thing and helping people. Being a copper seemed to be a good thing.' By July 1988, he was a police investigator with the Armed Robbery Squad. 'There was something about armed robbery,' he said. 'I had a penchant for it. I was fairly good at it, I knew that. And it was something I took a delight in. Each armed robber is quite unique and they leave their own calling card on particular jobs. So once you've been around a while and you've gone to a few crime scenes, you think, *Hang on, who're we looking at here? This is right up their alley.*'

There was a lot of surveillance involved but even that could be fantastic. 'I remember lying down in cars,' he said, 'and your heart is beating out of your chest as the crooks drive past. *Did they see us?* Because you try and get as close as you possibly can but not blow it.

'It's a great thrill,' he said. 'Sometimes you would see armed robberies go down and them preparing, and then the thrill of catching them in the act was just ... magnificent. It's something it's hard to compare with. I guess it's a bit like the crooks when they rob a bank. They get this great adrenalin run. Well, we have this great adrenalin run arresting them.'

Thirty-two years later, Ashworth could look back at that day in Doncaster as if it had been a movie. 'You've got cars squealing around carparks,' he said, 'you've got shots down the bottom, shots up the top, number-one crooks ... It doesn't get any better than that, when you're a copper investigator.'

It was a time of heightened alert for the Armed Robbery Squad. The Barkly Square fiasco had taken place only two weeks before and, a few days later, Ashworth had received a call from the NSW Armed Hold-Up Squad, offering descriptions of Denning and Carrion in case of an unrelated wave of stick-ups in Victoria.

Ashworth was out Doncaster way, on an unrelated surveillance job, when a call came over the police radio that a Brambles armoured security van had been followed into the Doncaster Shoppingtown complex by a New South Wales–registered station wagon. The police wondered if the guards were being tailed by the Barkly Square gang. While other police sealed off the scene and patrolled the crowded shopping centre for known faces, Ashworth's crew tracked down the Commodore to the upper-level carpark, where it sat silent and empty. An undercover officer opened the back of the car and found, among other incriminating papers, Ray Denning's prison library card. So Ashworth was confident he had the escapees' vehicle—which would effectively rule out any connection with Barkly Square, since the Brunswick bandits had hit Dominik Hefti and his team four days before Denning and Carrion had broken out of Goulburn.

The police drove to the top of the carpark, planning to flank the station wagon as it took off, then stop and intercept it. Ashworth, armed with a pistol-grip Remington 870 shotgun, was supposed to jump out and confront Denning, then cover him with the shotgun while he was arrested.

Denning returned to his car, which he reversed up the parking lane, mirrored by police on either side. But then a Ford Fairmont pulled up alongside the Commodore. 'Which is really odd,' said Ashworth. '*How do you secure a park in a shopping centre on a Friday afternoon?* Anyway, he pulls straight in and they start talking. And we couldn't get a good eyeball of who it is.'

The two men spoke for a while, then Denning went to drive off. He turned left, the cops turned right and blocked him in. Then Ashworth did something extraordinary. 'I jumped onto the bonnet of his car,' he said, 'and covered him with the pistol-grip shotgun, screaming, "Police! Police!"

'My adrenalin's up and running, of course, and I had a perfect view of him. So it was the perfect way to cover him. And if anybody did anything, well, you'd just shoot them straight through the windscreen.'

Meanwhile, the Ford squealed back to Ashworth's right and straight down the carpark. 'And I've got the best seat in the show,' said Ashworth, 'because I'm standing on the bonnet of the car as the other police have come in, extracted Denning, and got him down on the ground, handcuffed.

'And the next thing I hear is *crack-crack-crack-crack*. It's like cracker night down the bottom end of the carpark.'

Police were chasing the Ford on foot and shooting, as the driver, apparently, returned fire with a pistol.

Ashworth could only see the roof of the Ford as it screeched and turned.

'So I jump off the bonnet of the car and then run across back to the police car, past the police car and into the next lane,' he said.

The Ford threw a U-turn and roared straight up the lane towards Ashworth. 'Stupidly, I run right across in front of the car, to the right side of the lane,' said Ashworth. 'Another fella comes to the left side of the lane. Then, in the glinting, you could see the driver holding a handgun. And I still remember quite vividly that glinting. And the bonnet of the car lifted right up. And I thought, *Gee, he's gonna run us down or do something here*. So, with that, I unload two out of the shotgun to the windscreen. My offsider on the other side does the same thing. So we pepper the car.

'We smash the windscreen out, he loses control. He clips a car, spins that around—which fortunately was the last one in the row, which didn't hit anything else—right past us and smashes into the wall of Doncaster Shoppingtown. So I run up to the passenger side, and I can still see him going forward and slump down but still holding this chrome-coloured revolver. And I was raving at him, screaming at him, and there was no reaction—so I let another shot through the passenger's side of the car with the shotgun. It hits the lock mechanism and, on its trajectory down, smashes through the console on the left-hand side of where the driver's sitting.

'It's funny in those situations,' said Ashworth. 'Things are very slow and you can see them. You're aware of the bang, and you can smell the cordite, but some things you can't hear. I've been in other situations where shots have been fired, and one right past my ear—and the only thing I remember about that was a dull thud when it hit the bloke behind me.'

At Doncaster Shoppingtown, the second driver was lucky, said Ashworth, 'because I had a pistol-grip shotgun—because they're great for close-quarter combat but they're not very accurate over a little bit of a distance. If I'd had a normal shotgun—which would be at my shoulder and a lot straighter—he may not be here today.'

The driver had been shot at and shot. His car had been immobilised. His mate had been arrested. His windscreen spiderwebbed and he seemed trapped inside the threads. 'So he then sort of gives up and slumps completely down,' said Ashworth, 'and I'm screaming, "Gun, gun, gun!" And covering.'

The driver didn't want to get out of the car but, in the end, he surrendered. He was a movie-star bandit, caught after a car chase and a gun battle, and there were worse ways to end a career.

'Other Armed Robbery Squad detectives have come up to the right side of the car,' said Ashworth. 'They've dragged him out. We've got him down on the ground. And he's handcuffed and secured. He's wearing a white singlet, and he's got a shoulder holster on underneath.'

They bundled the two men to the offices of the Armed Robbery Squad for interview. 'We satisfy ourselves it was Denning,' said Ashworth. 'Searching the vehicle, we find sawn-off shotguns. There was also some money, and some paperwork from a bank they had robbed on their way down.'

But Ashworth still had no idea of the identity of the other driver—although he looked oddly like a bedraggled John Cleese. 'We're getting word back,' said Ashworth, 'we're trying to say, "Who is this fella we got out of this Ford?" And he had a driver's licence on him in the name of Rossiter, and a birth certificate in the name of Rossiter . . . and he says to the police taking him back to the Armed Robbery Squad that you'll be surprised who you got. And then he gets back there and the boys say, "We'll take your fingerprints. We'll find out who you are." And then he says, "Well, I'm Russell Cox."

'But that's all he said.'

In fact, it was all Cox ever said to police.

Back on Bowen Road, as police helicopters hovered over Shoppingtown, Deane and Mercuri hastily abandoned the house.

—

Cox still wasn't keen to have his picture taken, either.

Ashworth told me, 'The photographer who came out to Doncaster on the day, and who later came back to the offices and photographed all the exhibits: his car was broken into in the early hours of the next morning and all the equipment stolen. So all the official photographs were gone. But when we'd take crooks back, we would take what we'd call a trophy shot: we're standing in an interview room and Russell Cox is in the middle of us. He's got his head bowed down. And why he's got his head bowed down is one of the blokes had a .38 down the back of his trousers.'

Ray Carrion got away, but the cops caught Anne Denton as she tried to leave the shopping centre. Poor Denton—one third of Bonnie and Clyde and Cox. She rang home and asked her son to forgive her for being away for his birthday, and promised she would hold a little party in jail. Her mum, Elizabeth, was going spare. She was just a 62-year-old widow and she didn't have the money to bail out her daughter, who was a nice, quiet girl who'd had no idea that Australia's two most famous armed robbers were planning an armed robbery. But ever since Denton—her mum called her by her given name, Margaret—had borrowed that damn book from the library, it had been Ray this and Ray that and she couldn't get him out of her head. He'd become her world, said Elizabeth.

'It's crazy,' said Elizabeth, 'because Margaret has never done anything like this before.' She'd never once run off with a bankrobber and prison escapee, or gone along to a shopping centre with two blokes bent on committing a payroll heist.

'The man just had some sort of spell over her,' said Elizabeth. 'This past week has been a nightmare.'

Ken Ashworth was pleased not to have killed Cox and have to live with that memory for the rest of his life. 'I've been involved in other operations where we have shot and killed people,' he said. 'And, over the years, it's taken its toll . . .

'But I remember waking up on the Saturday morning after it all, and I could hardly walk. My legs were so sore, and that was from the jumping and the moving bits and pieces. And I could hardly talk, and that was from the screaming, "Police, don't move! Police, don't move!"'

22

Mad Dog Denning

Denning fell hard when the cops dragged him out of the Commodore. He later complained they had smashed his head into the cement. He was pulled up bleeding from the brow, with a scarlet trail running down his left cheek—the same wound that had opened when he'd escaped from Maitland in 1977. Not much had changed in eleven years, except his good looks had been battered further back into his face, and he'd lost a front tooth in a fight with another prisoner ('He used to flick his front falsie off with his tongue to make the tooth disappear,' Brett Collins told me).

Denning was stunned by the thunder of his arrest. 'They're mad down in Melbourne,' he later told his lawyer. 'When you have an argument, they shoot you—at least in Sydney they just break your leg.' Ashworth said when they first apprehended Denning, he was 'a loudmouth banging on about prisoners' rights' but neither he nor Cox would answer any questions.

Denning and Cox were held in Jika Jika, Pentridge's maximum-security wing, a sterile unit reached through a riddle of interlocking corridors, each entrance closing another door to the world outside. They appeared at Melbourne Magistrates' Court on 25 July 1988, two handcuffed bandits with bruises on their faces. Denning instructed his barrister to tell the court that his injuries had been sustained after his arrest. Cox's barrister, the well-known lawyer Frank Galbally, claimed his client had no chance of a fair trial since he had been branded 'Mad Dog' in the media and had his prior convictions broadcast on TV.

'He is not a mad dog,' said Galbally. 'He is a human being.'

It took police a few days to discover Cox's address, said Ashworth, 'because—again, this comes back to the cunningness and sharpness of Russell Cox—he didn't have anything on him to identify where he lived, what he did or whatever'.

Police found the business card for a lawnmowing service, called the proprietor and described Cox and his car: he said it sounded like a client at 52 Bowen Road.

'So a warrant's taken out and round to that address,' said Ashworth, 'and, sure enough, it had been cleaned out in a hurry, but it hadn't been cleaned out well enough. There, we find articles of disguise, make-up, hair colouring, gun magazines, a whole lot of notes relating to Armaguard deliveries, pick-ups and bits and pieces. We also find Cox's fingerprints, Mercuri's fingerprints, Helen Deane's fingerprints et cetera. And also, lying in the main room of that residence was a telephone book and it was open at Jenny G's details.'

The page including Jenny G's phone number and address was torn out and pushed into the toilet. 'And they'd obviously tried to flush that,' said Ashworth, 'but it didn't flush properly.'

—

Bernie Matthews was driving home on the day of the arrests, when he received a page asking him to ring Weir from a call box. On the phone, Weir told him to listen to the radio news—Cox and Denning had been pinched.

The first reports were that two men had been caught about to rob a security van in a shopping centre. 'Well, I knew that was shit,' said Matthews, 'because he went down there to meet Russell. He didn't go down there to do a stick-up. They might have done one a couple of days later, but not in the initial stages.'

Carrion fled to Sydney and went straight to meet Matthews in Bondi. 'He said he and Anne left Ray and Russell,' said Matthews. 'They went into the shopping complex to buy some clothes or whatever. Fucking next minute there's fucking gunshots! Anne's ran back to the carpark saying, "Listen, we've got to help them! We've got to help them!" And Ray's said, "How can we fucking help them? There's twenty fucking jacks there!"' Denton was arrested in the carpark. Carrion went the other way.

Matthews figured the disaster was probably down to Denton. 'I didn't think for one minute that she was a dog,' he said. He guessed Denton might have phoned her mum to ask about her kids, and police had intercepted the call and traced Denning and Cox from there. 'I thought, *It's got to be her*,' said Matthews. '*There's no other fucking weak link*.'

Denton was extradited to Sydney on 28 July 1988 to face charges of harbouring Denning. She sobbed through her court appearance. Ray Carrion was arrested in New South Wales on August 3.

Carrion's best mate, Mark Merriman, was still at Goulburn, killing time in A Yard, when another prisoner publicly read out a card from Denning, claiming Carrion had informed on their escape. Merriman swore he'd fight anyone who put Carrion on the dog and the other man backed down.

Meanwhile, Matthews took a call from Kevin Storey, who was then in Parklea.

'Listen,' said Storey, 'they reckon Russell's put a contract on Ray Carrion.'

'*Fucking what?*'

'Yeah, a couple of the boys want to knock him.'

'Listen,' said Matthews, 'fucking pull it up.'

Matthews drove to Parklea and told Storey what had happened, including his theory that Denton had slipped up. The murder was called off and 'Carrion was sweet', said Matthews. 'But apparently it was fucking Denning who'd sent the message, *Fucking Ray Carrion's left us posted—he's a cunt.*'

'I thought he was covering for his sheila,' said Matthews. 'I knew for a fact that Carrion hadn't done anything.'

But Denning wrote to Matthews from Jika Jika in September, 'Russell and I are only here because some CUNT who we went and got something for let us walk back into a TRAP without even trying to warn us he seen the police ... If anyone is to be judged it is that weak CUNT, to say the least, NOT ANNE.'

—

Helen Deane was Australia's most wanted woman until 20 September 1988, when she was arrested by detectives in Melbourne Magistrates' Court clerks' office, a few hours after Cox and Denning had appeared for a remand hearing. Police searched her handbag and found a 'pen pistol'—which could be lethal and accurate over a very short distance—along with ammunition and money.

Deane came to court the next day, wearing—modelling, maybe—a long, black hooded jacket, black pants and black ankle-length boots. She was Honor Blackman as Pussy Galore in *Goldfinger*, Diana Rigg as Emma Peel in *The Avengers*, and she was showered with serious charges—everything from the murder of Ian Revell Carroll to possession of a pistol to harbouring an escapee. At the end of the hearing, she said, 'Thank you very much. Goodbye.'

Russell Cox wasn't Ned Kelly anymore. Thanks to Helen Eva Deane, he was James fucking Bond.

'Russell really began to open up to me after Helen Deane was arrested,' said Denning later. 'He made one particular comment to me about seeing the identikit photographs in the newspaper regarding the Brunswick murder and armed robbery, and said to me that the first identikit he seen looked a bit like Sam Mercuri and the second identikit he saw looked more like Mark.'

In December 1988, Ray Denning asked Dot Bach to contact Aarne Tees for him. Dot had stayed in Denning's life to become his closest friend outside the jails, and she'd urged him to understand that his only option was to cooperate with the law. After Cox had told him the story of Barkly Square, Denning had something valuable to trade with police—Mercuri.

Mercuri was nobody to detectives, just a list of arrests to colour a chaotic life. Police thought the Barkly Square job was the work of a gang of crooks connected to the Pettingill family and nicknamed 'the Flemington Crew'. On 11 October 1988, officers of the Victorian Armed Robbery Squad investigating Barkly Square shot dead Graeme Jensen of the Flemington Crew. The next day, two police constables were murdered in retaliation, in what came to be known as 'the Walsh Street Police Shootings'. Then Jedd Houghton and Gary Abdallah, both of them thought to be involved in Walsh Street, were shot dead by police in separate incidents. The cops believed the Flemington Crew's Victor Peirce—who was charged but later acquitted over Walsh Street—was Dominik Hefti's killer. Denning knew this wasn't true, and the bloodbath had been sparked by misinformation.

Dot and John Bach met with Aarne Tees on 12 December 1988 and told him a confusing story about the wrong person being charged with the murder of two Victorian police officers. Tees wasn't sure what they were talking about or, indeed, what it had to do with them, but they gave him the name of a Victorian cop who they said knew all about the case. Perplexed, Tees flew down to Melbourne and visited Denning in Pentridge with a detective from the Victorian Armed Robbery Squad. Denning told them Cox was behind the Barkly Square job and somebody other than Peirce had shot Hefti. 'Reference was made to a reward which had been offered by Armaguard for information leading to the arrest and conviction of those responsible for the murder of their employee,' Tees said later. 'Denning indicated that he would be willing to give evidence against Cox in this matter—however, he was concerned for his future and his safety, and once he became known as an informant he would have to change his identity . . . He considered the reward money as being important in assisting him to set up a new life once he was released from prison.'

In other words, Ray Denning, the one-time prisoners' hero, promised to roll over on Russell Cox in return for a new identity and $100,000. Denning's public explanation for his sudden change of heart and mind was Cox's supposed indifference to the fact Victor Peirce had been charged over Hefti. He thought Cox had gloated over the police error, and Denning couldn't live with that. He felt Cox, who was going to be inside for life anyway, should have stuck up his hand for Hefti and let Peirce walk free. After all, by Denning's account, that was what he had done himself: he'd never dobbed in Warwick James for bashing Karl Faber, but he'd taken James's punishment. Denning said later he decided it was 'time to stand up and be counted because they had arrested someone who had not committed the crime, and to stop all the killing'.

Denning was a friend of Peirce's mother, Kath Pettingill—as, apparently, was Dot Bach.

—

On 10 February 1989, Cox and Denning were each sentenced to five years' imprisonment for going equipped to steal and using a firearm to resist arrest at Doncaster Shoppingtown. On the same day, Denning lodged an application to be transferred to a prison in NSW. During the next ten days, he alleged to police that Cox was involved in three murders—Brian Kane, Ian Revell Carroll and Laurie Prendergast—and had been caught in the midst of planning another killing. At first, Victoria Police simply didn't believe Denning. He was told, 'It's almost like Russell Cox came in to give you up. I mean, you could never picture that—and in the second breath you're tipping the bucket right on him.' It was as if Denning were the mad dog.

Denning later explained to police the significance of the scrap of paper the gang had stuffed into the toilet at Bowen Road—the telephone-directory page that included the details of Jenny G: 'It was decided amongst the three of them that they would try and find her home address and knock her,' said Denning, 'because she was the only one that Sam believed had identified him. They still had the car keys to the car, and on them was a key tag with the registration number. Russell had a contact at the Registration Office to find the name and address, and he told me that they also had a hole already dug for a bloke that they were going to knock.

'When I use the word knock,' said Denning, carefully, 'I mean murder the person.'

Reading between the lines of Denning's possibly unreliable story, the person for whom Cox's crew had supposedly prepared the grave was underworld hitman Rodney Collins (a.k.a. Rodney Earle), often held to have been the second masked gunman at the shooting of Brian Kane in 1982.

Denning had much more to say about Russell Cox and Mark Moran: 'Russell told me that he had a secret panel in the house at Doncaster where he kept personal items. He told me that there was a notebook in there of Armaguard stuff ... He said that this is where they put the key tag with the registration number. He also said that he had got the name and address and wrote it on a separate piece of paper and that there was also a book which had details of certain armed robberies that he had done and also [sic] going to do.

'Mark's father had contacts at the registration office and Mark would make the inquiries with his father . . . Mark's father wasn't to know that Mark was working with Russell because Mark's father had been a close associate of the Kanes over the years.'

Denning gave police other information about the Moran family, described the way Cox disposed of a stolen car, said there had been an argument between Cox and Mark over Cox's suggestion they should kidnap a doctor to look after Mercuri's hand, and alleged that Moran, Mercuri and two other men had drugged and 'terrorised' Helen Deane to find out where Cox's money was hidden. He also told police how Cox relayed messages to the fugitive Mercuri.

Why would Denning roll over on Cox, of all people? Billy 'the Kid' Sutton had a theory: 'Russell helped the guy out many years ago,' said Sutton, but Denning had always resented that Cox had escaped from Katingal without him. In addition, 'Between the 1981 capture and the latest escape, there was a great deal of bitterness about Russell—the fact that Russell didn't do anything for him. He thought Cox should look after him.'

There was also a certain professional jealousy, nursed during Denning's many years behind bars. 'There was Russell still out there doing it,' said Sutton, 'and he blew the game himself. A great deal of people were jealous of Russell. They wouldn't have envied his position, but they would certainly have liked the notoriety, or the alleged wealth.' According to Sutton, Denning would have liked to be Public Enemy

Number One, but the title was always given to Cox: 'It did piss him off.'

Within a week, Tees had organised Denning's transfer to Long Bay, where he later gave two long interviews to Ron Woodham, superintendent of the Internal Investigations Unit, and a Detective Sergeant Ian Teasdale. Woodham addressed Denning as 'Raymond'; Denning called him 'Mr Woodham'.

In the course of these interviews, Denning gave up Ray and Roy Carrion. He gave up Brett Collins and Bernie Matthews. He gave up the old crim who'd sold him the guns in Bondi. He gave up the woman from the PAG whose home he had visited unannounced. If he didn't give someone up, it was generally because he could not remember—or had never known—their name. He gave up people for crimes they hadn't committed. He had witnessed more uncorroborated confessions than Roger Rogerson. He claimed Bernie Matthews had admitted to a murder (he had not). But the focus of the interviews was not so much crimes but prisons. Woodham asked Denning if he knew how escaped prisoners might be safe-housed—specifically by the Prisoners' Action Group—and Denning gave up the Blockhouse Network.

'Say, for instance, that somebody escaped today and they went to the halfway house,' said Denning, 'they'd probably know Bernie Matthews or somebody like that, and they'd contact him to somebody else they know and through friends, and friends of friends. It just works that, *Oh listen, I know somebody who lives in South Australia—we'll give them a ring and see if they can put somebody up for a couple of days.* There's no one person that they use all the time. It's a matter of who's around at a certain time, what places are available, who they feel they can trust and who they can't. It's not just

Australia-wide, it is probably worldwide. They know people in different countries.'

When Woodham asked if Denning was aware of any prisoners who had escaped from NSW jails and used the safe-house system, Denning gave up armed robber and fugitive Ian Steele. He alleged that, 'When he escaped, he went and seen Brett Collins and Brett put him up in a couple of places and got him a passport. From what Brett told me, he sent him over to England.'

The network would help 'anyone that they'd think won't say anything' said Denning. 'They work on their past record, whoever they believe is not an informer.'

Woodham wanted to know how prisoners exchanged messages with the PAG—and it turned out that they talked to each other. 'It usually works through visits,' explained Denning. 'For instance, you could tell your visitor to go and see Bernie and say, *Oh listen, I'm fucken, I've had enough of this. I'm going to piss off next week and can you fucken arrange a place for me to go or fucken get me a gun or fucken fix up a car?* Things of that nature. Your visitor then goes and sees Bernie or Brett, or whoever it may be, and you get the message back. It usually takes a few weeks, and it all gives them a bit of time to work out what they're going to do with you.'

Woodham asked Denning if he knew of any prisoners in NSW who were planning to escape, and Denning shopped Ron Chester for something he hadn't done yet, and Steve Sellers for something he couldn't possibly do, since he'd been dead for almost a year: 'Before I left Bathurst,' said Denning, 'Ron Chester told me that if I knew any goes up there to fucken tell him, because he wanted to escape from Bathurst, because apparently the police had come and see him from South Australia and told him that he'd be wanted on extradition over armed robberies over there, and he told me that he was arranging a gun with a bloke by the name of Steve Sellers. Apparently, Steve Sellers come up and visit him in gaol and he was arranging an escape with him and he asked me if I wanted to be involved, which I said no.

'Well, I'm going back probably nine or ten months now,' Denning admitted.

Chester had been looking at going over the pottery shed roof at night, said Denning, and he felt he could pull it off with a makeshift ladder.

Denning gave up gangster John Visser—a close friend of Denning at Parklea—and said 'he's always trying to go'. He threw in a crim from Katingal: 'Jockey Smith was always talking about it too,' he said, 'but nothing ever seemed to eventuate.'

Woodham was less interested in Denning's 1980 escape, but Denning still casually gave up Brett Collins for taking a phone call from him, and Billy Sutton for shooting his first video. Woodham wanted to know if poor Peter Livesey had helped him, but Denning said no—he'd had no assistance from any lawyer. Woodham asked if he had stayed at a farm near Port Macquarie (Livesey's). Denning said no, but later annotated the record of interview to give up Billy Sutton for staying there legally.

When Woodham asked Denning if he'd ever been contacted by the heroin Mr Big asking for information about senior officers in Corrective Services, Denning said the request had come from Mr Big and another prominent Sydney identity, who'd promised prisoners that 'they'd be given money and drugs in exchange for any information that they could come up with and that they'd be well looked after if they could sign a statement—anything especially to do with Ron Woodham.

'Which is you,' added Denning, helpfully.

Occasionally, Denning baulked. He would not give up Carrion's female relative who had been in the car that picked him up outside Goulburn. He told Teasdale, 'I really don't want to fucken get her in to trouble, the female you know it's just a fucken . . . it's a close relation of Ray Carrion. It's never been in any trouble, I think it would be pushing, you know a bit over the fucken the limit I would be prepared to go to actually.'

The other person Denning refused to shop was himself.

When Woodham asked if, while he was an escapee, Denning had driven past Parramatta and 'fired a couple of shots at the tower'. Denning replied, 'Ah, well I was never found guilty of it. I know something about it, I can't say nothing further about that particular incident at this stage. There was a note left in one of the screw's letterboxes to do with it, and that was proven to be in my handwriting.'

Woodham asked Denning if he knew of any corrupt prison officers, and Denning hesitantly named a couple of men in Parramatta whom he had heard might have been working for Neddy Smith. Woodham asked about George Johnson, the Katingal guard who had unwittingly allowed Cox to escape. Denning said he'd never heard of Johnson bringing anything into a jail. Teasdale asked if Denning had been 'involved in drug trafficking or drug use' while he was a prisoner. 'Ah, I wouldn't like to talk about that at this stage,' said Denning.

—

Nobody in the milieu had any idea where Denning had gone. A woman phoned Bernie Matthews and told him Denning was no longer in Victoria. When Matthews couldn't find Denning in NSW either, he assumed he must have been taken to Queensland in connection with the Zillmere robbery—so he rang Boggo Road Gaol and said, 'My name's Jack Denning. I want to visit my son, Raymond John Denning.'

'He's not here.'

'Listen, mate,' said Matthews, 'if I had to front a Brisbane Court, what other jails would I go to?'

'This is the only jail—Boggo Road.'

In the end, it was a prison officer who let the secret out. Matthews was visiting a mate in Long Bay when he saw 'the old screws' union rep', who pulled him up so they could complain to each other that things weren't like the old days anymore. The prison officer told Matthews that Denning was right behind him.

'I looked over my shoulder,' Matthews told me, 'and I looked at the Special Purpose supergrass jail'—the informers' prison.

Matthews went back to Glebe House, rang around and warned everyone, *Fucking something's going on. He's in the supergrass jail. He's talking.*

Matthews thought, *I've helped him here, I've helped him there. He's gonna put me in jail, this cunt. It's got to be me.*

'I went home,' said Matthews, 'and I was like a bear with a sore tooth. My missus—she was a squarehead—asked, "What's wrong with you?" "I've got a funny feeling I'm gonna get pinched." "Why?" I said, "You wouldn't understand." I was dirty on the world. I just saw bad things.'

His wife coaxed the story out of him.

'She's looked at me,' said Matthews, 'and I guess this is the wisdom of women who fucking just don't know anything—and she's said, "Bernie, you're not important enough." And, of course, that hurt my ego. She's said, "Bernie, if they're going to go to all that trouble to roll him over, it's not for you—it's for something big." I'm thinking, *Well, fucking I'm big. I'm involved in all this fucking shit*. But she was right. It wasn't me at all. It was the Hilton Bombing.'

23

Giving the Dog a Bone

In June 1977, Detective Inspector Paul Delianis of the Victorian Armed Robbery Squad described armed robbery as 'a form of terrorism no different to the forms we see occurring on television in other countries'. In February 1978, international terrorism jumped out of the TV and onto George Street, Sydney, when a bomb in a garbage bin exploded outside the banal and brutalist Sydney Hilton Hotel, disrupting a regional meeting of Commonwealth Heads of Government. Three people were murdered by the bomb and—as is the drearily predictable way with terrorism—none of them was a Commonwealth head of government. Two council workers who emptied the bin into their truck were blown apart as the device detonated when compressed. A police officer guarding an entrance died later from his injuries.

It was widely believed that the target of the bomb was the prime minister of India, and his would-be assassins were connected to the Ananda Marga (or 'path of bliss') movement, whose leader, known as Baba (father), was in jail in India. Unusually for a Hindu sect, the Ananda Marga had a public relations secretary in Australia, the determinedly cool-headed and relentlessly articulate Timothy Edward Anderson. On behalf of the movement, Anderson denied responsibility for the attack.

In June 1978, Anderson and two other margis, Paul Alister and Ross Dunn, were loaded up with dynamite by a Special Branch informer and arrested by Roger Rogerson of the Armed Hold-Up Squad. Rogerson bashed Anderson, called him a 'fucking cunt' and charged him with plotting the murder of Australian Nazi leader Robert Cameron. In a masterfully imaginative verbal, Rogerson claimed Anderson 'did not reply in English but shouted out something in a foreign dialect'.

Each of the 'Ananda Marga Three' was jailed for sixteen years. The flimsy case against them was probably accepted by a jury in part because the informer said they'd also confessed to the Hilton bombing. A campaign to free Anderson and his friends focused on the corrupt police practices that had led to their convictions. They were eventually released, pardoned and compensated in May 1985. In their seven-and-a-half years in prison, all the margis had befriended Ray Denning, and Anderson had taught Denning meditation. Denning had supported the margis when they were bashed in the yard, probably on the say-so of Neddy Smith.

Anderson stayed intermittently involved with the flagging prisoners' movement through the PAG and pursued a stubborn crusade to have bravery rewards withdrawn from police who had arrested and verballed him. The PAG was briefly re-energised in early 1989, and Anderson again became associated with public criticism of the police. This may have been a catastrophic error of timing.

On March 1, Denning made a statement to Aarne Tees in Long Bay. He claimed he had first met Anderson at the MRP in 1979. They became 'close friends' and had 'hundreds of conversations', many of them 'through the toilet system'. 'That worked,' he explained, 'by banging on the pipe of the toilet system to attract the attention of the person above you. When you hear the banging back, you empty the water from the bowl' and shout into the toilet. 'During one of these conversations,' said Denning, 'he said words similar to, "We might go under on this charge even though we have been verballed ... But the main thing is that we won't go under on the Hilton." I said, "Are you talking about the Hilton bombing?" He said, "Yes, I and some others did it but one of them had a good alibi, so I won't go under on that." ... He said, "I put the bomb there."'

When asked why Anderson would confess to him, Denning later explained it was because of his own ongoing campaign against police verbals. 'I believe he thought that getting me on side—by saying, "Here's my credentials, I bombed the Hilton, and that makes me somebody in jail."'

In fact, Anderson—who denied the crime in every other arena—simply couldn't stop giving himself up in jail. 'He confessed to me on the actual Hilton bombing on three separate occasions,' said Denning later. 'He seemed to me the sort of man that I would consider, as a crim, a bit naïve. Because he trusted quickly.'

Denning gave a second statement on 22 May 1989, in which he revised the circumstances of one of Anderson's confessions and 'remembered' Anderson's sinister promise: 'The placard era finished during the Vietnam War, and it is time to get fair dinkum. Like we did at the Hilton.' The most notable difference between Denning's two statements was that he had at first claimed Anderson had confessed to him in Long Bay in the 1980s. By his second statement, Denning—who had been told by Tees that Anderson hadn't been in the Bay in the 1980s—was saying, 'I now remember it was at Parklea.'

As it turned out, prison records showed Denning had arrived for the first time at Parklea in June 1984 just after Anderson had left for the last time.

Of course, the statements against Anderson may have been Denning's idea, but not much else ever seems to have been Denning's idea, except for robbing banks and escaping jails. On May 30—and solely on the basis of Denning's statements—Anderson was arrested by Aarne Tees, who didn't bash him or call him a cunt and who promised there would be no verbal this time. The day after Anderson was charged with the Hilton bombing, former margi Evan Pederick came forward and claimed he had planted the bomb on Anderson's instructions. Pederick was the latest in a long, pathetic queue of curiously motivated individuals who sought to associate themselves with the atrocity. The police helped talk most of them out of it. Aarne Tees helped talk Pederick into it—and polish his testimony into a brightly shining turd.

Denning had also provided Tees with a statement about the ANZ Bank hold-up in Zillmere. He gave up Carrion as his co-offender, and he even gave up poor Anne Denton as having bought a rifle for him. Denning's cooperation with the police paid off. When Denning was eventually sentenced for the Goulburn escape, the cops didn't raise the Zillmere robbery (Denton did time for the gun, Denning didn't). The court was led to believe Denning had made a spur-of-the-moment decision to jump the fence and had more or less behaved himself until he met Cox, whereupon he had committed an unspecified firearms offence. The judge added only 30 months to Denning's sentence.

In the travesty that followed the charging of Anderson, a new Campaign Exposing the Frame-up of Tim Anderson (CEFTA) was formed by activists including Brett Collins. Outside the courts, CEFTA both defended Anderson and attacked his accusers with extraordinary rigour.

Pederick was found guilty of the murders at the Hilton and sentenced to twenty years. As Denning gave evidence at Anderson's committal hearing, a former prisoner—some say it was Billy Sutton—dipped into a white plastic shopping bag and pulled out a fresh bone.

'You forgot your lunch, Denning!' he shouted.

The man left the bone on the rail of the court and ran out of the building.

Collins went along to watch Denning testify, and he made a point of standing so Denning had to look at him on his way into court. At first, Denning kept his head down and wouldn't look at Collins. Later, Denning would stare Collins directly in the eye and walk through. Collins felt Denning was taking responsibility for what he was doing, that he'd found some pride.

The holes in the story that Denning and Tees had fashioned for the Goulburn-escape sentencing had to be papered over for the Anderson trial. In November, Tees wrote to the Criminal Investigation Branch, Brisbane, explaining, 'During the committal proceedings against Anderson, Denning gave evidence over 3 days. He was cross examined concerning his spending and his lifestyle whilst he was an escapee between 2 April 1980 and 8 November 1981. He lived off the proceeds of armed robbery offences, some of which he was convicted of and some he had not been charged with. In reply to a large number of questions he refused to answer on the grounds he would incriminate himself.'

Denning's evasions made him seem shifty, untrustworthy, and left open the possibility that he'd earned his money selling drugs. To quash these misconceptions, he had to admit to the 1981 Brisbane Railway Centre hold-up. In capital letters, Tees wrote: 'IF HE IS GRANTED AN IMMUNITY CONCERNING THE RAILWAY ROBBERY HE WILL BE ABLE TO SAY THAT HE OBTAINED HIS FUNDS FROM THE ROBBERY.' Tees returned to the lower-case to add, 'The same situation applies to the Zillmere bank robbery.'

And, of course, there were the old scores still to settle. 'There are numerous inquiries still in train in this State,' wrote Tees, 'the main one will relate to the Prisoners' Action Group who have been forging identification documents and have assisted escaped prisoners to leave the country . . . It is of vital importance to us that Denning be granted an immunity in Queensland in respect to offences he committed up there. His continued cooperation both in this State and Victoria is essential if we are to succeed in convicting persons such as Anderson, Mercuri and others who have been responsible for some of the worst crimes committed here and in Victoria.'

Denning's indemnity from prosecution for offences in Queensland was later granted by the Queensland Attorney-General, another benefit for Denning from his decision to switch sides. But as Anderson's case progressed, Tees became the target of a slanderous CEFTA street-poster campaign and several investigative stories in CEFTA's newsletter, *Framed.* A poster was printed with a picture of a twisted two-cent piece and the slogan 'Aarne Tees is a bent copper too': Tees put it up in his office.

At Anderson's trial, the defence argued Tees had first negotiated a deal with Denning in the early 1980s, to give a positive character reference to the judge at his sentencing hearing (and drop the 'interstate blues'). Many of Anderson's supporters believed Denning's side of the bargain was to promise good behaviour in jail and pay $20,000 to the police. The money, they thought, came from the sale of the vehicles—including two cars and a boat—that Tees had allowed Dot Bach to retain. Tees admitted he had gone to Goulburn to have Denning sign over the property, and at first said he thought the proceeds from the sale had gone into consolidated revenue. Later, he said, he'd checked it out and he didn't sign any boat into consolidated revenue. So your guess was as good as his, really.

Despite the contradictions in Evan Pederick's ever-changing evidence, Anderson was convicted. This time, he was sentenced to fourteen years in jail. On 28 October 1990, the law firm Blessington Judd lodged an application on Denning's behalf for a $250,000 reward for information leading to the conviction of the Hilton bombers, and Tees made what he later agreed was a 'very, very strong recommendation' to the Reward Evaluation Committee that

Denning should receive the full amount: 'At the time the reward was offered ($250,000),' wrote Tees, 'it was a very large amount of money, today inflation has eaten into it and the whole amount would only purchase a home in most Sydney suburbs . . . Denning is in need of reward money in order to re-establish himself in society. He has no credit rating and life would be difficult for him without the reward money to assist him . . . He would not be in this position if he had not offered assistance and given evidence for the prosecution at the Anderson committal and trial.'

However, Anderson served only seven months before his release following an appeal in June 1991. Chief Justice Gleeson offered the leading judgment on the appeal case. 'A jury, acting reasonably, would give Denning's evidence little or no weight,' said Gleeson. Anderson accepted some police didn't like him, but said he was 'still shocked to the extent which they go to pursue their grubby little vendettas.

'There's a lot of malice in the minds of police who have been promoted since 1978 and who are now in a position where they are able to make strategic decisions in relation to major prosecutions,' said Anderson.

On the morning of Anderson's acquittal, Aarne Tees received crime reporter Lindsay Simpson in his office. 'It's just another day,' said Tees. 'I am not jumping up and down about it.' With the oblique hardman half-humour characteristic of the NSW Armed Hold-Up Squad, he said, 'As far as I'm concerned, the Hilton bombing still remains solved. Pederick is convicted.'

Pederick later appealed against his own conviction, on the grounds that he could not have been telling the truth if Anderson was not guilty. Stranger legal strategies have succeeded, but only for Russell Cox. Pederick served eight years before he was released on parole.

As well as his statements against Anderson and the various people who had helped him throughout his life in jail and on the run, Denning said he was 'supplied a list of prisoners' names that were in jails and asked if I could mark next to those names anything I knew about them—whether they were drug users or potential escapees or whatever: there was hundreds of names'. While sceptics, cynics—and the entire criminal world—believed Denning had rolled over to get out of prison and claim rewards, Denning stuck to his own explanation.

'I've never been one for sitting on the fence,' he said later. 'I've always taken a stand on what I believe in. And I was 100 per cent against authority and the system at one stage. And then I jerried that justice works for everybody, not just for the one side. And I was prepared to stand up and be counted and inform on other prisoners who I believed had done the wrong thing—and to give the victims a chance for once.'

The Anderson acquittal proved that Denning had finally turned into the creature he had once reviled: a verballer. But Denning had even come to terms with unsigned statements and fabricated interviews. 'The crims had a pretty good run in the past,' he said. 'Sure, we've had the verbal to contend with, but in 99 per cent of those cases the crim was guilty anyway.

'I've put my life in danger,' said Denning. 'I know that. The Prisoners' Action Group and all that gang, they once used to say "Free Ray Denning", now they say "Kill Ray Denning". I'm prepared to live with being called a dog. It doesn't worry me one iota.'

With the rage of the righteous, even Jack the Hat broke off contact with his son.

On an ABC Radio show about Denning's change of heart, a man who was introduced to listeners as 'Eddie', but who was plainly Billy Sutton, credited heroin with Denning's transformation. Sutton called Denning 'a junkie waiting to happen': 'He's got an addictive personality,' he said. 'He can be addicted to a substance or an involvement or anything else, as long as it doesn't go out of his control. However, once he'd found heroin, heroin does control very quickly and very powerfully. His main sense of being was directed to heroin. Occasionally, there'd be this moon-talk about escape or this, that or the other, a little bit of surface radicalism, but basically it was chasing the arm.

'I've used a lot of restricted substances with Denning over many, many years,' said Sutton. 'He had a constant supply.'

Sutton believed Denning's politics had always been a sham. 'Ray had no political conscience,' he said. 'He would not have been able to articulate or even comprehend any political ideologies. If something sounded decent to him, or concerned him, or was relevant to anything he was after or involved in, then that would be embraced. If it wasn't, well, that would be superfluous background noise . . . The major aim all the way through was just getting a break in the traffic and escaping.'

Sutton thought the latest Denning was no more real than the last Denning. 'If his loyalties lie with the other side,' said Sutton 'I'm sure he'd have no problem giving the $100,000 [sic] reward to the victims of the bombing: the two garbagemen's families and whoever else was involved. I don't think he'd have any problem with doing that, since his loyalties are now with society and its structures. As a matter of fact, I think that perhaps he may wake up tomorrow morning and say, "Gee, I think I owe the ANZ four or five hundred thousand dollars. I think I owe the Commonwealth Bank about a quarter of a million dollars. I think I'll give them all a proportional split."'

—

The Greiner government's truth-in-sentencing laws were passed with the crowd-pleasing conceit that an offender sentenced to life might die in jail. This created a problem with the case of every NSW prisoner who had previously been given 'life' by a judge—since His or Her Honour could reasonably have expected them to be out in eight years with good behaviour. So a transition period was announced, in which all current lifers were to be brought back before their original judges to review their cases and re-sentence them from scratch.

Towards the end of 1989, Dot Bach, a regular, persistent and enthusiastic litigator, had approached her lawyer Denis Mockler at Blessington Judd, to represent Denning for his re-sentencing. 'I'm not a criminal lawyer,' the dapper, amiable Mockler told me. 'I did mainly insurance litigation for insurers. Don't ask me why I stayed involved. I suppose, with hindsight I wouldn't have done so. I had no idea it was going to develop into this ongoing shemozzle.'

Many criminal-law firms might have been reluctant to act for Denning, as others in the milieu would probably be unhappy about discussing their cases with a counsel who was also acting for a supergrass. Mockler felt there would be no prejudice to any of his clients—although it turned out that insurers weren't especially thrilled to share their representation with an armed robber.

Since the judge in the original Faber case had retired, Mockler had to go to the Supreme Court for the redetermination of the sentence. He asked Arts/Law student and family friend Daniel Hanna to research cases similar to Denning's, when offenders had been given life for crimes other than homicide. It turned out there were hardly any.

The young and personable Hanna went to see Denning at the Special Purpose Prison (SPP). 'I'd never seen inside a prison,' he told me, 'never seen anyone convicted of a serious offence. I didn't know what to ask him because (a) I wasn't a lawyer; (b) I wasn't a criminal lawyer; (c) I hadn't even read the legislation that we were supposed to be meeting the requirements of. So I absolutely knew nothing about what I was doing there.

'He struck me as a gentle person,' said Hanna, 'which I wasn't expecting. He had scars more than tattoos, like he'd been beaten a lot. His eyes were bright, they were sparkling, he had a sense of humour and he didn't seem dumb at all: he just seemed focused on getting out of jail legitimately.

'I questioned him on his change from being crim to informant,' said Hanna, 'and he kept on using this term, "I was the meat in the sandwich." He'd shunned the idea of being the PAG hero. At the end of the day, he realised, *I'm the only one copping the beatings. And I'm the only one copping the false accusations and staying in jail. So these people really don't have my interests at heart. I was just their vehicle.*

'He'd traded all his old friends for a very limited circle of new friends,' said Hanna, 'which was the police he was informing to, who seemed to be friendly with him. Aarne Tees did like him. Denis Mockler was his friend. Dot Bach was his friend. So I guess I became one of this circle of friends,' said Hanna.

Over time, Denning spoke to Hanna about his family. 'He'd rob a bank,' Hanna told me, 'and word would go around the underworld that Denning had some money, and then Dad would show up, cry poor, and Denning would give him money.' Hanna said Denning had a bunch of hangers-on who did the same thing. 'He robbed from the rich, but he gave to anyone.'

Hanna thought Denning's crimes had helped a rudderless man-child navigate the turbulent waters of his life. 'He wanted to be loved,' said Hanna. 'He wanted to be needed. He wanted to be relevant in someone's life. And the only real way he could do that was fall in with criminals who'd welcome him—because no one else would welcome him—and do things that they wanted him to do. And he'd get his pat on the back and he'd get his affection from them. I think all his criminal life came from that mentality of *I never belonged, I want to belong. I never had a home—can I live in yours for a while? Yes, if you give me this money.*

'He was trying, I suspect, to use the proceeds of bank robbery to buy what he never had. He never had a family. Never had a place to go . . .'

Blessington Judd later recruited former NSW attorney-general John Dowd as Denning's barrister. Denning would not admit to the Faber bashing—so they couldn't argue he felt remorseful about it—but, in his incarnation as a pro-authority figure, Denning accepted that the process of his conviction had been fair. It was difficult to know what he could possibly have meant by this.

Blessington Judd commissioned a report from a psychologist, who found Denning 'friendly, cooperative, good-humoured and open' and wrote that he had 'good insight into his past behaviour and expressed regret over it'. He had stirred up trouble after the Faber conviction 'partly because he felt that he had "nowhere to go"'. The psychologist wrote it seemed that Denning's anti-social behaviour 'began to decrease in 1981-2', which was true only in so far as he stopped robbing banks once he was back in jail. She administered tests that showed him to be a 'dominant, rather outgoing and sensitive person who is self sufficient and resourceful' with 'a mild tendency towards craving excitement'. If he were to be released, he told her, he would like to go into farming, small business or building. He was studying agriculture by correspondence, and his academic results were very good (although it later became apparent that his marks had been boosted after he'd written to his tutor to explain that he was hampered in his study because he'd suffered brain damage in a car accident).

There were further reports from other experts, different opinions and a lot of help from Aarne Tees. It seems that Denning said he had never had a lasting relationship with any woman except Dot Bach. Dot had been responsible for much of his change in attitude over the years, and she planned to leave John and buy a farm—perhaps growing avocados or macadamia nuts in northern New South Wales—to help set Denning up on the outside.

Denning accepted his fate. 'I suppose one way you could look at it, the first half of my life I've been running from the police,' he said later. 'The second half I'll be running from the crims.'

He wasn't to know there'd be no second half.

24

Death of a Marked Man

Roy 'the Red Rat' Pollitt was one of the staunchest mates Denning ever had. In his *Diary*, Denning wrote that Pollitt was no help 'in anything to do with thinking' but 'the best when it comes to being solid in his support for me'. 'I have known him for about the last 20 years,' Denning told police in May 1990. 'We were close friends. I have even escaped from jail with him.' Denning said he had been in the yard with Pollitt in 1988 when Pollitt had told him that one of Kath Pettingill's sons, the late Dennis Allen, had asked him to murder the drug dealer Alan Williams (who had been involved in the shooting of Michael Drury). Pollitt had taken the job, but shot dead a squarehead named Lindsay Simpson instead.

'He said to me, "Oh, you wouldn't believe it," said Denning, "'I got the wrong bloke.'"

Pollitt had already been arrested for the crime, so Denning wasn't giving police anything they didn't already have—but Denning tried to cut off his mate's best line of defence when he said Pollitt had been writing to Pettingill 'to get her to say that her son Dennis had confessed to her on his deathbed'.

Denning's life sentence was redetermined in April 1991, weeks before the Court of Appeal quashed Tim Anderson's conviction. He appeared in court in a blue suit and tie, his long hair tied back in a ponytail. He had pledged to make videos to deter young offenders from falling into a life of crime—and, fantastically, 'a video for the recruitment of prison officers also'. He said he had been told that, upon his release, he would probably have to be relocated overseas. Aarne Tees insisted Denning had not been promised a life in another country but that he had reached a point of no return. 'He cannot go back associating with any of the people he was involved with,' said Tees. 'He will be looking over his shoulder in his new lifestyle and he has got the added problem that should he ever return to jail he would virtually have to be placed in isolation—that is the only way they would keep him alive in the mainstream.'

The judge was impressed. 'It is exceedingly important to be able to demonstrate to other prisoners that a man once considered intractable and beyond redemption is capable of mending,' he said, and ordered that Denning be released in November.

He was all set for a new life. 'As Raymond Denning, he will cease to exist,' promised Tees. 'Even I won't know what the identity is.'

He was half right. Raymond Denning soon ceased to exist.

—

In October, Tees' old mate Roger Rogerson made his famous declaration that NSW Police bricked and verballed suspects all the time. Tees said Rogerson was 'obviously around the twist'. And, of course, he was right. Rogerson was raving mad. He'd been batshit crazy since at least 1981, when he'd been lecturing bank tellers about their duty to help foil bandits at the same time as he'd been skimming the takings from bank robberies, and describing heroin as society's greatest scourge while stuffing drug money into his own back pocket. Roger Rogerson was mad with the idea of himself. He thought he could do anything, because he always had. He always tipped a bucket of shit and walked away whistling.

But you couldn't think the worst of Rogerson because anyone could see he was a knockabout bloke who loved to have a laugh. Like the time he said Steve Sellers had murdered Sallie-Anne Huckstepp over her 'lesbian affair' with Wendy Bacon, when every man and a good few dogs knew exactly who'd had Huckstepp murdered. Like the time he'd called up John Dowd, then Leader of the Opposition in NSW, and told him, 'I am accepted as a decent and honourable person by people I have been with such as banking people.' Like the time he lied to Mike Willesee that the incorruptible Michael Drury was corrupt. Fuck the hold-ups, Rogerson should've had a career in stand-up—as, in fact, he did in later life.

By the time Rogerson tipped the bucket on his former colleagues, the police verbal was falling out of fashion. It had become easier and cleaner for detectives to use prisoners to verbal suspects, since a confession to a cellmate didn't require a signed record of interview or a video tape of the whole fucking charade just to waste everybody's valuable time. The rapid growth of the practice came to the attention of the NSW Independent Commission Against Corruption (ICAC), which provided a stage for an Investigation into the Use of Informers, presided over by ICAC Commissioner Ian Temby, QC.

The inquiry's attentions were specifically directed at prison informers and particularly in relation to nine separate 'matters'. It was the November 1991 hearings into the matter of the Sydney Hilton Hotel bombing that brought together some of the surviving cast of the Golden Age of Armed Robbery, including major players such as Ray Denning and Aarne Tees, and supporting characters Dot and John Bach. Cox did not attend in body, but he was there in spirit, referred to in evidence as 'Williams', because he was still facing charges. The ICAC wasn't concerned with the credibility of individual prison informers. Its brief was to examine the actions of public officials—in this case, in NSW Police and Corrective Services—and the way the informers had been used.

Incredibly, activists in the prisoners' movement—at least one of whom was philosophically opposed to the entire concept of incarceration—took legal steps to ensure Denning stayed a sentenced prisoner throughout the hearings and beyond. He remained at the SPP—where he was prisoner P44, 'Massey'—under the oversight of Dave 'Emu' Farrell. 'I wouldn't trust him one little bit,' Farrell told me. 'If he said the sun was shining, I'd take a fucking look. He was a manipulator, a nasty bit of gear.'

Denning was almost friendless, but he still had charm. He began to hear again from Rosalyn—now Robyn—Lawson, his girlfriend from the Kings Cross days who had been charged with harbouring him after his escape in 1980.

Sue Jefferies, a nurse who had first met Denning at the Bay in the late 1970s, looked after him at the SPP. 'He was a bit more withdrawn,' she told me, 'harder in his countenance—when he was a kid, he had a bit of joie de vivre—but he was still friendly, still quite a personable man. Jail's full of arseholes and he definitely wasn't one.'

But he was a heroin addict. 'Ray was on methadone and I was coordinating methadone,' she said. 'We were allowed to put them on because there was a high possibility that they'd relapse on release or that they'd picked up some sort of habit inside.'

Farrell said Aarne Tees came to the jail and tried to give Denning a carton of Benson & Hedges, but Farrell wouldn't let the cigarettes in or allow the inmate any special treatment. 'Old Aarne went off,' said Farrell. 'He was a big guy, and I don't think anyone ever knocked him back. A few months later, he comes up again and he says, "Oh, Ray, he's a good informer. I've got an old video recorder I want to give him. He knows all the criminal networks all around Australia, and if he had a video recorder he could record the news in Western Australia and all around the place and let me know who he thinks could be involved." I said, "No, that's not happening. I don't do that for other prisoners, I'm not doing it for him."' Farrell thought Denning was lazy and only wanted the machine so he could record late-night movies to watch during the day.

At the ICAC inquiry, Commissioner Temby asked why Tees had acted so favourably to Denning after his capture, and Tees burned a barrel of credibility by insisting Denning had only wanted to do the right thing. Temby later described this as 'an absurd proposition'. He wrote, 'Prisoners give information, and on occasions become witnesses, for a range of reasons. However a sense of good citizenship does not loom large.'

Temby questioned a police statement of the facts about Denning's most recent escape—the evidence police had presented at Denning's sentencing hearing: 'The prisoner travelled to Wollongong, from there to Sydney and then to Queensland where they remained for a few days. From there they travelled to Melbourne arriving there on 22 July 1988. He was recaptured only a few hours after his arrival.'

This was true as far as it went, but neglected to mention that Denning had held up a bank when he arrived in Queensland, as evidenced by Tees in his application to have Denning granted immunity for the Zillmere robbery.

Temby suggested to Tees, 'It should be relevant for a sentencing judge dealing with a man for escape to know . . . whether following his escape he spent all his time looking after his sick mother or whether on the other hand he was roaming around holding up banks.'

Tees said there was no evidence that Denning had been holding up banks.

'But he had admitted holding up banks, hadn't he?' asked Temby.

'When?' asked Tees.

'To you,' said Temby.

'No,' said Tees, brilliantly.

This argument, once again, seemed founded in epistemology as much as the law. Although a layman might believe Denning had accepted responsibility for the Zillmere hold-up, he had not signed a sworn statement and therefore the idea that he had done it could not be used as evidence against him and he had not 'admitted' it.

Temby was also interested in the fact that, way back in 1983, Tees had told the sentencing judge at Denning's earlier escape case: 'He has had little time at liberty during the past decade. In this time, it cannot be said he is an associate of the criminal element.'

But Denning had spent almost all of his adult life in prison, except for the period when he escaped and robbed banks with other criminals, including Cox. This raised the interesting possibility that Australia's once most-wanted criminal, Russell 'Mad Dog' Cox—who, as we've established, was neither a Russell nor mad nor a dog nor a Cox—was not even a criminal.

Temby asked Tees if he considered Cox belonged to the criminal element.

'Well, I consider him a criminal,' Tees conceded.

Uncharacteristically, Tees went further, and even accepted that Cox was the kind of criminal who 'belonged to the criminal element'.

'How can you say that [Denning] was not associated with a criminal element in those circumstances?' asked Temby.

Tees replied with a jumble of words that meant that, although he'd held suspicions about what Denning had been up to, he couldn't be certain.

Temby felt Tees might have hinted at selfish motivations for Denning's change of heart when he had written to the CIB: 'It is of vital importance to us that Denning be granted immunity in Queensland in respect to the offences he committed up there. His continued cooperation both in this State and in Victoria is essential . . .'

In a highlight of his often counter-intuitive testimony, Tees argued that the important feature of these two sentences had been the 'full stop'. He had never meant to imply Denning should be given immunity in exchange for his cooperation.

'So you're saying that ... those two sentences that I'm seeking to link in fact contain unrelated thoughts?' asked Temby.

Tees agreed this was, in fact, the case.

He had been understood at last.

Tees also reprised an idea he had aired at Denning's 1983 sentencing hearing that Denning's armed robberies were not very dangerous. Denton had obtained a rifle but no magazine for the Zillmere job. Tees speculated—'and this is only a presumption,' he stressed—that Denning had only wanted a gun that *looked as though* it could shoot people.

'Your thinking being that if he was waving around a weapon that didn't have a magazine he might be doing that in a threatening manner toward a gun expert who would think, *Aha, there's no magazine there, I'm safe*?' asked Temby.

'*And he could fire one shot, and if he misses me, we'll rush him*,' Tees expanded.

'It's pretty close to ludicrous, isn't it?' asked Temby.

'Well, it can be,' said Tees, a man of the world, 'but people do some awful silly things when they've got guns pointed at them.'

In his final report, Temby wrote: 'One has to ask whether Tees performed his duties in a somewhat sloppy manner, or is he a very clever man who set out to create a position in which Denning could be helped and he (Tees) could not be blamed. This is tantamount to asking whether Tees is a fool or a rogue. Anybody having dealings with Tees would hesitate long and hard before calling him a fool.'

As an interested party, Tim Anderson was permitted to put questions to both Tees and Denning. Tees told Anderson it had been a major blow to 'your people' when Denning had pleaded guilty in 1983.

'What do you mean by "my people"?' asked Anderson.

'Well, the anti-verbal campaign,' said Tees. 'Prisoners' Action Group; you were writing that literature in those days.'

'Is that how you saw it?' asked Anderson. 'You saw it as a political statement, did you, his plea of guilty?'

'In part, it was,' said Tees. 'Yes.'

The Anderson case had always been about politics, but not the politics imagined by the public. The police didn't know who had bombed the Hilton, not really. It was probably one margi or another. But everybody knew exactly which fucking shouting-something-in-a-foreign-dialect former-margi banged on and on about police verbals, would never accept that he had it coming and would never cop it sweet.

—

A sideshow at the ICAC was the appearance of Dot and John Bach. It seemed Tees didn't know about the Bachs' trip to Hong Kong; at the ICAC hearings, he appeared genuinely surprised to learn of it. And Temby noted, 'Tees struck me as a man who is surprised neither easily nor frequently.'

Until the ICAC, Denning didn't know that Dot had signed a statement against him two years earlier, telling police Denning had suggested the heroin deal, assured her it was safe, that it was an ongoing arrangement and nobody had been caught yet—and, if they were arrested, they'd get the best representation money could buy. While the Bachs maintained they had thought they were being dispatched to Hong Kong to bring back money or gold, Temby noted that John had tested his smuggling singlet by filling the pouches with icing sugar. 'This is of course, very similar to processed heroin,' Temby pointed out, 'and quite unlike either gold or money in any form.'

Temby wondered why Ron Woodham, who knew some of the details of the Hong Kong debacle, had not prevented Dot from visiting Denning in jail. 'It must have crossed your mind, at least,' said Temby to Woodham on the stand, 'that Dot Bach was not simply a good-hearted woman who had befriended Denning, with a view to his rehabilitation, but was also somebody who had . . . been involved in a serious criminal conspiracy with him.'

Woodham accepted that it had indeed crossed his mind.

'Which casts doubt upon her credentials as a rehabilitator, surely?' pressed Temby.

Woodham said Dot had been involved with several prisoners in the past and he didn't know anything about that, and he didn't know what the police knew about Dot and Denning—epistemology again—but imagined the police would be able to find out about it without asking him. Woodham agreed that it would have been desirable for the judges to have been 'appraised of the fact that the Bach family were not pillars of rectitude' (as Temby put it to him) but argued that it wasn't his role to let them know.

'I can't see where I could be held accountable for not doing that,' said Woodham, having weighed up the evidence in his own mind and decided it was only reasonable to exonerate himself.

It also came out at the ICAC that Dot, now a familiar figure in ex-prisoner circles, had been paid small sums by police to inform on Bernie Matthews and the PAG, and been registered as an informer for her own safety—although it was not entirely clear (as always) in what way being a registered informer might keep Dot safe. In fact, the ICAC probably heard more revelations about the Bachs than about any sentenced prisoner. It turned out Denning had initially planned to share his reward money with Dot, and that John now made his living as a pathology courier for NSW Police.

The state delayed Denning's court-scheduled release, but his lawyers took out a writ and Denning moved into his safe house, with 24-hour police protection, on 21 April 1993. His new name, said Hanna, was Bill Johnson.

But much of Denning's evidence had been discredited and it was no longer clear what he had done to justify a claim on the taxpayers of NSW. A faintly ridiculous report was produced for the NSW Police Commissioner arguing that Denning might well reoffend and thereby jeopardise the witness-security program. This idea was visually expressed in a risible bar chart, which showed one very tall column illustrating the risk posed by Denning to 'witsec', next to a tiny stub representing the dangers faced by Denning himself. Two weeks after he was released from jail, Denning was removed from witness protection.

It was a massive, catastrophic betrayal.

'We were told money had been put in a bank account in the name of Bill Johnson,' said Hanna, 'but they cut it off just before Ray was going to get his ID as Bill Johnson.

So he couldn't get at the money. And then the accommodation went.'

Denning had received none of the goodies he had been promised—no reward for the Hefti matter, no reward for the Anderson verbal, no new identity, no witness protection. Yes, he was out of jail, but he would have had to have his sentence redetermined anyway—and it might have been easier for him to secure his release if he hadn't jumped the fence with Carrion.

'The times we met him afterwards, it was sort of like the sightings of Christ following the resurrection,' said Hanna. 'It was only to limited people and it was in very confined conditions. The police who'd worked with him as an informer were trying to look out for him a little bit, but they couldn't just stand guard on him. One day he was in our office and we had a police person at reception, making sure everything was okay.

'John Dowd was absolutely pissed off at the then Liberal government for cutting the witness protection,' said Hanna. 'We all thought it was abominable—cutting him off, *see if he lives*, sort of thing. Dowd rang up and said, "Come and have lunch with me." I said, "John, I'm busy." He said, "No, no, no. See you at my chambers." So I go back to his chambers and there's Ray Denning sitting on the lounge. He said, "Let's go to lunch."

'So, for the first time ever really, I saw Ray just walking the streets of Sydney with no guard, no witness protection, no anything. Just John Dowd and myself. We march up to Parliament House, and I'm asking, *What're we doing here*? And he says, "Well, I've still got rights at the parliamentary dining room for lunch, so I thought we'd eat there."

And then it dawned on me that basically Dowd was rubbing Denning in Parliament's face, saying, "You don't give him witness protection, we'll come in where you are and show you what it's like to be exposed to the risk of danger." So we took the middle table—it was a table that would probably have sat eight, but it was just us three. The food was standard fish and chips but it was super cheap. So we ate like kings, and Ray was having a good time, nodding at people as they passed and waving . . . And I think Dowd said, "I'm gonna bring him here for lunch every day."'

'Denning had a good sense of humour,' said Denis Mockler. 'He came to a birthday party for me in the office, and he was laughing, saying when he got out of jail he went to buy a stocking to put over his head and he discovered that, in the meantime, they'd gone from single stockings to pantyhose. So he said he felt like a goose when he put the stocking over his head and he had a spare leg as well. Which shows how long he'd been in jail.

'He laughed about Mad Dog Cox,' said Mockler. 'He said in Queensland it was like getting lollies from a lolly shop, it was so easy to rob them. But he said it was funny getting a fortune and they had to go back to some room and they had a twelve-inch black-and-white television set, when they could've afforded to buy a large colour television set, but Cox was pretty tight.'

Denning moved in with Robyn Lawson, who had been arrested twelve-and-a-half years before for allegedly harbouring him in Chippendale. They lived together in a shabby, lime-green terrace in Little Comber Street, two blocks from Oxford Street in genteel, gentrified Paddington, but Denning felt more comfortable 45 kilometres to the west, at the Mount Pritchard & District Community Club ('Mounties'), a temple to the clinical, efficient banditry of the poker machine. Denning drank at the club two or three times a week, with Lawson and a couple of mates. They were never any trouble, never rude or out of control. He turned up for one of the fight nights at Mounties, where club-level boxers fought mismatched battles for dubious titles, and men bayed like drunken donkeys at the strip-club-seasoned ring-card girls.

Denning told his most thorough interviewer, Janet Fife-Yeomans of *The Australian*, that he had a job lined up unloading trucks at Flemington Markets. He was getting to know his son, Ben, and had bought him a pet rabbit and taken him to the football. 'I don't know much about relationships,' he said to Fife-Yeomans, 'because I have been in and out of jail all my life. All I know is what I've read in magazines and seen on TV. I haven't got all my feelings where I can wrap my arms around him and say, "I love you, kid."'

But he thought the love would come. Denning was philosophical about the past and optimistic about the future. He had planned to be on witsec, living on reward money under a new identity. Instead he had been abandoned by the authorities, washed up and hung out to die. 'It's like the whole of my life, there's always been a twist,' he said. 'You try to do the right thing but nothing seems to run smooth. But it will, eventually.'

On 10 June 1993, Denning and Lawson went out looking at caravans for sale, then dropped in at Mounties at about 11 a.m. Denning drank steadily through the day and ate lunch at the club bistro, and he and his mates won $110 on the Keno. Lawson seemed happier than the blokes. Late in the afternoon, Denning called the office of the NSW Ombudsman from the foyer of the club. He wanted to make a complaint about being taken off the witness protection program. He said he was frightened for his life.

He and Lawson returned to Paddington, where they had dinner at the Dunbar Hotel on Renny Street. They went home but, late in the evening, Denning left the house again and did not come back until 2 a.m. He climbed into bed with Lawson and wrapped his arms around her. She asked if he was okay and he told her he was. He had stomach pains, his fingertips turned blue, and then he died.

Lawson later told Fife-Yeomans, 'This last month we had together was the best of my life, I will cherish it always. I have always loved him.'

Denning's death was a lead item on the TV news. 'Dowd rang and was almost silent on the phone,' said Hanna. 'I said, "Look, I'll come up." There he was, sitting in his chambers, on one of the ornate couches, just crying. And I sat down and cried with him. We'd become very fond of the poor bloke.'

Brett Collins cried too, when he heard the news. Donna—now married with children—screamed.

'I was very upset,' said Hanna. 'As was Denis. But for me, it was technically my first client. Really, you can almost track my entire history in the profession—which is mostly in insurance law—from this one criminal case. And I go to school reunions and people say, *Ah, the famous bankrobber!*

You acted for the famous bankrobber! Have you acted for any more robbers recently?'

One schoolfriend, Richard Ruppas, was particularly disturbed that Hanna had represented Denning. 'It's been a bone of contention between him and me,' said Hanna.

At eighteen years old, Ruppas had been living in Gosford and working as a junior bank clerk at the National Australia Bank in Hornsby. 'I loved it,' he told me. 'It was my first full-time job.' On 4 August 1987, the day after the bank holiday weekend, 'everyone was pretty happy', he said. All the business customers who did their banking on the long weekend had deposited their takings in locked wallets in the bank's night safe. 'Not everybody was in as yet,' said Ruppas, 'because it was still quite early.' The main safe had been opened, but nineteen-year-old Jason Avery was emptying the night safe. Suddenly, 'I heard this tremendous crash,' said Ruppas. 'I turned around and a car was coming in! I saw all this glass and everything coming in and I was stunned for a moment. I'm going, *What's going on here?* Nothing made sense.'

All Ruppas could think was that it must be an accident, so he moved to go and help the driver.

'The next thing you know, the car door flies open and this guy gets out with a gun and tells me to get on the ground or he'll fucking kill me. He's got a balaclava on. He has a pistol taped to his hand. I didn't know what to do. I hit the carpet like everybody else. I crawled forward and tripped the alarm button under the counter, and then I've gone, *Ah shit—was that the right thing to do or the wrong thing to do?*

'This guy was yelling, absolutely going off his nut, swearing and carrying on. It seemed to go very, very quiet. I could hear him walking around on the broken glass, and then I could hear Jason—and he was drowning in his own blood. Because when Jason was servicing the Flexi Teller, he had the door open—he was behind the door and he had his head down inside the machine. As the car came through, that steel door slammed into his head.

'He was on the ground and the idiot was yelling at him to get up and give him the money. And I thought I was going to die. I thought I was a goner. Because he said he was going to shoot everybody. I was panicking, just going, *Oh shit! Oh shit! Look what's happened.*

'All I could hear was Jason trying to breathe, and people started to look around a bit. We were having the branch painted at the time, and the painter came around and said, "They've gone. You can get up." Nobody moved for probably a couple of minutes, then we got up. The first thing I did was run around to Jason and he was in a very bad way. So we rolled him over onto recovery position so he could breathe—because blood was coming out everywhere—and we called an ambulance. The next thing we know, police come barrelling in with their guns drawn, going, "Where is he?" And we're, like, *He's gone! He's gone.*

'"Which way did they go?"

'We've got no idea.'

The bandit took all the night wallets. Ruppas only saw one gunman but, as he waved his weapon, he threatened, *My mate's outside and he's going to come in and kill you all.*

The raider wore a black balaclava, but police guessed who it might be. The headline in the next day's *Daily Mirror* was '"Mad Dog" Cox Link to Raid'. 'It was a very professional job,' said Detective Sergeant Dennis O'Toole of the Armed Hold-Up Squad. 'He was in the bank for about 60 seconds.'

At a training course the next year, Ruppas was shown pictures of a bank robbery—flickering images captured by a CCTV camera, an animation of still photographs taken once every two seconds. 'They made a big deal of it on the course,' said Ruppas, 'saying, *Things can go wrong, and this is the sort of thing you can be exposed to.* And I've gone, *That was me!* I think in one of the pictures, you could actually see me.'

The training staff told Ruppas the robbers were Cox and Denning—although Denning was in jail at the time of the raid and Cox has not since been accused of the crime.

Ruppas returned to work within a day of the hold-up. 'There was a big patch of red carpet with blood everywhere,' he said. 'It was very sombre and very sad. Everyone was worried if Jase was going to be okay because they didn't think he was going to survive. Thank God, he did. He got deafened in one ear permanently and cracked his skull. One eye was turned, as a result of it. The good thing about it was I saw him many years later, and I said, "Do you remember that day?" And he said, "No, not at all. I can't remember anything."

'For a little while,' said Ruppas, 'I was very jumpy about a lot of things. In that time, bank robberies were very, very common. Before we got hit, pretty much every branch down the North Shore had got hit. The National Bank across the street got robbed, the Commonwealth down the road got robbed, the ANZ literally across the street got robbed. Like any job, it's always the case that something could go wrong. But in our case, things went wrong all the time.

'When Dan came on television—that was not long afterwards—I've gone, *I went to school with Dan! What the hell?* I crossed paths with Dan again about three years later.

And the funny thing was, Dan was going, *Ah, he was an alright bloke*. And I said, "I don't think so. I'll have to sit down and talk to you about what happened to me that day I met him . . ."'

—

After Denning's death, Hanna's first comments to the media were that Denning had 'always had one eye over his shoulder' and that he believed Denning had been murdered.

He told a journalist that Denning was a 'magnet for a bullet'. 'I then got dragged down to Paddington Police Station,' Hanna told me. 'They said, "You've got to come in and make a statement." And at the end of the day, a fairly senior cop who I don't know, after giving me a real scare, said "This 'magnet for a bullet stuff . . .'" He wanted me to stop saying that. And I did what he said—I did stop saying that. He charged me with nothing, he threatened me with nothing, he didn't say I was there for any particular offence. At the end of the conversation he said, "Well, you won't be doing that again in a hurry, will you?"

'Someone in the cops was trying to shut us up and get rid of any allegation of foul play,' said Hanna. 'And it's easy enough to conclude why. They'd cut the guy off witness protection, then he dies. They don't want to be held responsible for that. They'd rather think it was self-inflicted or Denning having too much of a party once he was out and then getting himself killed. *What a shame, but what an idiot and we couldn't have prevented it anyway*.'

Denning had promised to make videos aimed at steering kids away from a life of crime. Tim Anderson told television reporters, 'These are the videos that have been made. These are the examples to young people. He died alone and friendless with a needle in his arm.'

Except, it turned out, Denning hadn't died with a needle in his arm. At the inquest, said Hanna, 'We saw photos of things we just didn't want to see, like they'd dismembered him and put his brain in a jar. They were looking for physical evidence of drugs and anything else. But the only place they found a needle mark was in his back.'

An informant given the unimaginative court name 'Mr Smith' furnished evidence in exchange for immunity. He admitted selling Denning heroin on the night of 11 June 1993. But police refused to allow Mr Smith to be cross-examined. Denis Mockler told me, 'I'd got a call the morning he died from an informant called "Smith" who wanted to know where Aarne Tees was. I'd been told the previous day that Aarne would be down in Albury. To my knowledge, he didn't travel a great deal, but unfortunately he was out of Sydney that day. So we were very keen to call Mr Smith to give some evidence. Without this evidence from Smith, we really couldn't raise a lot of the allegations that we wanted to maybe raise about what may have happened.'

In the Coroner's Court, Denning was verballed for the last time. In an event beyond irony, the statement came from an informer, an ex-prisoner (brilliantly described in *The Daily Telegraph* as a 'former Long Bay jail colleague') whose name was suppressed and who said he had seen Denning in early 1993 shoot up 'about nine or 10 times, easy' with heroin smuggled into Long Bay in balloons by another prisoner's grandmother. Denning and the informer would swallow the balloons and later vomit them up and inject the drugs with a syringe they kept hidden in the garden.

Denning supposedly told the informer that he wanted to taste the 'pure stuff' and, in perfect sympathy with the event, the man recalled him saying, 'When I get out, I'm going to have a shot I'll remember for the rest of my life.'

Magnificent.

Nurse Jefferies told me Denning had stayed on the methadone program. 'He was on it when he got released,' she said. 'He was fine on that. He was quite happy on that.'

Outside the Coroner's Court, Jack the Hat stood with Linda Jobson and poor little Ben. They still wanted to know where Denning had been when he'd left Robyn Lawson in Little Comber Street. Lawson had said it was not unusual for Denning to go out at odd hours to use a nearby payphone. But who did he call?

Denning had gone out with $100 in his pocket and come back with five cents.

Every prisoner in jail thought Denning had been given a hotshot, but the coroner found he had died of acute narcotism from a self-administered heroin overdose. The needle marks on his back were held to come from the needles used by the ambulance paramedics as they struggled to revive him.

Denning's funeral was held at Pinegrove Crematorium in Minchinbury, near Mount Druitt, NSW. Robyn Lawson was there and so was Dot Bach. Denis Mockler turned up to farewell his client. Janet Fife-Yeomans covered the service for *The Australian*. Frank Sinatra's 'My Way' played Ray out as the curtains closed behind his coffin, when Jack the Hat halted the service. 'It turned out, unbeknown to me, that there is provision to stop a funeral for a limited time,' said

Mockler. Jack the Hat wanted to ask the Coroner's office to check again for evidence of poisoning. 'But the toxicology had been done,' said Mockler. 'I think we stopped him being cremated for about five hours.'

Linda Jobson spoke at the funeral. She said she was heartbroken to have to tell Ben, now nearly eleven years old, that his father had died just as they were getting to know each other. Charmaine remembered her brother: 'It was like he carried a tinkling of magic dust with him and, when he sprinkled it on you, he brought life and happiness to your life.'

Publicly at least, Jack the Hat drew only one lesson from his son's death: 'I would advise anyone else considering becoming a police informer to remember the three wise monkeys—don't look, don't see and, above all, don't speak.'

Jack the Hat later contacted Denning's lawyers. 'The only time I ever heard from him, I think he sent me a letter,' said Mockler. 'He asked for details of what money Ray had and could he get some of it, basically.' But Denning had left little behind. 'He certainly had no money,' said Mockler. 'He didn't pay his lawyer, I can assure you.'

25

The Aftermath

Russell Cox and Ray Denning were once Public Enemies Numbers One and Two, Australia's most wanted fugitives. Each had his moment—in different but overlapping circles—as the most admired criminal in Australia. While books were written and movies made about lesser men with smaller reputations, the lives of Cox and Denning remained largely unexamined.

Denning was difficult, in death as in life, because it was hard to see where he fitted in. He was no great gangster, but he worked with the best of them. He was no symbol of rebellion—he would've had to die young and unsullied for that. He could hardly be claimed by the authorities, when his evidence against Anderson was discredited and he died of a drug overdose within weeks of his release. Some people who helped Denning in his campaigns felt betrayed (in part because they were, in fact, betrayed) and that perhaps they had wasted their time. Denning's *Diary* was re-edited in 1994 and repackaged as *Ray Denning: My life and time* by Donald Catchlove. The new edition, published by Pan Macmillan, bookended the diary extracts with two blocks of short, biographical chapters written by a well-liked but low-key screenwriter in the hollowed-out style of someone more used to providing only dialogue and stage directions.

There are narrative problems with Denning's story, too. How do you portray events that are disputed? Whose 'facts' do you believe? The question that Catchlove felt still needed to be answered was: did Denning kill Willy Karl Faber? In the two years I've spent writing this book, I've changed my mind repeatedly. Yesterday, I thought Denning didn't do it. Today, I think he did. For all Denning's faults, he didn't seem like a killer to me—on paper, on tape, in the memories of his one-time friends. But Billy Sutton and Bernie Matthews held that he was guilty, and they had both met more killers in one day than I'll know in my life (hopefully). Denning's lawyers, Daniel Hanna and Denis Mockler, genuinely believed their client was innocent. But whatever he did, Denning was obviously verballed and, as Brett Collins told me, being verballed made a criminal feel as if he was the real victim.

In 2011, long after Denning's death, the Denning story was made into an episode of a curious TV show called *Tough Nuts: Australia's hardest criminals*, which included dramatisations of key scenes, in which Denning was played by character actor Wayne Bradley—whose peculiar grooming left Denning perhaps the only criminal in history to have been better looking in life than his on-screen counterpart. Among the commentators featured on *Tough Nuts* were Chopper Read, who had never met Denning and who made some barely coherent noises about hating prison reformers, dogs and everyone else—but, uncharacteristically, stopped short of claiming to have killed Denning himself. Quite what Chopper made of Denning being described as one of 'Australia's Hardest Criminals' was not clear.

But even people who did know Denning continue to hold fanciful theories about him. Denning seems to have made some kind of deal with Tees in 1982, and another with Woodham in 1986. But most—if not all—of Denning's old friends and comrades think he struck a further bargain in 1988 to get out of Goulburn, in what Bernie Matthews called a 'Clayton's escape' to lead police to Cox. Roger Rogerson offered this story to journalist and author James Phelps, and it has enormous currency in the milieu. However, it's clear from the files of the Serious Offenders' Review Board (SORB) that many people over many years were responsible for the lowering of Denning's security classification—it wasn't accomplished by fiat of Ron Woodham. The Board's visiting committee saw Denning at Parklea in May 1986, when he had completed by correspondence a large part of a motor mechanics course and they were sufficiently impressed by his 'sweeping and lawn tending work' to recommend he be moved to Bathurst and reclassified as B. By November 1987, according to the SORB, 'He was a full time student, who also did general administrative duties in the office. The education officer reported that he was having a good influence on other prisoners. If someone with Denning's reputation as a "heavy" could do education then it was acceptable for others with lesser pretensions to do the same.' It was the SORB that decided to 'test his response to a different environment' and recommend his transfer to Goulburn.

It's not as if Denning was the only beneficiary of the SORB's largesse. Ray Carrion had a similar—and more recent—record of attempting to escape and seriously assaulting a prison officer and he had his classification reduced, too. And no one has ever suggested the law had a soft spot for Carrion. But if a deal was brokered for Denning, whatever amorphous authorities that were supposed to have been involved did not keep their side of the bargain. By 1988, Denning could've reasonably expected to serve another five years. When he was recaptured after his escape, he did another five years. There was no net gain for Denning. He might've gotten off lightly on the escape, but if he hadn't escaped there wouldn't have been anything for him to get off lightly from—and he would never have gone to Jika Jika.

Denning might have appeared blasé about being spotted when he drove up to Woolgoolga with Weir in 1988, but then he knew he was going to get caught—he always got caught. There was never any thinking behind his escapes, anything you could call a plan. And, when he arrived in Brisbane, it turned out he had travelled 1100 kilometres in the wrong direction. Denning didn't even know where Cox was.

It seems extraordinarily unlucky for Cox to have been arrested at Doncaster Shoppingtown while he wasn't even about to commit an armed robbery. At best, he was engaged in his usual careful surveillance—he just happened to have Denning with him. But that doesn't mean Denning alerted the cops. The police who arrested Cox and Denning in Doncaster Shoppingtown were certainly not aware they were supposed to be following a script. Ken Ashworth didn't jump on a car bonnet in a firefight believing he was among friends.

But then, why did Denning accuse Carrion of betrayal—if not to draw attention from himself? To protect Anne Denton? Whom he later implicated in crimes committed that same week?

Aarne Tees may have pulled every string in his puppeteer's kit to obtain better treatment for his ventriloquist's dummy, but Denning's solicitors at Blessington Judd had to fight hard to get Denning out of jail by 1993. Nothing was made easy for them and unexpected obstacles were put in their way by everybody from the state to Tim Anderson.

Denning's story is riddled with puzzles and anomalies and secrets taken to the grave. But of all the phantom conspiracies that haunt the case, only the intrigues against Anderson seem to have much grounding in reality. Although I have met Anderson once, he did not answer any of my phone calls or emails about this book, nor even reply to my requests for access to his papers at the State Library of New South Wales. I was not involved in any of his campaigns and, before I began this book, I guess I thought it unlikely that anybody could have been arrested, tried and convicted of two major crimes on the basis of fabricated evidence.

I now think that certain police at certain times would stop at nothing to convict a suspect—and if they couldn't get him for something he had done, they would settle for something he hadn't. Cops, crims and lawyers all knew that most crooks were only arrested for a small fraction of the offences they committed. If you looked at it that way, *everyone* had it coming.

And if the suspect was a smartie—if he tried to show off by keeping his mouth shut or gabbing off about a slap around the shoulders with a wet phone book—then he had to be shown that cleverness didn't pay. Smarties threatened everything. And Tim Anderson was the ultimate smartie. In the eyes of some police, he'd got away with the Hilton bombing then spent his time in jail banging on about load-ups and verbals and brutality and, even after he was released, he wouldn't fucking shut up.

Anderson acted as if everything that squareheads were told about the law was literally true. He tried to have police bravery medals rescinded just because those particular cops hadn't done anything brave. They couldn't let him get away with that. He'd get what was coming to him. But if the motive behind Anderson's prosecution was partly political, it was also viciously lazy police work. Sure, many police might have hated the left—but the right were given similar treatment. There is no longer any real doubt that the anti-communist 'Croatian Six', convicted in 1981 of conspiracy to commit terrorist attacks in Australia, were framed and verballed by corrupt NSW Police including Roger Rogerson. Once you start verballing one suspect, you end up verballing them all.

As to Denning's death, almost everyone I spoke to thought he had been murdered by other crims. 'I'm convinced they killed him,' said Daniel Hanna. 'He dobbed on so much of the underworld that it could've been any of them who did it. There were suggestions that the police did it, which I don't think are true. Because the police who had contact with him in those latter years all liked him. They'd actually become, not friends, but friendly with him, because he was this matter-of-fact likeable guy, really.'

The family apparently consulted a forensic expert who said there may not have been enough heroin in his body to kill him in the way he was said to have died. For what it's worth, I doubt that he was murdered—but that doesn't mean I'm certain he wasn't, or couldn't have been, or wouldn't have been if he had stayed alive for longer. Maybe Denning saw his murder coming and helped it along himself. Because Denning wanted to be whatever other people wanted him to be. Throughout his life, Hanna felt, 'He was gravitating to, and being influenced by, people who offered him love. And he was just easily led, on those very basic things that he never had—affection and whatever else. That seems to then gel in with the number of women he was apparently with, who took him in, or the people who thought he was a hero ... he was a guy who wanted to be loved and did some shitty things, some terrible things, in order to achieve that.'

That was the other difficult feature of the Denning story—the Woman Question. It's easy to hear a sneer when you read in *The Sydney Morning Herald* wrap-up of Denning's life that Denning was once the 'rebel pin-up of middle-class academics, journalists and lovesick girls'. Silly girls. A bloke's hero wouldn't let men down like that. And as for middle-class academics, what did they know? Only what they read in *The Sydney Morning Herald*. And journalists? Well, it was a journalist who wrote the story, but not the kind of journo who falls for crims. Not a lovesick girl. Not a clever woman. Not a successful social reformer. How we hate middle-class women, like the middle-class women who adopted the prisoners' cause. For 'middle class', read 'educated'—women who'd been to university. Why would anybody listen to them?

After all, nobody had ever paid any attention to their mums.

For Bernie Matthews, the tragedy of Denning was the destruction of the tracs' mutual-aid network. 'It's all over,' said Matthews. 'There's no network anymore. There's no solidarity. There's no trust. The old principles have gone.'

That was a win for Ron Woodham, Aarne Tees and the forces of order, if not law—and not too many squareheads would mourn the demise of a criminal conspiracy.

I wrote this book in the belief that Denning's life deserved more than an epitaph from Chopper Read. Because he was a villain, then a hero, then a traitor. For a while, he was a symbol of prison reform. And not many blokes born in the shadows of the smokestacks of Port Kembla become symbols of anything, eh? And if the maggots don't get bashed until they shit themselves at the reception biff at Grafton anymore, it's partly down to Denning.

The little fella led a big life.

The charges against Cox fell over one by one. On 24 May 1989, during Cox's and Deane's committal hearing for the murder of Ian Revell Carroll, a detective told Melbourne Magistrates' Court that Cox had admitted shooting Carroll in self-defence. Cox's statement had been tape recorded and transcribed. When asked why he had fallen out with Carroll, Cox apparently said, 'He was a friend of mine and some time during that day he proved to me he wasn't.' The detective described Cox as 'a deep thinker with a mind of his own and a very serious person'. The next day, the magistrate dismissed the case: she said there was no evidence of how or why the fight between Cox and Carroll had started so she could not conclude which one of them might have acted in self-defence.

Cox served three years and three months in Victoria for the Doncaster melee before he was extradited to Queensland in October 1991.

At Melbourne Magistrates' Court once more, Cox stood in the dock with his long hair tied back into a ponytail, and waved and blew a kiss to Deane, who sat watching the proceedings. Back in Brisbane, Cox first faced charges on the hold-up of police officers George Sharry and Kim Roylance. He awaited trial at the Sir David Longland (SDL) Correctional Centre in Wacol, where he was locked up in a maximum-security unit with Mark Carroll and Queensland armed robber Bart Vosmaer. 'Russell and Bart were real good friends,' said Carroll. 'He turned him into a vegetarian. When we'd get out to the oval, they'd just run for hours and hours and hours on end.'

Jail life was bearable at SDL, so long as the prisoners got on. 'There was only twelve blokes to a unit,' said Carroll, 'and it was pretty much locked down, but the standard of living was quite high—as far as prison can go. You'd get fresh food brought in every day, and every unit had a cook. And I was the cook.' Cox loved curry. 'Everything he ate had curry in it,' said Carroll.

'He was a guy who to be in jail with was a pleasure,' said Carroll. 'Very few people I've met are like that. I think at that stage, he was sick of it. He just wanted to do his time and be left alone.'

But there were younger, wilder men at SDL, prowling around the jail, looking for a war. 'Seven blokes, total fucking nitwits,' said Carroll. 'They were called the Angry Gang. Oh God, they were fucking angry too. But they were kids. They couldn't keep them in the boys' homes—they were too hectic—so they took them to SDL, had them locked in one of the units and that was it for them. There was no getting out.

'Russell was living in that unit with us,' said Carroll, 'and there were certain blokes that wanted to be in the unit, he didn't want to have much to do with them. And, you know, that's a hard thing to say: *We don't want you living here because you're too much trouble*. But if you've spent as much time in prison as him, why would you want people around you who want to cause trouble? Because it's one in, all in.

'They turned on us,' said Carroll. 'They were going to try and kill Russell but he got wind of it.' The Angry Boys were out to make a reputation. 'There's no rhyme or reason to any of it,' said Carroll. 'But I think the more notoriety you had, the more of a target you would be. Bart and I fell into it at the gym one day. We were training in the yard and they just came out to me and him and said, "Do youse want to go to the gym?"' It was 24 March 1993. 'They were seven-out on us and I got stabbed real bad,' said Carroll. 'I lost my spleen, one of my lungs, about a metre and a half of my intestines . . . and Bart died. They beat his brains out.'

Former professional footballer turned armed robber Gary Sullivan also did time at SDL. 'Gary Sullivan and Russell became very tight friends as well,' said Carroll, 'and they used to get together and talk for hours on end, very quietly. It wasn't long after that that Gary escaped . . .'

As for Cox's role in the death of Ian Revell Carroll, 'It wasn't something that I'd bring up with him,' said Mark Carroll. 'It's not conducive to being locked up with a bloke: talking about how he'd killed one of your relatives. What can Russell say about it? *I didn't do it, it was him*. Russell wouldn't tell the dentist what tooth to pull out.

'I know that they were very, very good friends,' said Mark, 'and there's a lot of stories in the family about what happened—Russell had gone to rob him and all this shit—but knowing what I know about Ian, I think the shoe might've been on the other foot.'

Denning died before he could give evidence against Cox on armed-robbery charges, so the big case against Cox was dropped—but Cox got three years for Sharry and Roylance when the matter finally reached court in October 1993. He'd already served two years in Queensland, so he was immediately extradited back to NSW.

He was given a glowing report by the Queensland Corrective Services Commission. As far as they were concerned, his time had passed 'without incident' and he had used his incarceration 'constructively to undertake activities and programmes which fostered his personal development and provided him with favourable skills for his eventual return to the community'.

The authorities found Cox to be 'cooperative, organised, punctual, industrious, clean and with an overall excellent attitude to both staff and inmates'.

In NSW, Cox went to trial on 8 May 1995 for escaping lawful custody at Katingal in 1977. His lawyer argued that he had not escaped from lawful custody because his confinement in Katingal had been unlawful. He claimed Cox's treatment in the jail had been 'cruel and inhumane', and he used the argument first raised at Steve Sellers' committal hearing in 1979—that Katingal had never been formally gazetted as a jail. The trial began on Monday and was over by Wednesday, when the judge found there genuinely was no documentation that showed Cox had been in legal custody at Katingal. In effect, Russell Mad Dog Cox, who was neither a Russell nor mad nor a dog nor a Cox, had not escaped from an escape-proof jail that was neither escape proof nor a jail. Mercifully, the question of whether he had tried to break in again never came up.

Cox never went to court for the Barkly Square job. Victoria Police eventually caught Santo Mercuri, who pleaded not guilty to armed robbery and murder but refused to make a statement: he got twenty-five years and eventually died in jail. The slow death of the terrified witness Jenny G ended when she went into witness protection and was born again with a new identity.

Cox continued his NSW sentence at Goulburn Gaol, where he successfully applied to have the alias 'Mad Dog Cox' removed from his prison record on the grounds that it was not a true alias—after all, he had never gone around calling himself 'Mad Dog': it would've likely got him killed. In Goulburn, he became head facilitator of the Young Offenders Program, where he counselled junior rough heads against a pointless life of crime and imprisonment. Johnny Lewis used to bring in boys to talk with him. Cox's security classification was eventually lowered. He could have transferred to a cushier life at Maitland but, when a prison officer asked him to stay on at Goulburn and keep up his involvement with the program, Cox said he was 'more than happy' to remain. Cox was grounded and encouraged by the regular visits from Lewis, who treated him as family and made him feel normal, not like a mad dog.

But Cox was always at his best in jail, biding his time between escapes. 'Other than the Paul Cafe escape and shooting,' said Dave Emu Farrell, 'he wasn't really a problem like so many others had been, for barricading cells and all this sort of stuff.' Cox was one of the smartest armed robbers of them all, but he was no smartie.

At least, not to your face.

In 1996, Cox made an application to the Supreme Court of NSW to have his sentence redetermined. Part of the argument put forward by his lawyers rested on the definition of the verb 'to serve'. The Supreme Court's Justice Badgery-Parker said that 'serve' in Australian law was 'arguably' intended to refer to the serving of a sentence in prison. Cox's lawyers said 'serve' could mean 'to go through' or 'be subject to' a sentence 'which continues to run from the time of its imposition regardless of the location of the person upon whom it was imposed'.

Under this definition, if a prisoner was absent from a prison but had not escaped from lawful custody, he should be regarded as serving his sentence. Since Cox had not escaped from Katingal because he wasn't legally held there, he might have been serving his sentence while he was on the run, shooting Ian Revell Carroll, assaulting Sharry and Roylance, taking a gun to Doncaster Shoppingtown and so forth. In another unlikely twist to the story of Melville Peter Schnitzerling, Badgery-Parker agreed with Cox's counsel that Cox had served his sentence 'throughout the time at large'. He acknowledged this was 'a peculiar loophole' but one which, nonetheless, 'given the ambiguities, ought to grant benefit to the applicant'. He was only prepared to follow this argument a certain distance, however. 'In order to obviate the ludicrous situation of ignoring the time at large,' he said, 'the nature of the time spent serving the sentence will factor significantly into any determination I should make.'

He re-set Cox's life sentence at a minimum of 29 years, dating back to 1975 and including his eleven years on the run.

Cox enrolled in a Bachelor of Arts in Communication at the University of Technology. He worked hard and studied and became a boxing trainer like his great mate Lewis. He started to grow into the man he always could have been. He married Helen Deane in prison. He was moved around the NSW system, through Lithgow, Maitland, Parklea, Parramatta and Cessnock, until he found himself back in Grafton—which was now a jail like any other.

Cox fronted the Serious Offenders Review Council, whose members included Steve Tandy, one of the Long Bay guards who had been held at gunpoint in the MRP during Cox's 1975 escape bid. But even Tandy felt that Cox deserved another chance. 'Initially and, I suppose, for a few years thereafter, he wasn't on my Christmas card list,' said Tandy. 'But after a while you think, "What good is there continuing the dislike?" I've seen him three or four times over the six-monthly periods we review them, and there's certainly no animosity. At least in me anyway. And I certainly don't think he harbours any grudge towards me.'

The NSW Parole Board agreed to release Cox on licence once he had served his minimum term. 'If I had any doubts about him reoffending, I would have opposed release to parole,' said Tandy. 'It's as simple as that. I just think he's had enough and he deserves a go.' Grafton governor John Heffernan, who had also been a prison officer at the Bay in 1975, also supported Cox's application unreservedly. Even Paul Cafe, shot twice in the leg by Marko Motric, has since said he doesn't carry a grudge.

Cox heard about his release from his legal aid solicitor—who, gloriously, was the one-time prison-reform activist Jack 'the Hat' Grahame.

In a spectacularly opportunistic intervention, Grafton-area MP Steve Cansdell said he thought Cox should be made to go back home. 'It should be like years ago when they put them on a one-way train out of here,' he said, as if Cox—or any other recently released prisoner—had ever threatened to stay in Grafton. Queensland Premier Peter Beattie didn't want Cox in his state, either: 'I wish he'd stay elsewhere,' said Beattie—but he stopped short of nominating Grafton.

It was said that Cox had a job as a builder's labourer. Terry Tye, Sunshine Coast organiser of what remained of the BLF, said, 'If Russell Cox decides the Sunshine Coast is where he wants to live, then we'll give him every assistance. Russell will be welcomed on the work site, and his wish for privacy and getting on with normal life will be respected.'

On the morning of Cox's release on 8 December 2004, a handful of locals turned up to see him off and offer the gathered media someone to talk to while reporters and photographers waited for the opening of the gatehouse door. A man named Andrew Taylor predicted, 'Eventually they'll have to make a movie or a mini-series about him ... I might get to be an extra because I was here.'

First out of the jail was the prison chaplain, former speedway driver Ian Bailey, wearing sunglasses, a red beard and a clerical collar, like a bikie in fancy dress. Cox followed him, under a straw hat and a jail-issue bomber jacket, its belly bulging with whatever small possessions he carried. Cox covered his face with a large manila envelope. He looked like Guy Fawkes heading for a British bonfire night, or a fat scarecrow escaped from his field.

Bailey climbed into his Corrective Services car and accelerated out of the carpark with Cox in the back seat. A couple of media vehicles gave chase but—predictably—Cox's getaway driver shook off his tail. Once they had lost their pursuers, Cox jumped into a back-up vehicle and was driven to meet Johnny Lewis and his wife, Ingreed Rojas. According to Lewis's biographer Paul Kent—who seems to be the only writer ever to have interviewed Cox—Lewis, Rojas, Cox and Deane took an evening stroll along Brushgrove, on the southern tip of Woodford Island in the Clarence River. 'It was a warm evening in a lovely summer and they walked for more than an hour,' wrote Kent, then Lewis and Cox talked long into the night, before Cox headed to Queensland the next morning.

—

In 2010, the Russell Cox story had featured in an episode of *Tough Nuts: Australia's hardest criminals*, where Chopper Read weighed in for his 'mate', calling him 'a bloody good bloke . . . a real Australian, the last of the true bank-robbers'. More obscurely, Chopper added. 'He'd be the Banjo Paterson and Henry Lawson of bankrobbers.' Russell Cox, said Chopper, was 'the only yoga-loving, peace-freak, hippy, gunman, bankrobber, alleged killer, I've ever met . . . he was into all this touchy-feely save-the-world sort of stuff, but he liked armed robberies and carrying guns'. It's possible that, by 'touchy-feely save-the-world sort of stuff', Chopper meant vegetarianism.

The smug, sly, murderous Roger Rogerson appeared on *Tough Nuts* too. Rogerson was the anti-Chopper Read: rather than admitting to the murders of people other men had killed, he killed people then blamed other men. Another guest, Michael Drury, who still believed Rogerson had tried to murder him, said, 'He was an extremely active and violent criminal. He had to be quarantined from the community. And the best way to do that was put him in jail . . . He was *mad*.' Drury was talking about Cox, but the words better described Rogerson.

The actor James Lugton represented Cox in the dramatisations and played Cox in exactly the same way as Wayne Bradley was to play Denning. Cox's fictional criminal mentor was the same actor as Denning's fictional criminal mentor—Matt Potter—but wearing a smarter shirt. And, yes, there were similarities between the two men. Of course there were parallels. But Cox was the cleverer man, the harder man and—if you can put a value on a life, like you can put a price on a head—maybe Cox's life was the bigger waste. Cox was an athlete, a thinker and a fantastically professional armed robber. He was a gentleman, a loyal friend, a faithful lover and a fearless enemy. And it's easy to judge others when, like me, you didn't grow up in boys' homes and you weren't tipped out into the world to fend for yourself. But you can be the greatest gangster on earth and the only thing you'll ever be known for is taking money you didn't earn and murdering your mates.

Like a mad dog.

Afterword

The Golden Age of Armed Robbery may have died between the security screen and the ceiling of the St Leonards branch of the Advance Bank in 1991, but it reeled around headless for almost a decade. Veterans Bernie Matthews and John Killick still had some heists to pull off and Norman Lee, the last surviving Bookie Robber, was shot dead by police as he attempted to rob the Ansett freight office at Tullamarine Airport in July 1992. But the great majority of hold-ups in the 1990s were the work of hapless, hopeless junkies waving syringes, sticks or knives. The number of offences kept on rising until about Christmas 2000, when the heroin drought cleaned up the streets faster than any Dirty Harry or Rotten Roger.

The banks installed armed guards, security screens and CCTV, then stopped handling large amounts of cash when most people turned to credit cards. Branches disappeared as quickly as they had once multiplied. These days, it's hard to even find a bank to rob. Companies began to pay wages and salaries by direct bank transfer, and the big payroll loads disappeared from the armoured vans.

Professional criminals got out of the game. It's almost unheard of for anyone to hold up a business with a gun in Australia. The pistol would be worth more than the takings. Today, 'organised crime' is just another word for the drugs trade. The heavies and the smarties all smuggle and deal—or stand over or protect smugglers and dealers.

The clever, charismatic, wounded outlaws of the 1970s and 1980s have all but disappeared. Jails have become dumping grounds for addicts and the mentally ill or overcrowded holding centres for Indigenous despair. The supermax units are filling with Islamists, who are recruiting from the drug gangs to form bonds in captivity that might survive long after their sentences have been served. And the bad old days may really seem like a golden age, once they all get out . . .

Acknowledgments

I was fantastically lucky to benefit from the generosity and wisdom of a generation of armed robbers, detectives, lawyers and prison officers. Among the ex-crims who helped me, first and foremost was Bernie Matthews, whose book *Intractable* was an invaluable resource. John Killick was also extraordinarily helpful, as was his book *Gambling for Love* (Killick has also written two other memoirs, *On the Inside* and *The Last Escape*). Mark Carroll was fantastic. Mark Merriman was generous. Ray Brownlowe was very helpful. Ray Pedrana cleared up a mystery for me. I spoke only briefly with Carl Synnerdahl, but he helped. Alan Weir was great. Phil Player was gracious and supportive. Garry ('the Hand of Death') Page told some great stories. Graham Henry (subject of my mate Jay Pring's *'Abo': A treacherous life*) set me to rights on a couple of points. Every one of those guys has a book (or another book) in them. Thanks also to 'Unknown': you know who you are.

Cheers also to former prisoner—and deft, prolific writer—Ray Mooney.

Among the police, Ken Ashworth obviously stands out, both as a source and a human being. Thanks also to Kim Roylance, who answered the phone to a bloke he didn't know and told a story he needn't have told. Michael Kennedy was great. Chris Fraser helped as much as he could.

For the prison officers, Dave Emu Farrell (author of *Old Screw*) was terse and funny. Richard Osborne explained the perspective of blokes on the job and shed new light on Katingal. George Eastham told me about Maitland. Peter Egge (author of *It's All in the Fall*) helped with great courtesy. William Dodson (author of *The Sharp End*) put in time and effort for me.

I must also thank Keith Bush for his eye-opening tour of Maitland Gaol and Andrew Weglarz for his helpful and informative tour of the NSW Corrective Services Museum at Cooma.

Patrick Kennedy, author of *Long Bay*, was fantastically helpful and his book was a vital resource. Prison nurse Sue Jefferies was lovely. Tim Watson-Munro, author of *A Shrink in the Clink* and other books, offered fantastic background.

As for lawyers, past and present: Denis Mockler, Daniel Hanna, Peter Livesey—obviously, I can't thank you enough. Ron Driels, Tom Kelly, Joe Weller, Robert Richter and David Buchanan all helped a lot. Thanks also to Frances Gibson.

Andrew Sergeant at the Petherick Reading Room at the National Library of Australia went far beyond the call of duty in his help with the book. Jane Griskaitis at the Law Society of NSW was equally helpful. Almost everyone at the State Library of NSW gave me a hand (most often in an attempt to show me how to use the microfiche reader). The staff at UTS Library were very helpful too.

A few former (and current) activists helped a great deal—Vivien Altman, Brett Collins, Meredith Burgmann, Irina Dunn and Michael Matteson were all brilliant. Wendy Bacon, Linda Funnell and Chips Mackinolty also did their bit.

The criminologists Donald Weatherburn and Russell Hogg helped me see sense.

Richard Ruppas was tremendously generous in giving me a victim's perspective. Gary Waddell was fascinating.

Among my fellow journalists (including, of course, Bernie Matthews), special thanks to the marvellous Andrew Rule, who suggested I write this book, and to Janet Fife-Yeomans (who was a great help even though we've never met), Warren Gibbs (who was a great help even though we have met) and Stephen Gibbs. Also respect to Frank Robson for his forensic work on Russell Cox in *Underbelly: The golden casket*, even though I question some of the information Frank was given. Thanks to Roy Eccleston and the librarian at the Adelaide *Advertiser*. Thanks to John Silvester for looking for a document. Thanks to Neil Mercer for looking for people. Thanks to Kate McClymont for pointing me towards Neil Mercer.

And special thanks to Michael Robotham.

Several people spoke to me on condition of anonymity. Thanks to all of you—most of all to Donna.

Other works consulted include *Ray Denning: My life and time* by Donald Catchlove; AIC Seminar: Proceedings No. 26, *Armed Robbery* edited by Dennis Challinger; *The Long Bay Oral History Project* by Corrective Services, NSW

Department of Justice; *Johnny Lewis: The biography* by Paul Kent; *Maximum Security* by James Morton; *Shotgun and Standover* by James Morton and Russell Robinson; *The Profession of Violence: The rise and fall of the Kray Twins* by John Pearson; *Australia's Hardest Prison* by James Phelps; *A Tale of Two Cities* by John Silvester and Andrew Rule; *For Simmo* by Jan Simmonds with Anne Gollan; *Wilful Obstruction* by Tony Vinson; and *Chopper from the Inside* by Mark Brandon Read.

Special credit must go to the excellent Radio National *Background Briefing: A break in the traffic* by June Pritchard, which answered a lot of my questions before I had even asked them.

In a former life, I met Roger Rogerson, Tim Anderson (author of the excellent *Take Two: The criminal justice system revisited*), Johnny Lewis and, indeed, the late Chopper Read.